THE FUTURE OF HUMAN REPRODUCTION

THE FUTURE
OF
HUMAN
REPRODUCTION

EDITED BY

CHRISTINE OVERALL

women's
P R E S S

CANADIAN CATALOGUING IN PUBLICATION DATA
The Future of Human Reproduction
Includes bibliographical references.
ISBN 0-88961-132-7

1. Human reproductive technology — Social aspects.
2. Childbirth — Social aspects.
I. Overall, Christine, 1949 —
QP251.F87 1989   362.1'98   C89-093888-1

Cover design: Sunday Harrison
Copy editor: Nuzhat Amin

Printed and bound in Canada
First printing 1989; Second printing 1994

Published by Women's Press
517 College Street, Suite 233
Toronto, Ontario M6G 4A2

This book was produced by the collective effort of Women's Press
and was a project of the Social Issues Group.
Women's Press gratefully acknowledges financial support from
the Canada Council and the Ontario Arts Council.

CONTENTS

For Devon
who thinks "philosopher" and "feminist" are synonymous

ACKNOWLEDGEMENTS

My first and greatest thanks go to all of the contributors; their excellent work, their co-operation and their patience have made the task of editing this volume a rewarding experience.

I am also grateful to the women at The Women's Press, particularly Maureen FitzGerald, who was always available to provide information, advice and reassurance at the right moment.

Ann Liblik, my secretary at Queen's University, has helped by taking care of many of the time-consuming tasks that erode my blocks of time.

I also wish to acknowledge the financial assistance of the Ontario Arts Council.

Finally, I want to thank Devon, Narnia, and Ted Worth, who have graciously tolerated and supported yet another year of my preoccupation with reproductive issues, Winnie MacInnis, my loyal and thoughtful co-counselor, and Dorothy Overall, the best possible role model.

INTRODUCTION

Eve be / got the Womb
Adam be / got the Word
now man discovers reproductive technology
now woman dis / covers the word
this could be wholeness
this could be war

in vitro, in glass reproduction
glass penis womb

glass tube longing
for return of His sparerib
ex-, out + jaculari, to throw, from jaculum, dart ejaculate

     jaculari

   throw, ter-, return of his

           dart, sper, spareribs

man's throwback to Adam – *test(icle)* tube babies
trei-, three, testament, contest, trine (trinity)
Yahweh procreating with Adam
it's a man's wor(l)d
Paradise
yet something had been missing
the *miss, mei-, mistake?*
the little Missus

Betsy Warland,
from *serpent (w)rite (a reader's gloss)*
(Toronto, The Coach House Press, 1987)

Louise Joy Brown, the world's first "test tube baby," was born in July 1978. Conceived through the process of in vitro fertilization (IVF), the infant was watched by a divided world at once fascinated, awed and fearful of the possible meanings and implications of this new reproductive technology. Four years later, in 1982, Canada's first "test tube babies," twins Colin and Gregory Rankin, were born in Oakville, Ontario. Subsequent world developments have included the freezing and successful thawing of human embryos, the preselection of the sex of embryos, and the "lavage" or washing of embryos from the uterus of one woman for implantation in that of another.

Despite these developments, and the practical, moral and social questions they raise, in Canada the debates about the brave new world of reproduction are still in their infancy. *The Future of Human Reproduction* is the first collection of papers to examine a broad range of issues in reproduction and reproductive technology within the Canadian context. In particular, it focuses upon contraception, abortion, prenatal diagnosis and treatment, donor insemination (DI),[1] "surrogate" or contract motherhood, in vitro fertilization, midwifery and birthing.

The working assumption behind the inclusion of all of these topics is that seemingly familiar issues such as abortion and birthing cannot be neglected for the sake of apparently more glamorous techniques like IVF. In none of these areas do medical developments and social policy questions remain static. Just as there is no Canadian consensus on the value and uses of IVF, so also there is no consensus on the proper place of birth or the availability of abortion. Issues in reproduction cannot be treated in isolation from each other: a decision about, for example, embryo research or fetal surgery is bound to have implications for abortion policy and IVF treatments.

The areas of research of the contributors to this volume are diverse and multi-disciplinary in nature; they include law, medicine, philosophy, sociology and political science. In the area of reproduction and reproductive technology, disciplinary boundaries are inevitably and productively crossed: the philosopher learns from the sociologist; the political scientist shares with the legal theorist; and all of them rely upon information from the field of medicine. Hence the organization of this volume is predicated neither upon rigid academic specializations nor upon narrow delineations of the reproductive processes themselves. Instead, the papers are grouped into four general categories.

Section I, Current Medical Perspectives, provides background information about reproductive processes and reproductive technologies from contraception to the freezing of embryos. Section II, The Social and Political Context of Reproduction, examines both the current societal assumptions and values that frame reproduction, and the more specific politics involved in particular reproductive services such as donor insemination and midwifery. Section III, Social Policy Questions, analyzes in a more explicit way the question implicit in the previous sections: what general principles and legislative forms are appropriate to regulate reproductive practices in Canada in the late twentieth century? Section IV, Looking to the Future, presents a vision of reproductive health care in the future, and discusses ways by which changes in reproductive practices could be evaluated.

What unites all of the contributors to this volume is their shared feminist perspective. Issues in reproduction are pre-eminently women's issues; so whether we discuss prenatal diagnosis or contract motherhood, contraceptive devices or the place of birth, it is always essential to examine women's experiences, beliefs, needs and activities in connection with these topics.

Moreover, human reproductive behaviour is by no means just "natural" or merely "biological." Our ways of conceiving, gestating and birthing babies are subject to the pressures and constraints of social construction. And the cultural shaping of reproduction contributes to the social construction of women. This anthology helps to show how the oppression of women is manifested within the supposedly "private" arena of child-bearing. As many of the papers in this volume demonstrate, reproduction by women has been and is being gradually arrogated by men and by patriarchal institutions. So reproductive relations and structures are political in nature; that is, they both reflect and preserve the power inequities between men and women.

This anthology is like a collection of snapshots, sometimes overlapping and sometimes quite different, taken by a specific group of women and men at a particular point in time. Like any group of photographs, it cannot pretend to be all-inclusive, nor to represent the viewpoint of all people, or even all women, with regard to reproduction and reproductive technology. In a field as rapidly changing as reproduction, we can communicate only from a particular place and point in time, the late eighties in Canada. And as professional academic women and men, the contributors speak from a position of relative privilege.

Nevertheless, while avoiding over-generalizing, all of the contributors, as feminists, have tried to think beyond their own perspective to consider the implications of current reproductive practices for other Canadian women. The focus is not only on the present but also on the future: the contributors examine both reproductive practices and issues as they are now, and their possible implications and the social policy questions they raise. This orientation towards the future has resulted in both a deeply critical dimension and a more optimistic element throughout the papers in this volume. New and existing reproductive technologies, along with the practices associated with them, can be neither wholeheartedly endorsed nor totally condemned. Instead, it is necessary to explore their meanings and implications for women and children, and the social context in which they are used.

Of course, the benefits of reproductive technology may already be fairly familiar. Reports in the popular media stress the positive outcomes: the beautiful babies, happy mothers, proud fathers, brilliant scientists, physicians, technicians. The disappointments, the failures, the health costs, the emotional pain are seldom the focus of front-page stories. Even less visible to the general public is a political analysis which would ask who has access to reproductive technology, who makes decisions about its research and development, and what are the long-range costs to the women who are involved in this medical management of their "problems" of fertility and infertility.

A feminist approach to the debates about reproduction requires that we look critically and sceptically at the ostensible benefits of reproductive technologies and practices. In this anthology four general themes woven through the different papers are related to some of the apparent benefits of the developing reproductive technologies, and the reasons for which feminists must be cautious about accepting them at face value.

I THE DESIRE FOR HEALTHY CHILDREN

First, at its most positive, the justification for the technologies is based upon the desire to have healthy, strong, happy, thriving children. This is a desire that surely no one could quarrel with; we all want the best for our children, and we all have high hopes for the children of the future. Thus, the story goes, prenatal diagnosis helps us to know more about the condition of the fetus as it develops, and birthing technology permits the survival of imperilled infants. IVF, DI and contract motherhood enable persons with problems of infertility to obtain the child they have been longing for.

Nevertheless, the apparently straightforward desire for

healthy children is not a datum, a given which must simply be accepted for its own sake. In her paper, "Reproductive Technology and Social Policy in Canada," Deborah Poff argues that it is important to examine the origins of the desire to have children, and the ways in which that desire may be constructed so that only certain kinds of children will be acceptable. To a large degree the apparently natural "need" for children is socially created.

In addition, we cannot take for granted the idea of family which seems to provide the context for this desire for a child. There is no universal and unchanging form of the family. The methods by which new reproductive technologies fulfil the desire for a child help to create and define new varieties of family. For example, in "Donor Insemination: The Future of a Public Secret," Rona Achilles discusses the ways in which making use of donor insemination redefines family relationships and requires a new understanding of the ways in which individual family members are linked to each other.

A significant effect of reproductive technologies is that they seem to enable us to make more and more detailed specifications of what kinds of children we do and do not want to have. The apparently innocent goal, the positive goal, of having strong, healthy, thriving offspring, changes into a more negative goal of avoiding or getting rid of children with certain supposedly undesirable characteristics. The implicit attitude towards children is that they are products, artefacts, which can be made better and better, even at the stage of embryonic and fetal development.

Earlier in this century, eugenic programs, founded upon the belief that technology can be used to improve human beings and to weed out undesirable ones, used coercive sterilization in the attempt to control poor people and people of colour. In the late twentieth century eugenic values are manifested in the growing and extensive use of diagnostic tests during pregnancy. As Abby Lippman explains in "Prenatal

Diagnosis: Reproductive Choice? Reproductive Control?" these prenatal tests are directed primarily towards the detection and elimination of a variety of fetal disabilities, but they can also be used to select offspring on the basis of sex, and they have the potential to be used for eugenic discrimination founded upon other physical characteristics.

Given the historical connection between the status of children and the value attributed to mothering, there is also a connection between the treatment of embryos and children as consumer products and the promotion of a role for women as reproductive entrepreneurs. As Somer Brodribb shows in "Delivering Babies: Contracts and Contradictions," women can perform a "job" involving the lease of their uterus; they produce child-products for sale to wealthy men. Thus they are co-opted to continue the patriarchal tradition of mothering as work performed for men.

In general, the social uses of the new technologies appear to increase the patriarchal misuse of women and women's bodies. Thus in "Of *Woman* Born? How Old-Fashioned! New Reproductive Technologies and Women's Oppression," Kathryn Pauly Morgan explores the ways in which reproductive technologies and the practices associated with them contribute to women's psychological oppression through processes of stereotyping, cultural depreciation and sexual objectification. What all of these papers indicate is that it is essential for feminists to be critical of the ways in which the desire for healthy children is misshapen and misappropriated within a patriarchal context.

II PROVIDING INFORMATION

A second apparent benefit of some reproductive technology is that it provides information about women's reproductive systems, about the course of gestation and about the state of the fetus as it develops. Knowledge is, itself, a positive thing, and the decisions that we make are likely to be better decisions, the more information we have. But as Cynthia Carver's discussion in "The New – and Debatable – Reproductive Technologies" shows, while much is known about treating and compensating for infertility, there is a lot which is still unknown. Moreover, what gets researched and explored – as well as what is ignored and overlooked – is at least partly a function of political and social pressures that are not always sensitive to the real needs of women.

In addition, unfortunately, the information we have is not always one hundred percent accurate, and, as the diethylstilbestrol (DES) debacle demonstrates, often reproductive interventions in women's bodies are undertaken without adequate knowledge of their outcomes. DES is a drug that was given over the course of several decades to pregnant women in Canada and elsewhere in the hope of preventing miscarriage. Its legacy, years later, is sometimes severe reproductive abnormalities in many of the offspring of the women who took the drug. In her paper, "1938-1988: Fifty Years of D.E.S. – Fifty Years Too Many," Harriet Simand argues that we must learn from the hard lessons of DES, and give serious thought to the possible effects of present reproductive interventions such as in vitro fertilization. They too may involve taking risks with the health of women and their children without adequate knowledge of the possible long-term effects of the treatments.

We also need to consider what is the goal of the new knowledge about fertility and infertility. Abby Lippman's paper shows us that there are many possible uses for the collection of technologies known as prenatal diagnosis; so far there has not been adequate thought given to what those uses should be. One problem lies in the fact that prenatal diagnosis is not, of course, omniscient: it is not totally error-free, it cannot always tell the degree of seriousness of a disability, and it cannot guarantee that a child will not be born with disabilities.

Another problem is that the use of prenatal diagnosis may encourage us to see all human beings as divided into two classes: the disabled and the non-disabled. And this distinction gets translated into a distinction between those that are considered undesirable human beings and those that are considered desirable. In addition, the standards for a "desirable" human being, i.e., a non-disabled human being, may seem to get raised higher and higher, or become more and more specialized, as technology enables us to learn more and more about the developing embryo and fetus. Thus there are reasons to be anxious about what messages are conveyed by this escalation: What do they say about disabled people who exist now or who may be born in the future, or persons who may become disabled later in their lives? What do they say about our attitudes towards children?

One very obvious example of the misuse of reproductive knowledge is the practice of sex selection. When female children are considered less desirable than males, prenatal diagnosis may be used to find out the sex of the fetus, for the purpose of aborting it if it is female. In North America there is extensive evidence to suggest a preference on the part of future parents for male offspring, particularly as firstborn or only children. The recent development of sex *pre*selection methods, which permit the determination of the sex of offspring at conception itself, will permit some people to continue to treat femaleness as if it were a disability to be avoided if possible.

In sum, the quest for healthy children and the quest for greater information about reproductive processes may work together to reinforce the eugenic impulse in the social uses of reproductive technologies.

III REPRODUCTIVE CHOICE AND CONTROL

A third apparently positive aspect of new developments in reproductive technology is that they seem to expand the amount of control and the number of choices that women have with respect to having children or not having children. On the one hand, sexual intercourse is becoming separated from reproduction, through the development of more efficient contraception and the availability of abortion, and on the other hand, reproduction is becoming separated from sexual intercourse, through woman-controlled access to donor insemination. How and when we conceive, the process of gestation, and the course of birthing itself all appear to provide more options for women than ever before.

Nevertheless, feminists have urged that we rethink how much our reproductive freedom is enhanced by current reproductive practices. As Thelma McCormack warns in "When is Biology Destiny?" we need to look more carefully both at what "reproductive choice" means and at what it includes – and excludes.

For example, Nikki Colodny's paper, "The Politics of Birth Control in a Reproductive Rights Context," clearly shows that while heterosexual women are apparently blessed with an array of contraceptive choices, these methods are not entirely reliable or safe, and women may not always be provided with an adequate understanding of them. To what extent, then, do heterosexual women have genuine reproductive freedom with respect to birth prevention?

In "Small 'p' Politics: The Midwifery Example," Patricia O'Reilly shows that with the development of sophisticated birthing technology, the processes, rituals and practices surrounding birth have passed out of the hands of midwives, and birthing decisions are now thought to be the responsibility of members of the medical profession rather than the parents, and the mother in particular. This system of controlled procreation is being enhanced and extended by the addition of complex and invasive infertility treatments such as in vitro fertilization. In Linda Williams's paper, "No Relief Until the End: The Physical and Emotional Costs of In Vitro Fertilization," we see that women subjected to IVF become absorbed into a complex, demanding and often painful set of no-exit procedures, with "no relief until the end."

Women's reproductive freedom may be further compromised by processes such as fetal surgery and prenatal diagnosis, which set the stage for a potential conflict between the alleged rights of the embryo/fetus and the rights of the woman. Lip service is paid to the rights of the woman, but appeal is made to her capacity for unselfishness, and to the alleged needs of the fetus. In "Pregnancy as Justification for Loss of Juridical Autonomy," Sanda Rodgers explores the legally sanctioned manifestations of the maternal/fetal conflict in some detail. As Rodgers shows, correct moral behaviour for the pregnant woman is claimed to involve the sacrifice of her own wellbeing and autonomy for the sake of the wellbeing of her fetus, and that sacrifice has often been enforced through juridical mechanisms. Pregnant women are assumed not to be entitled to make decisions on behalf of themselves or their fetus – even though, as Paul Thompson's paper, "The Home Birth Alternative to the Medicalization of Childbirth: Safety and Ethical Responsibility," argues, these sorts of decisions are similar to the kinds that parents are justifiably entitled to make in connection with their older children.

Hence, the proliferation of new reproductive practices and technologies has provided opportunities for the narrowing, rather than the broadening, of women's reproductive freedom. Many current reproductive practices are presented with a sort of veneer of apparently pro-women, pro-liberation language; when that language is peeled away, what we find is the appeal to more traditional moral behaviour for women. Although there may be little in the technologies themselves to limit women's reproductive choices, the patriarchal ideology which governs the use of those technologies dictates the further aggrandizement of control over women's bodies.

A sensitivity to this ideology leads some feminists to

emphasize and explore the growing victimization and oppression of women through the medicalization of reproduction. Other feminists stress instead the importance of women empowering ourselves to resist the takeover of our bodies, through community and collective education and the development of alternative health care systems. These two approaches are not incompatible: it is essential both to understand the ways in which women's self-determination is eroded through the extension of reproductive control by the medical system and the state, and to explore the different possible paths to the reassertion of women's self-determination.

In light of the Canadian history of state-sanctioned limitations on procreative freedom, there is good reason to be sceptical about the future of social policy formation with respect to reproduction. Some recent gains – such as the 1988 Supreme Court decision on abortion and the move to recognize midwifery in Ontario – are more than balanced by the potential dangers of further state regulation of abortion, contraceptive choice, contract motherhood and the new reproductive technologies. Moreover, there is no consensus among feminists as to the role the state should play, and the degree of regulation that is appropriate.

One example concerns in vitro fertilization. Some feminists regard IVF as essentially an experimental technique so ineffective and so potentially dangerous to women that it should no longer be offered as a "medical" treatment for infertility. By contrast, other feminists argue that no women who need the procedure and are fully informed about it should be prevented from obtaining access to it. Behind a disagreement of this sort lie diverse assumptions not only about the degree to which women's health is threatened by IVF but about the allocation and social control of reproductive resources and services. The issue here is not one of protecting women but of empowering women, and the means by which that goal can best be achieved. More feminist debate is still needed concerning whether and to what extent the health care system and the law can be used to genuinely address women's needs and concerns, and to enhance rather than curtail our reproductive freedom.

IV MINORITY GROUP WOMEN
A fourth potentially positive aspect of reproductive technology is that it may be especially important to so-called minority group women – disabled women and lesbians in particular – as mothers and as potential mothers. Disabled women who are mothers or who are contemplating becoming mothers may have special interests and needs, and the information and choices offered by reproductive technologies, particularly prenatal diagnosis, may turn out to be especially helpful to them. For lesbians, on the other hand, the women-controlled use of the very simple technique of donor insemination makes motherhood a real possibility without heterosexual intercourse or a relationship with a man.

Unfortunately, however, the medical institutions which dispense reproductive services and technologies function in a gatekeeping capacity to ensure that prospective candidates for prenatal diagnosis, DI and IVF fit what are thought to be appropriate criteria for motherhood. The institutional uses of these technologies typically stress conformity to the requirements of stereotypical womanhood – heterosexuality, marriage, absence of disabilities – and to the personal attributes associated with that role: passivity, nurturance, orientation towards men. The screening process controls access to reproductive technologies and contributes to the social shaping of individual women and families, excluding some from access and pressing others into conformity with the stereotype. Often, neither lesbians nor disabled women are found to fit the "requirements" for access to technologically assisted motherhood.

There are, in addition, other ways in which the present social applications of reproductive technology may be harmful to the interests of Women of Colour, poor women and lesbians. For example, racist elements are present in some of the social practices related to reproduction. Couples hiring a contract mother, who are usually white, invariably seek a white woman to bear "their" baby, and white customers for sperm specify that the product must be from a white man. Yet reproductive entrepreneurs in the United States are also looking to meet the demand for white babies by exploiting the procreative labour of poor Women of Colour, who would be hired to gestate fertilized eggs produced through in vitro fertilization using gametes from white women and men.

Classism, moreover, is a ubiquitous part of some reproductive services: for example, since in vitro fertilization is rarely covered by public health insurance (Ontario is the one province that pays for part of the costs), IVF is open only to those women who can afford the huge price tag and, often, the time away from work. Finally, the heterosexist bias of high-tech reproductive health care is evidenced in the requirement at most IVF clinics that prospective candidates be married or in a "stable" heterosexual relationship.

It should by now be clear that existing and new reproductive technologies and services are easily co-opted for sexist and androcentric purposes. Hence, rather than falling for a simplistic patriarchal construction of the issues, feminists must continue to explore the development of women-centred and women-aware social policies for reproduction. This volume includes several thoughtful and careful discussions of policy development and analysis, discussions that are particularly concerned with the issue of access to, and responsible use of, reproductive technology. In "The Future of Abortion in Canada: A Legal Viewpoint," Sanda Rodgers discusses past abortion legislation and judicial decisions, and assesses future policy possibilities and prospects. In her paper, "Reproductive Technology and Social Policy in Canada," Deborah Poff examines the issue of accessibility with regard to IVF and DI. In "Some Minimal Principles Concerning the New Reproductive Technologies," Margrit Eichler outlines basic ethical precepts suggested by the Canadian Coalition for a Royal Commission on New Reproductive Technologies to guide future policy with regard to research, development and availability of services in reproduction. Feminist discussions of reproductive policy provide a crucial voice that needs and deserves a greater audience in the Canadian political arena.

V WOMEN AND REPRODUCTIVE FUTURES

What is the future of human reproduction? More specifically, what is the future of reproduction for Canadian women? Emphasizing the dangers of reproductive technology projects one sort of future; emphasizing the benefits projects another. "Principles into Practice: An Activist Vision of Feminist Reproductive Health Care," by Vicki Van Wagner and Bob Lee, depicts an inspiring reproductive future in which women of all races, sexual orientations and abilities work collectively to acquire the knowledge and control to choose whether, when and how to birth healthy strong children. Susan Sherwin's paper, "Feminist Ethics and New Reproductive Technologies," presents some of the feminist ethical criteria by which we, as women, can seek to prevent an oppressive reproductive future and to facilitate an empowering one for women and children.

As feminists, our critique of present reproductive practices aims towards a future in which women are no longer the victims of oppressive practices and institutions. Through your thinking and political activism, the readers of this volume are invited to join with the contributors and to participate in the formation of a future for reproduction which is feminist both in its means and in its goals.

Christine Overall

NOTES

1 Until recently this process was commonly referred to as "artificial insemination by donor" or AID. However, because the acronym AID is so close to AIDS or acquired immunodeficiency syndrome, the name has been changed to "donor insemination" or DI. Current medical literature usually uses TDI or "therapeutic donor insemination." This term implies that the procedure must be performed by a physician, and it reinforces medical control over the process. Some feminist literature uses the term "alternative insemination," which is appropriate to describe donor insemination outside clinical settings. The term "donor insemination" or DI is used in this anthology because it applies to all situations, both medical and non-medical. (Thanks to Rona Achilles for clarifying these terms.)

I
CURRENT
MEDICAL
PERSPECTIVES

The Politics of Birth Control in a Reproductive Rights Context

Nikki Colodny

At the core of the politics of birth control are issues of power and control. The power (or lack of power) occurs in two areas. One is in the development of contraceptives and the other is in access to existing birth control information and options. Technology and access determine the parameters of an individual woman's choice.

The history of who has access to existing information and technology is telling. For example, in the Museum of the History of Contraception at Ortho Pharmaceuticals, Toronto, there is an example of a device known as a stem plug. A forerunner of the IUD used in the early 1900s, the stem plug was a silver or gold rod, about four centimetres long, with a flat button at one end. It was placed in a woman's cervical canal by a physician. The button blocked the cervical opening (os). Infection, cervical erosion and other complications often followed. The stem plug at the Ortho Museum is silver and rests in an elegant leather silk-lined box with a silver clasp. The grandchildren of the *gentleman* who had owned the plug donated it when they discovered what it was. They had found it with his duelling pistols. Fertility control in whose hands? Certainly not the woman's.

The movement for women's reproductive rights has a larger agenda than simply birth control options. It has taken up a series of demands that relate to the issues of control of information and access to technology. The implementation of these demands would make it possible for all women in this society to take greater control of whether, when and under what circumstance to have children. The list of demands is long and would include accessible sex education and birth control information; non-directive contraceptive and sexuality counseling; the development of safer and more effective contraceptive technology for women and men; the development of reproductive technologies in the interests of women's liberation and under our control; an end to forced and coerced sterilization of Women of Colour, Black women, Native women, Asian women and disabled women; the right to make our own choice about abortion and to have full access to free abortion; the right to have universal publicly funded daycare and paid parental leave; the right to information and choice about birthing options, including legalization of independent midwifery; the right of native peoples to keep their children and not have them forcibly removed by government agencies; the right to economic security and equal pay for work of equal value; an end to violence and the threat of violence; an end to discrimination against gay and lesbian people; and sexual self-determination for everyone.

These demands grow out of our fundamental right as women to control our bodies, our reproduction and our sexuality. We organize to seek the recognition of these rights, which are our birthright, from governments and from the institutional infrastructure of the state, including the medical establishment and the educational system.

As long as governments do not include women's liberation as part of the basic framework for their political goals, we will only gain such recognition piecemeal. But it is still important to organize for the small bits that governments can be compelled to give us for two reasons: First, even small gains are a tremendous contribution to women's autonomy in society. Second, participating in the women's movement teaches organizing skills to many women and gives us a sense of our own power. It also teaches us that it is possible to win concessions from reluctant governments when we organize. We will need such skills and knowledge in order to continue to maximize what we can get from reluctant governments and also to eventually bring about a change to a government which has, as part of its basic framework, the liberation of women and of all peoples.

For example, DES (diethylstilbestrol)[1] is still used in many Third World countries. If we succeed in stopping the use of DES all over the world, it would be a small achievement compared to our ultimate goal of full control of pharmaceuticals that affect women. We do not want such drugs and devices to be developed according to colonial and racist population control ideologies. Nor do we want them developed to profit big-business multi-nationals. We want them developed according to the best interests, well being and aspirations of women who use and are affected by them. That level of control is part of our ultimate vision.

Yet the banning of DES, though only a small part of what we need and deserve is extremely valuable in and of itself. DES is dangerous. Women's groups who have stopped its use in their countries have prevented untold tragedy and harm to women's lives.

Many of us are involved in trying to change some aspect of women's oppression or exploitation. It is discouraging to work hard and still achieve only a small bit of our ultimate vision of a society, difficult even to imagine in its entirety, where we, as women, could live rich and productive lives with economic security, without fear of violence and in full control of our reproduction and sexuality. Still those small gains, hard won, are essential, both for the bits themselves and for the lessons we learn while organizing to win them.

There are always two levels of organizing: for the immediate demands, around which we can gather the broadest and therefore the most successful coalitions; and for the long term principles or objectives, which have, in this time and place, fewer supporters. So we continue to educate ourselves and others in order to expand the pool of supporters of women's liberation. Someday we will realize our vision.

An important precondition for that vision of our liberation would be a society that provides the cultural and material support for us to have children if and when we want them; and to not have children and still be heterosexually active, if we so choose, without the risk of pregnancy. That cultural support would include social mores that allowed frank and easy discussion of sexuality, fertility, birth control, pregnancy and childbirth. Material support would include easy and free accessibility to contraceptive information in our own languages and to feminist reproductive healthcare and better birth control options.

TYPES OF CONTRACEPTION

Today's contraceptives can be divided into five categories: pharmaceuticals, devices, barrier methods, fertility awareness and surgical methods.[2]

Pharmaceuticals are oral contraceptives: combined estrogen plus progestin; progestin only; the morning after pill, including DES; injectable hormones, including Depo Provera; hormonal implants under the skin (subdermal); vaginal rings that release hormones; and spermicides in the form of foam, gel, or cream, which are used alone or in combination with barrier methods. Pharmaceuticals in the research stage also include hormone nasal spray (LHRF analogs), birth control vaccines and self-administered abortifacients like RU486 (a pill that causes an abortion).

Devices include three types of intrauterine device (IUD) also known as loop or coil, "inert" plastic, copper wrapped and hormone releasing.

Barrier methods include the diaphragm, the cervical cap,

condoms which are placed on the penis and sponges which are placed in the vagina over the cervix.

Fertility awareness methods are methods of determining ovulation. They include mucous observation, taking one's oral temperature and testing urine.

Surgical birth control includes vasectomy, tubal ligation and abortion.

With the exception of hormones, all of these forms of contraception had been "invented" by 1880. They were, however, extremely unavailable until the birth control movement of the early 1900s forced their introduction to a wider population.[3]

FACTORS AFFECTING SELECTION OF BIRTH CONTROL METHOD

There are a number of factors that affect the selection of a birth control method. These include cost, convenience, flexibility, safety, effectiveness and availability.

Cost

Cost can be an impediment to the use of contraceptives and also limits contraceptive choice. The cost of foam (twenty-five dollars for fifty grams in Toronto pharmacies) leads some couples to use condoms alone, a far less effective option than foam and condom in combination. The yearly cost of the birth control pill is higher than the yearly cost of condoms and foam, but most pharmacies will allow women to purchase one month's supply of pills at a time, thus eliminating the requirement for a large lump sum payment, whereas the purchase of foam requires a lump sum. This poses an economic barrier to many people in this country and influences the type of birth control used.

Some family planning clinics are able to sell birth control pills at cost by special arrangement with the pharmaceutical companies. However, the companies will not make this arrangement with most clinics or doctors' offices because the companies do not want to antagonize pharmacies, which are their major customers. Pharmacies lose their dispensing fee when pills are bought elsewhere by patients.

Most provincial funding that covers patients' medication costs, including some medicare plans and most family benefit and general welfare assistance programs, does not cover the cost of non-prescription medications. This can limit real choice in the selection of contraception. Some women's groups, including Toronto's Jessie's Centre for Teenagers, are lobbying provincial governments to begin providing full coverage for non-prescription contraceptives under existing health benefits.

Convenience
The perception of convenience is related to the extent to which something has to be done at the time of sexual intercourse to prevent pregnancy. This seems like a rather straightforward variable until one examines some underlying cultural assumptions. The IUD is high on the convenience scale as defined above. Once it is inserted in the uterus it is always working to prevent pregnancy. Aside from checking the string to ensure that it is still in place, and from getting regular check-ups to detect non-symptomatic infections early, nothing else is required for the two or three years before it should be replaced.

However, the IUD is often inconvenient for women in other ways, at times other than during heterosexual activity. Women who use the IUD often have crampy lower abdominal sensations that range from mild to uncomfortable. While using the IUD menstrual periods are often affected: we discharge more blood for more days with more cramps. Is this really more convenient?

Similarly, the pill is rated high on the convenience scale. But anyone who has had to take any kind of medication on a regular basis knows how annoying and difficult it is to do so.

The medical community calls pill taking "compliance" (that is, doing what I tell you) and it is well studied and reported in medical literature. In fact, physicians as a group are particularly unreliable about taking their own medication when it has been prescribed for them.[4] This, unfortunately, does not prevent them from heaping derision on women who forget to take a pill and conceive as a result.

Taking a pill every day, whether for ten days or several years, is not easy. Nor is it comfortable to experience the myriad of so-called "nuisance" side effects of the pill which many women tolerate in order to take advantage of its apparent convenience. But it is removed from the event of heterosexual sex, and that seems to be the operative value.

The cultural norms of romantic love contribute to this particular perception of convenience. Romantic love attempts to shape women as passive recipients in heterosexist sex thereby maintaining the patriarchal view of women as sexual victims. It assumes women's easy and spontaneous availability to a particular form of sexual activity: the placing of penis into vagina. As Rose Shapiro describes, "The fact that a contraceptive 'does not interfere with intercourse' and allows sexual 'spontaneity' is presented as an unquestionable 'advantage'. It is assumed that our priority is to be protected against conception in such a way as to ensure that we can be swept off our feet according to the rules of romantic love."[5]

Women need to be in control not only of our fertility but of our sexuality as well. That means determining what kind of sex we have, and when. Redefining our sexuality as autonomous women means developing our own criteria for convenience. We are not only warm vaginas waiting to sheath excited penises or fertile vessels waiting to hatch patriarchal progeny.

Another aspect of the perception of convenience has to do with our socialization about our bodies. Barrier methods seem inconvenient partly because they involve looking at and touching the genitals. This looking and touching ourselves and / or our lovers, or being touched, to put a contraceptive in place contradicts the ethereal, non-corporal notion of romantic love. It can also bring up feelings of humiliation and revulsion that we are taught to have about our bodies. The oppression of women distorts our worth in all society's institutions – a distortion that ranges from omission to degradation. We are socialized to view ourselves, in the distorted mirror of society's institutions, as worthless, incompetent, smelly, leaky, difficult and on and on. It is a challenge to reclaim the affirmation of our erotic and woman-bodies from the conditions of sexist society.

Flexibility

Flexibility depends on how easy or difficult it is to start or stop using a particular method. This often boils down to whether the method requires a physician. A diaphragm is very flexible – to stop using it, the woman or her lover simply doesn't insert it before intercourse. The IUD is relatively inflexible – it needs a health practitioner, in this country usually a doctor, to place it in, or remove it from, the uterus. A long-acting injectable hormone such as Depo Provera is even more inflexible. Women have to wait the months required for it to completely finish releasing from the site in the muscle where it has been injected. Even a healthcare worker cannot remove it.

The safety of various birth control methods has been, and will continue to be, well aired by the feminist press and the women's healthcare movement. (For a review of the safety and side effects of various methods see *A Book About Birth Control*,[6] *The New Our Bodies, Ourselves*[7] or *Immigrant Women's Health Handbook*[8]). It was the women's movement of the 1970s that forced the recognition of safety issues in oral contraception. Indeed, it was the gathering of women's experiences with oral contraception and their publication by feminists that helped build the women's healthcare movement in North America.

Effectiveness

Effectiveness is a very important factor for most women selecting a form of contraception. Its importance accounts for much of the popularity of oral birth control pills. (For information regarding the relative effectiveness of various forms of contraception see *The New Our Bodies, Ourselves.*[9]) But the theoretical effectiveness of the pill is not the same as its actual effectiveness. As an abortion provider, I have seen many pill failures. Some we cannot account for. Most can be attributed to missing a pill, taking it later in the day than usual, conception during the first month of either beginning to use the pill or changing from one pill to another, concurrent illness with vomiting, or concurrent use of an ever growing list of medications, both prescription and over-the-counter, that interfere with the availability of the pill's hormones in our bodies.

Most of these pill failures could be prevented if women were given appropriate information. Knowledge *is* a kind of power. But most doctors who prescribe oral contraception do not provide patients with the information necessary to prevent these kinds of pill failures. In my experience, most doctors do not have accurate or complete information about contraceptive options. In any case, comprehensive contraceptive counseling does not accompany most pill prescribing. Handing out booklets just does not work as well as talking to people.

The effectiveness of any particular kind of birth control is also influenced by the rate at which women stop using it because of uncomfortable or dangerous side effects. For example, some researchers argue that the effectiveness of the pill and the IUD are greatly reduced by the fact that their discontinuation rate may be as high as fifty percent.[10] This is certainly borne out by the experience of patients I have seen. We know from numerous studies that the majority of abortion patients were using birth control at the time of conception. But many women who were not using it at that time *were* using it just a few months prior.

The discontinuance rates of the pill and the IUD seem to be a major causative factor in unwanted pregnancy. When women stop using one form of contraception they often do not have, and / or are not given, sufficient information about alternative methods.

Safety and Effectiveness

Safety and effectiveness are inversely related (as one increases, the other decreases, and vice versa). Barrier methods and fertility awareness rank among the safest of birth control methods. Even including the risks associated with abortion as back-up, they are still safer than either the pill or the IUD. However, these forms of birth control are somewhat less effective than the pill. (This may, in fact, not be true for an individual woman. Since the range of effectiveness of the symptothermal methods is so wide, an individual who has a lifestyle that makes it relatively easy for her to take her temperature every morning may, in fact, be less likely to conceive than a woman who works shifts and is attempting to take a birth control pill at a regular time every twenty-four hours. But the statistical generalities of effectiveness for large groups still hold.)

Another example of the inverse relationship between effectiveness and safety is the combined oral contraceptive pill. It is high on the scale of effectiveness but lowest on the scale of safety when compared with methods commonly used in Canada. Its side effects range from uncomfortable to life threatening.

It is important to note a significant exception to these inverse relationships: the combination of foam and condom is high on both the safety scale and the effectiveness scale; in effectiveness it ranks just below the combined pill.

Availability

The availability of particular forms of birth control is influenced by a combination of factors including government provision of healthcare, the regulation of substances and devices by governments, the financial decisions of big-business pharmaceutical companies, and the biases of the medical establishment.

The lack of access to medically insured abortion is a fundamental example of how government regulation, including criminal law, limits the availability of our options for reproductive control. Unless the federal government is forced to keep abortion out of the criminal code and provincial governments are forced, under the Canada Health Act, to provide access to safe, free abortion, abortion will be more available to some women than others. Availability of abortion depends on geography, class, race, age and immigrant status. These are the same barriers to availability on which the Supreme Court of Canada based its decision to quash the old abortion law.

Two decades of tireless organizing by the pro-choice movement, in combination with the courageous stand taken by Dr. Henry Morgentaler to defy an unjust law, focused public attention on the very real lack of availability of abortion. Growing public awareness and Morgentaler's repeated jury acquittals (in spite of the letter of the law) led, finally, to the Supreme Court of Canada's ruling on January 28, 1988, that the abortion law, Section 251, was a violation of women's rights as embodied in the Canadian Charter of Rights.

As we know, governments are not neutral on questions of reproductive rights. There are numerous examples of government regulation of substances and devices that reveal the reluctance of the state to help make reproductive choice a reality for women. A good test of this reluctance as it applies to the availability of substances will be the future availability of RU486, a pill which causes abortion if a woman is no more than eight or nine weeks pregnant.

In the last couple of years, all IUDs (with the exception of the hormone-releasing Progestasert) were removed from the market in the U.S. The decision to do so was made by the companies that manufacture IUDs and was precipitated by the Dalkon Shield horror story.[11] The women's healthcare movement forced the recognition of the dangers of the Dalkon Shield. The resulting lawsuit against A.H. Robins Company, the company that manufactured the Shield and knowingly withheld information about its dangers, made other companies worry that their potential legal costs would cut into their U.S. profit margins. Although many of us have serious concerns about the risks of IUD use (for example, infection, infertility and chronic pelvic pain), the removal of a birth control option on the basis of profitability is unacceptable.

Availability is also significantly limited by the content of contraceptive counseling. For example, most physicians do not know that condom and foam used together have an effectiveness rating, among reversible methods, that is second only to the combination pill. Since they do not have this information, they do not convey it to patients and this option becomes "unavailable" because of lack of information. This applies to information about fertility awareness as well. If women are primarily dependent on physicians for contraceptive information (as most women are), then the norms of medical practice crucially affect what is available to us. The sexism embedded in the culture at large thrives in medical patriarchy. Women are seen as childlike at best, stupid and uncooperative at worst. So in general, physicians are uncomfortable with barrier methods and disapproving of fertility awareness because these methods depend on women's involvement or responsibility.

The class bias, racism and prejudice about disabled women

exhibited by most physicians crucially limits the contraceptive information and birth control options provided to working-class women, disabled women, Black, Asian, Hispanic, and Native women and Women of Colour; to say nothing of the disrespect shown to, and the indignities inflicted on, these women by their doctors.

A clear example of these striking limitations of the medical establishment are the medical norms of IUD use. The IUD is largely reserved for those whom doctors see as particularly irresponsible with other forms of birth control. This includes Black, Asian and Hispanic women, Women of Colour, Immigrant Women, economically disadvantaged women, Native women, disabled women, women who have had an abortion and, in a perverse turn of logic, women with large families. It is an outrage that many of us from these groups are coerced into using the IUD. Women identified as belonging to one of these groups are also the most likely to be coerced or forced into being surgically sterilized.

It is unacceptable that the facts concerning the risks of IUD use are not presented in an understandable fashion with the result that many women with IUDs are not aware of the risks of infection and infertility. Information is a crucial component of women's ability to assess the effectiveness and safety of contraceptive options. Information, or lack of it, can also produce or obliterate availability. The politics of information has real meaning in this context. Where is the information? How can we get it?

It is the telling of women's own lived experience and the women's healthcare movement that provide us with our best information. Wide dissemination of this information means letting women know where we can find it on our own. It also means establishing autonomous, feminist healthcare providers and centres as well as influencing the existing medical system.

The medical model of contraceptive selection is one of

informed consent. Informed consent requires that a patient be informed of risks that could result from a particular medical intervention and what the risks are if nothing is done. Informed consent has largely been pushed on an unwilling profession by patients' rights and consumer advocacy pressure. Patients and doctors alike know that this requirement is seldom fulfilled. Some doctors are concerned that they will worry their patients excessively about something that is unlikely to even happen. Others believe that if they mention a side effect, it will cause the patient to experience it. Still others are more interested in doing things to patients than in talking to them. Even at its best, informed consent is a one-way conversation, with the power all in the doctor's hands. The doctor *tells* the patient certain things about the method she / he (the doctor) is *telling* the patient to use. The patient then consents, that is, *acquiesces*, to the good doctor's *advice*. Questions from the patient are perceived as a sign of uncooperativeness, an interruption of the fundamental process of giving advice. In the medical model, the doctor takes responsibility for the patient.

A feminist model of contraceptive selection or abortion decision counseling is one of *informed choice*, not informed consent. Birth control counselors using a feminist model may be physicians or nurses, but many are non-medical caregivers, historically related to witches and midwives.[12] The women's healthcare movement has a strong tradition of so-called "lay" counselors and caregivers. In addition, independent midwifery is alive and growing in Canada.

A feminist model of birth control selection and abortion decision counseling assumes that as women we are the experts of our own experience. Counselors may have the information that patients don't have. That information needs to be communicated in understandable non-medicalese in the patient's own language. Counselors may express opinions and disclose a bias, but they do not tell the patient what she should do. Specific information about the patient's life and circumstances is taken into account so that the form of contraception selected, or the decision made regarding abortion, can fit the reality of each woman's life as far as the available options allow. Questions and comments from patients are welcome, rather than being seen as a sign of uncooperativeness. The model is one of interaction and dialogue. The goal is to provide the woman with information so that *she* can make a choice. In a feminist model the patient is encouraged to take responsibility for herself, her body, her fertility and her sexuality.

Until we live in that society of the future where women are truly autonomous, women will not have full choice. Our choices will be limited by the sexism, the racism and the classism of the society in which we live. But we can push our society to the limit. We can maximize and defend our gains. And we can organize to make a non-capitalist, non-patriarchal, non-racist world a reality. None of us, as individuals, can finish our own personal work of resocializing ourselves until the society as a whole is reorganized. The objective reality of sexism simply creates too many barriers. And society, as a whole, can't be reorganized unless we undo the oppressive aspects of our female socialization and claim our power to criticize, to stand up for our rights and to organize with others to achieve the recognition of those rights from governments.

NOTES

1 Anita Direcks and Ellen 't Hoen, "DES: The Crime Continues," in Kathleen McDonnell, ed., *Adverse Effects: Women and the Pharmaceutical Industry* (Toronto, Ont., Women's Educational Press, 1986), p.41.

2 More expansive definitions and explanations of these various birth control methods are available in numerous sources including Susan Bell, "Birth Control," in *The New Our Bodies, Ourselves,* by The Boston Women's Health Book Collective (New York, Simon & Schuster, 1984), p.220; and in Donna Cherniak, *a book about birth control* (Montreal, The Montreal Health Press / Les Presses de la Santé de Montreal, 1988) and in Erica

Mercer and Patricia Murphy, eds., *Immigrant Women's Health Handbook: A Book By and For Immigrant Women* (Toronto, Immigrant Women's Centre, 1981).

3 There are many accounts of this remarkable period of women's history. One such account is Rose Shapiro, "The Early Birth Controllers: Where do they come from ... what do they want?" in *Contraception: a Practical and Political Guide* (London, Virago Press, 1987), p.3.

4 M. Pinner and B.F. Miller, *When Doctors are Patients* (New York, W.W. Norton and Co., 1952).

5 Ibid., p.41.

6 Cherniak, op. cit.

7 Bell, op. cit.

8 Mercer, op. cit.

9 Bell, op. cit.

10 Bell, op. cit., p. 224

11 Ann Pappert, "Dalkon: Shielded by the Law," in *Healthsharing*, vol. 7, no. 1 (Winter 1985) p.8; Vancouver Women's Health Collective, "Dalkon Shield Action Canada" in a special Dalkon Shield issue of *Healthmatters*, vol. 2, no. 4 (November 1986); Morton Mintz, "At Any Cost: Corporate Greed, Women, and the Dalkon Shield" (New York, Pantheon, 1985).

12 Barbara Ehrenreich and Deirdre English, *Witches, Midwives and Nurses: A History of Women Healers* (Old Westbury, New York, The Feminist Press, 1973).

The New
– and Debatable –
Reproductive
Technologies

Cynthia Carver

Assisted reproduction dates back centuries to the potions, chants and manipulations of midwives, herbalists, medicine women and men, and other traditional healers who aided the infertile and impotent, warded off miscarriages, and helped those who wanted children. Physicians have been assisting reproduction too, but only in recent decades has medical science brought extensive clinical and laboratory technology to bear on the multifaceted problem of infertility.

Infertility may be defined as the inability of a couple to produce a live infant after a certain period (often taken as two years) during which intercourse has occurred with reasonable frequency and in the absence of contraception. Infertility can be due to a host of physical, physiological and probably psychological factors, but in many cases its specific cause cannot be determined with certainty.

The desire to have a child, whether inherent or induced by societal expectations, is strong in many infertile individuals and couples. In the past two or three decades, the medical community has become deeply involved in the pursuit of ways to deal with or compensate for infertility, and the era of medically-assisted reproduction is now well established.

EARLY ASSISTANCE

Ovulation Charting –
Waiting for the Egg to Pop

With the knowledge that ovulation, the production of an egg ready for fertilization, occurred midway between two menstrual periods, women learned that they could use their normal body rhythm to achieve conception (or alternatively, contraception). The woman having difficulty becoming pregnant was instructed by her physician or midwife to engage in intercourse predominantly during the midcycle. This was the beginning of cycle slavery.

Additional information, that body temperature and cervical mucus altered just before and during ovulation, refined the use of the body cycle to predict the "right time" to have sex. Women found themselves touching their cervical mucus and taking their temperatures daily to ascertain the "right moment." Other therapeutic manipulations accompanied the use of cycle timing. These included the woman having her hips on a pillow during intercourse, remaining on her back with legs in a knee-chest position for half an hour after intercourse and refraining from sex during the non-fertile times of the month.

While some women improved their chances of becoming pregnant by planning intercourse, many others were spending their waking moments with a thermometer in their mouths or vaginas, and turning sex into a therapeutic exercise rather than an expression of love or desire. An interesting observation made by some physicians was that after months of sex-by-cycle, many couples would say, "Forget it," go back to intercourse-by-desire and find themselves pregnant a few months later. Was this success due to return of spontaneity? to reduction of stress? to coincidence? No one knew.

Artificial Insemination by Husband (AI-H)[1]

The most clearcut indication for undertaking artificial insemination with the husband's / male partner's sperm has been in cases where he, for organic or psychological reasons, is unable to ejaculate inside his partner's vagina. If his sperm are normal in number and function, and her anatomy and physiology are also normal, the introduction of ejaculate into the vagina or cervix with a syringe at the time of ovulation should produce conception with about the same rate of success as intercourse.

AI-H has also been used in situations where pregnancy has not occurred despite apparent regular ovulation, good sperm count and normal anatomy in both parties. In these cases, the sperm may not swim normally, the cervical mucus may be inhospitable to sperm or there may be antibodies which kill or damage sperm.

The discovery of a means of separating sperm which produce females from those producing males has led to the use of AI-H to avoid transmission of sex-linked diseases to offspring. For example, the genes for certain types of muscular dystrophy and bleeding disorders are found on half of the X (sex) chromosomes of women who are called "carriers." (Carriers do not themselves have a disease, but can transmit it to their male children.)[2]

The separation of X (female producing) from Y (male producing) sperm in the husband's ejaculate permits the sperm introduced into the woman to be mostly of the X variety (a hundred percent separation is not possible), thus greatly increasing the likelihood that a female, and therefore unaffected, child will be born.

The ability to separate male-producing from female-producing sperm has led to doctors offering, and couples demanding, the right to choose to have children of a preferred sex. Since our society tends to favour males over females, it can be expected that more couples will opt to have male children, thus altering the sex distribution of society. In 1987 this technique, to which there had been limited access, became available in community-based clinics for a modest fee.

AI-H is not risk free. For some of the conditions mentioned above, the sperm must be injected directly into the uterus and this poses a risk of uterine infection. The psychological effects on the couple – of repeated visits to the gynecologist for "procedures" to make the woman pregnant, and multiple ejaculations by the man into bottles to produce usable sperm – are not well established. But AI-H may well have a negative impact on self-image and sexuality.

AI-H has not yet been adequately studied and hence its success rates cannot be reliably predicted for individual situations. A fairly new development, introducing sperm directly into the fallopian tube through a catheter (a long, thin, flexible tube), might improve success rates in the future.

Donor Insemination (DI)
Using the sperm of an anonymous male donor to impregnate a healthy woman has been done predominantly when the husband does not produce sperm at all, has had a vasectomy which cannot be reversed, has abnormalities in the semen or has a known hereditary disease. More recently, DI has been used to impregnate single women who wish to bear a child.

The major biological risk to the woman using DI occurs when the donor has a communicable disease in which the infecting organisms are found in the semen as with hepatitis B, other viral diseases and acquired immunodeficiency syndrome (AIDS). There is also risk to the offspring if the donor has a genetic disease such as a blood disorder or hereditary high cholesterol. The risk of such disorders being present in the semen inevitably increases when donors are paid, since they will be less likely to admit to having symptoms or a history of such diseases.

In Canada, sperm donors have usually been medical

students or staff physicians who are either volunteers or are minimally paid, so the infection and hereditary disease problem has not been a major one. It is now possible to test for viruses in semen, and all donors should be quizzed extensively on their medical history. Despite such precautions, the risk – however small – is present.

There are potential psychological risks to both partners and to the child in the use of DI. There is no agreement as to whether it is better to tell the child that her biological father is not the same as the father she knows and loves. Parents handle this issue as they see fit. The male partner may, in time, resent the child, knowing she is not biologically his. This might be more likely if the child is difficult, handicapped or otherwise not "perfect." The anonymity of the donor can pose problems if the child develops medical problems and it becomes important to know more about the health or heredity of her biological father.

Far more research into the various risks and benefits of DI is needed. Nonetheless, it remains the best alternative for a single woman or for a couple wishing to have a baby when the male is incapable of producing sperm or presents a very high risk of disease to his offspring.

Pre-embryo Transfer – Donor Egg

When the male partner is fertile but the female is incapable of producing eggs, pre-embyro transfer with a donor egg and the male partner's sperm is a possibility. In this procedure, a volunteer egg donor agrees to be artificially inseminated by the sperm of the male partner from an infertile couple.

The insemination is performed at the time of the egg donor's ovulation, and five or six days later the pre-embryo (a very early stage of development) is lavaged (washed out) of the donor's uterus and implanted into that of the infertile woman. Repeated lavages may be required for several days in succession until the pre-embryo is retrieved.

The introduction of the pre-embryo into the recipient woman must occur shortly after her ovulation so that her hormone balance will be capable of supporting a pregnancy, and her uterus is ready to accept implantation. If she is not ovulating, then hormones are used to stimulate ovulation.

There are potential risks of infection, including AIDS and herpes, to both the donor and recipient women. Other risks include failure to retrieve the pre-embryo, resulting in a (probably unwanted) pregnancy in the donor woman. Ectopic (tubal) pregnancy may also be a risk. A thorough screening of the donor woman is essential, to ensure against genetic disorders in the infant. One or both women may require drugs to synchronize their cycles, and these drugs may also carry some potential risk.

There may be psychological effects on the donor woman as well. She is, in effect, a surrogate mother for a brief period of time, and is also giving away her egg as part of a future child which will be loved and raised by others.

In cases where the male partner of the recipient couple is sterile or has a low sperm count, a male sperm donor can be used to artificially inseminate the female egg donor. In this situation the infant will be genetically unrelated to either parent, although the infertile woman will undergo pregnancy and birth.

There are not enough data as yet to evaluate the success rate of pre-embryo transfer using uterine lavage.

THE NEWER REPRODUCTIVE TECHNOLOGIES

In Vitro Fertilization (IVF)

In all the methods of infertility management discussed above, the egg and sperm unite within a woman's body. With in vitro fertilization (IVF), this union occurs in a laboratory. In the simplest case, when a couple is unable to conceive, eggs are obtained from the female and sperm from the male partner. The eggs and sperm are placed together in a laboratory for twelve to eighteen hours to allow fertilization to occur. Two to three days later, the pre-embryo is placed in a catheter which is inserted through the cervical canal into the uterus. Two weeks after that, it is possible to tell whether pregnancy has occurred.

Even in this basic case, the procedure is not risk free. Until recently, the woman required a general anesthetic for a tube (laparascope) to be inserted through an incision in her abdominal wall and down into her pelvis, where the ovaries are located. Instruments fed into the pelvis through the laparascope could then "harvest" the ripe eggs from her ovary. With this surgery there is the risk of damage to ovary, pelvic and intestinal structures, and excess bleeding. General anesthetics occasionally cause major problems and sometimes (although rarely) cause death. Drugs must be given to the woman to encourage several eggs to ripen simultaneously (normally only one ripens each month) so that the "harvest" will be worthwhile. These drugs (for example, Clomid) can have negative side effects.

A new procedure involves obtaining the eggs by inserting a long needle through the vaginal wall into the pelvis. No general anesthetic is required, which removes one risk. But the needle is guided by ultrasound imaging and it seems likely that occasionally it will hit something major, like a blood vessel, and cause serious problems.

In most cases, an attempt is made to fertilize several eggs with sperm, and three or four pre-embryos are then inserted into the woman's uterus. There is a potential risk of infection being inserted along with the pre-embryos, the likelihood of pregnancy is poor and, if pregnancy occurs, there is a relatively high risk of a multiple birth. (Anyone with twins or triplets can attest to the risk to the mental health of the parents of multiples.)

There is also a theoretical risk of abnormality in the off-spring, resulting from manipulation (touching, artificial environment, temperature changes, infection, etc.) damaging the eggs, sperm or pre-embryo. But, to date, the risk of abnormality in the children of IVF does not appear to be higher than in any other children.

IVF with eggs and sperm from the infertile couple is most often used when the woman has damaged fallopian tubes which prevent sperm and egg from meeting, or the fertilized egg from entering the uterus and implanting itself. A low sperm count is also an indication for IVF. The eggs and sperm are in close proximity in the laboratory and fertilization is more likely to occur than after intercourse. IVF has also been used when the true cause of infertility is unknown.

IVF – Donor Sperm, Eggs and Pre-Embryos

When the male has a low sperm count, but tests indicate that his sperm are able to penetrate the outer layer of an egg normally, then artificial insemination is usually attempted for several ovulatory cycles, after which IVF may be considered. If, however, the sperm are also unable to penetrate eggs, then IVF with donor sperm for backup might be the treatment of choice.

The rationale for donor sperm backup is that the woman has had to undergo a major procedure to obtain her eggs, and therefore every attempt should be made to fertilize them. Both partners must agree in advance so that when fertilization appears not to have occurred with the husband's sperm after twelve to eighteen hours, the eggs may be exposed to donor sperm.

Unfortunately, the determination of fertilization is not always accurate, so there may be doubt as to who the biological father is.

Where the woman requires IVF and her partner is sterile, donor sperm is used for the fertilization.

Since the donation of eggs is much more complicated and more risky than sperm donation, it is not likely that many women will donate their eggs for infertile couples (except perhaps for friends and relatives). However, if a woman is having eggs harvested for her own IVF and there is a surplus, she may be willing to donate the extras to another woman's IVF. Similarly, women having pelvic surgery might be willing to have eggs harvested at the same time for donation to an IVF program.

Historically, doctors have not always asked permission for what they wanted to do to patients. As IVF programs increase, safeguards may be needed to ensure that egg harvesting is not done without a woman's permission.

Donor eggs are most often used for IVF when the recipient woman has no ovaries, no eggs, or carries a hereditary disease. When an infertile couple can produce neither eggs nor sperm, pre-embryos from others can be implanted in the woman's uterus. Pre-embryos become available when more eggs are fertilized than anticipated in an in vitro program, and couples are willing to donate the extra pre-embryos. When a donor pre-embryo is used, there is no genetic relationship between the parents and the child.

Another technique which has been used increasingly in recent years is gamete intra-fallopian transfer (GIFT). In this technique eggs are harvested as in IVF, but they are then placed into a catheter – usually along with the partner's sperm – and inserted through the cervix and uterus into the fallopian tubes. Fertilization, if it occurs, happens in the tube, and the fertilized ovum (egg) enters the uterus for implantation just as in a normal pregnancy.

Cryopreservation – Preserving Through Freezing

Since the 1950s, it has been known that frozen sperm can be thawed and still retain the ability to fertilize an egg. Experiments with animals have shown that the progeny produced from previously frozen sperm are perfectly normal. The freezing of eggs has only recently been achieved, and success rates are not yet known. The freezing of pre-embryos has been successful in a few cases, with normal infants being born. However, the attempts have been few, and the risk of abnormality cannot yet be quantified. Further development of the freezing technology will permit banks of sperm, eggs and pre-embryos to be established, making reproductive material available "on demand" for couples requiring it.

Cryopreservation of sperm has been used when the male partner is planning a vasectomy, if he requires radiation treatment, if the testicles must be removed because of malignancy, if he requires other treatments that might destroy his sperm-producing capacity or if there is a likelihood of abnormal sperm.

Cryopreserved sperm do not fertilize eggs as well as fresh sperm, and multiple attempts at insemination may be required to achieve fertilization. An advantage to freezing is that it kills the organisms which cause sexually transmitted disease, thus reducing the risk of infecting the recipient woman.

Cryopreservation of eggs will probably be utilized for the same kinds of indications as for sperm, namely when the woman has a disease requiring the removal of her ovaries or when she requires treatments which may impair her ability to produce normal eggs.

Pre-embryo freezing will probably be used primarily to save any excess pre-embryos from an IVF program, either for subsequent use by the same woman or as donations to other women in IVF programs.

There are potential problems with cryopreservation, including possible abnormalities produced by the freezing-and-storing process and ensuring the health of the donors and the genetic normalcy of the reproductive material. There are also legal problems especially with regard to pre-embryos.

Are they able to inherit? Who are their "real" parents? Whose responsibility are they? and so on. In this area, the technology is far ahead of considerations about legal status and ethics.

DILEMMAS ARISING

There are moral and ethical questions about much of the technology and its use; many of these will be dealt with in subsequent chapters. There are also questions about the utilization of resources to achieve pregnancy. Should millions of dollars be expended on achieving pregnancies in infertile couples when there are many diseases and conditions affecting much larger sectors of the population that are underresearched and underfunded? The use of expensive, time-consuming technology to achieve pregnancy in a few may be preventing resources from being applied to disorders affecting many more people.

Infertility programs raise an interesting question about the notion of "success" in medical treatment. The success rates in IVF and many of its associated techniques are not well established, but clinics performing them have reported success rates ranging from zero to twenty percent, which means that for every one hundred women entering the program, anywhere from zero to twenty may actually give birth to a liveborn infant.

The risks of procedures in fertility programs are rarely publicized, but there are many potential negative effects, both physical and psychological.

Are we as a society promoting these procedures, fostering a fanatical need for pregnancy, exalting the desirability of a "child of one's own" no matter now tenuous the connection of that child to the "parents," and thus creating a research and technological monster with large expenditures and little potential gain to society as a whole?

Finally, and perhaps most importantly, are we concentrating on ways to offer children to the infertile while ignoring questions such as: Are more men and women becoming infertile than in the past? What are the underlying causes of this infertility? Can it be prevented? Are we perhaps impairing the future of the species through our twentieth century environment?

Many such questions need to be answered. Some exploration of these questions is undertaken in this book, but much more is required.

NOTES

1 The term 'husband' in this essay is used in a generic sense to mean male partner.

2 During conception, the egg from the woman contributes an X chromosome to the fertilization and the sperm contributes an X or a Y; in the former case (XX) producing a female offspring, and in the latter (XY), a male. Thus female children receive one X chromosome from the mother and the other from the father. It is very unlikely that both parents (unless they are close relatives) will carry the gene for the same disease on their X chromosomes. Since the normal gene is dominant over the disease-producing one, female children of carriers are usually normal.

However, half the carrier's male children will inherit an X chromosome containing the disease gene. This will be unopposed by a normal gene from the father because he contributes a Y chromosome (which has no gene for the disease) to the male child. As a result, half the male offspring of female carriers are affected by the disease.

II
THE SOCIAL AND
POLITICAL
CONTEXT OF
REPRODUCTION

OF WOMAN BORN? HOW OLD-FASHIONED! – NEW REPRODUCTIVE TECHNOLOGIES AND WOMEN'S OPPRESSION

Kathryn Pauly Morgan

CONSIDER THIS PASSAGE:

> All human life on the planet is born of woman. The one unifying, incontrovertible experience shared by all women and men is that months-long period we spent unfolding inside a woman's body. Because young humans remain dependent upon nurture for a much longer period than other mammals, and because of the division of labor long established in human groups, where women not only bear and suckle but are assigned almost total responsibility for children, most of us first know both love and disappointment, power and tenderness, in the person of a woman. We carry the imprint of this experience for life, even into our dying.[1]

Now consider this one:

> ... if we continue in this framework, sex preselection, cloning and ectogenesis, combined with surrogate motherhood, will ensure that the fragility of woman's power is worn to gossamer and finally fades. Much as we turn from consideration of a nuclear aftermath we turn from seeing a future where children are neither borne

nor born or where women are forced to bear only sons and to slaughter their foetal daughters.... The future of women as a group is at stake and we need to ensure that we have thoroughly considered all possibilities before endorsing technology which could mean the death of the female.[2]

Reproductive technologies are already with us and have become part of the fabric of everyday consciousness about childbearing. The media are filled with pictures of beaming heterosexual couples bearing their tender one (or, often, ones) in their arms. Their bliss is taken as unconditional testimony to and endorsement of the deeply humane, life-oriented motivations of the theorists and empirical scientists who make the exciting breakthroughs and discoveries which enable the reproductive technologists to bring into existence new life on their behalf.[3] While not wanting in any way to call into question the authenticity of the bliss – the anguish of infertility can be one of the deepest sources of pain to sear a woman's soul – I want to argue that this image calls for further analysis. While the technology, in principle, might make it possible for women to exercise collective and individual autonomy over their fertility, it is both described and carried out in ways whose misogynistic import cannot be mistaken. What women are exposed to are: illusory images of success which camouflage high rates of failure; iatrogenically induced disease and loss of life resulting from procedures allegedly done in the name of "safety"; and coercion and loss of control masquerading as "enhanced reproductive choice." Such mystification is central to the oppression of women in the area of reproductive technology.[4]

My purpose in this paper is to explore how internalizing the language, beliefs and values of the patriarchal reproductive technologists contributes to a profound experience of psychological oppression for women.[5]

In analyzing these forms of oppression, I propose to use the categories of institutional, systematic psychological oppression developed by Sandra Bartky in her paper, "On Psychological Oppression."[6] Three categories which apply to virtually all women in mediated forms are stereotyping, cultural depreciation and sexual objectification. Living under psychological oppression, women come to feel fragmented, devalued, infantilized, dehumanized, degraded, and rendered invisible. One dangerous effect of psychological oppression is that when these feelings have become internalized, other political and economic forms of oppression come to be seen as normal, justified, or our "problem," and fail to be identified as oppression.

STEREOTYPING

The stereotyping of women in the context of the new reproductive technologies is leading increasingly to the invisibility of motherhood. It may well lead to its very annihilation. As Rich argues, the complex history of symbols surrounding motherhood marks the conspicuous deterioration of the actual status of women as well as providing a mythic rendering of the male medical takeover of the entire process of human creation. Rich cites this passage from the work of Frieda Fromm-Reichman:

> ... there is a Persian myth of the creation of the World which precedes the biblical one. In that myth a woman creates the world, and she creates it by the act of natural creativity which is hers and which cannot be duplicated by men. She gives birth to a great number of sons. The sons, greatly puzzled by this act which they cannot duplicate, become frightened. They think, "Who can tell us, that if she can **give** life, she cannot also **take** life." And so, because of their fear of this mysterious ability of woman, and of its reversible possibility, they kill her.[7]

Even when a woman's creative power is seen as a magical force, the fears which fuel reigns of mysogynistic terror lead, wherever possible, to the controlling and harnessing of that power of fertility. Often, although the primary metaphors are naturalistic, it is assumed that Nature is there to be used, albeit with some respect. As Raymond points out, woman is seen as a fertile domain in need of seeding, ploughing and harvesting in order that her "fruit" may come forth from her womb.[8] While this cluster of metaphors clearly underscores the "incompleteness" of the reproductive process apart from the "seeder / plougher," it can carry with it a sense of affiliation with the growing child. The poet Erica Jong describes her growing baby as a "little rose blooming in a red universe," as "an avocado pit almost ready to sprout," as a "little swimming fish."[9] Obviously, these are metaphors of delight and pleasure for the future mother. Again, while it is important to resist the over-romanticization of an experience which leaves many women vomiting, weak, physically unbalanced, and facing potential death, it is just as important to listen to and fight for the right to use these metaphors; for they are endangered linguistic species. And they are not without merit in the sense that they are supportive of women as the bearers of children. That is what we are in danger of losing.

In many western cultures, in particular, the situation of women has been dominated by the psychological (if no longer legal) premise that women are chattel, that is, articles of personal moveable, animate property legitimately controlled by men. As Gena Corea points out, traditions and laws regarding the ownership, possession and control of women's reproductive and sexual powers continue to pervade the lives of many women.[10] But this is taking a new twist in the context of reproductive technologies, particularly in the context of in vitro fertilization, embryo transfer and "surrogate" motherhood. Instead of being the complex, powerful, natural setting in which the vulnerable seed can be nourished, protected and loved, a woman is coming to be seen as analogous to a kind of animate semi-precious mineral, the ovum. Women are no longer valued as biological mothers, as integrated (albeit inferior) human beings, but as ova caches and dubiously valuable receptacles. As Dworkin and Corea have noted, this is fundamentally a continuation of the chattel premise transformed by modern technological advances in the aptly named field of animal "husbandry."[11]

In "Egg Farming and Women's Future," Julie Murphy argues that in the context of the new reproductive technologies, women are seen as egg farms and men as the egg farmers.[12] Here it is imperative to understand the term "farm" as referring to the modern farm, a highly technologized form of livestock exploitation rather than the notion of the cosy "family farm" of wintry greeting cards. In this context women are seen as agricultural "primitives," as a kind of vast, natural resource to be exploited since each woman stores virtually two million ova at the onset of menstruation.[13] According to this way of looking at things, the only process that affects a woman (and which is virtually outside the domain of her agency as an active subject, unless she is taking ovulatory drugs), is this ripening of the eggs. Where the language of agency occurs, it is in reference to the men who describe the *removal* of eggs as the "recovery" of the eggs. As Murphy points out, this term is a complete misnomer for women.[14] On the one hand, the woman herself isn't recovering anything; she is losing something. The agent and recipient here must be identified: he is male. Secondly, one can only "recover" what one has lost, misplaced or lost control of. What are we to think about men who take ova from women and describe it as their "recovery"? Only some objectifying notion such as the chattel assumption allows us to make sense of this.

Further linguistic usage that is documented by Murphy includes the following: the description of spontaneous abortion as "embryonic wastage" and the description of the ovaries of a mature woman as a "production line" of eggs. It is men who remove eggs; men who fertilize eggs; men who transplant embryos; and men who are the primary recipients of the harvest in the context of "surrogate" motherhood. As Murphy notes, women are increasingly coming to be seen through the dominant ovarian ideology as egg storers, egg layers and egg hatchers in a larger eugenicist context of genetic engineering.[15] Where women are referred to at all, they are referred to by such terms as "the uterine environment," "the maternal milieu" or "the embryo carrier." Such metaphors are, of course, consistent with the somewhat older metaphor applied to women entering menopause, viz. "the empty nest."

What is the import of these new metaphors? It is the psychologically oppressive reduction of biological motherhood to a genetic primitive coupled with a mediocre incubator function. It is the annihilation of anything recognizable as an integrated, human, woman-focused experience of conception and maternity. Seen in the light of the patriarchal hope for complete ectogenesis, I believe it is a crucial ideological step in the direction of destroying the desirability and powerful symbolism of biological motherhood altogether.

CULTURAL DOMINATION

In this context, cultural domination takes place in at least three major ways: (1) through the direct devaluing and dehumanization of women, (2) through the transformation of reproduction as a patriarchal artefact, and (3) through the experience of coerced voluntariness.

Devaluation of Women

Direct devaluing of women is most graphic in the context of sex predetermination / sex selection procedures. Whether it takes the form of using sex-targeted douches, refusing to implant female embryos in the context of in vitro fertilization, electively aborting female embryos after chorionic villi sampling or amniocentesis, or killing healthy female embryos in the context of anticipated multiple births so as to give male fetuses a greater chance of survival, the message is clear: females are not wanted. While there may be particular genetic medical conditions where knowing the sex of the fetus is crucial in one's decision-making, these are not the situations I am speaking about. I am speaking about the elimination of healthy future women. Future daughters, sisters or mothers are not as valued as future sons, brothers or fathers. Raymond describes this as the "previctimization" of women.[16] Powledge refers to this as "... one of the most stupendously sexist acts in which it is possible to engage. It is the original sexist sin ..."[17] I agree.

Further evidence of the devaluing of women comes from the testimonies of women who undergo the invasive procedures associated with infertility testing, in vitro fertilization and the monitoring of "surrogate" mothering. As one woman put it, "You feel like a piece of meat in a meat-works." Another remarked, "Our generation were guinea pigs for the Dalkon Shield and now we're guinea pigs for a new form of modern technology."[18] In addition to the lack of respect represented by the absence of explanations, counselling, discussion and political analysis of the social construction of motherhood by the reproductive technologists, I believe it is fair to say that, as in the discussion of ova importance, women are valued primarily in this context as raw experimental data. A number of medical ethicists and feminists have noted that no proper primate studies have been carried out prior to the implementation of the new reproductive technologies. *It is my conviction that women are the primate studies,* that actual practice between technologists and women does not support a perception of this as a genuinely reciprocated human encounter. "Egg farms," "guinea pigs," "piece of meat" – these are the terms the women use to describe their experience. These are deeply oppressive terms and reflect oppressive practices.

Fears about women's capacity to bear children are also translated into misogynistic language which strengthens the reproductive technologists' program to take motherhood out of the bodies of women.[19] In the influential book, *Birth Without Violence,* Dr Frederick Leboyer says,

> One day, the baby finds itself a prisoner ... the prison comes to life ... begins, like some octopus, to hug and crush ... stifle ... assault ... the prison has gone berserk ... with its heart bursting, the infant sinks into this hell ... the mother ... she is driving the baby out. At the same time she is holding it in, preventing its passage. It is she who is the enemy. She who stands between the child and life. Only one of them can prevail. It is mortal combat ... not satisfied with crushing, the monster ... twists it in a refinement of cruelty.[20]

While other theorists do not characterize biological mothers as monsters engaged in mortal combat with their babies, the central sentiment is still there albeit in somewhat muted form. Consider the remarks of Edward Grossman who, in an article entitled "The Obsolescent Mother. A Scenario" remarks that among the advantages of a "glass womb" would be the "fact" that the environment would be safer than a woman's womb, that women could be "spared the discomfort" of childbirth, and that women could be permanently sterilized.[21] Similarly, in 1983, world-famous geneticist Jerome Lejeune discussed the possibility of men being pregnant. He "told the court human embryos rely on their mother only for shelter and sustenance. He said a fetus is so independent it could be implanted in a man's abdominal cavity and grow to maturity."[22] Again, whether one considers the biological mother to be a monster, or to be an unsafe environment, or dispensable altogether, it is impossible to experience any feeling of being valued as a woman. Women are oppressed by the frame of reference, by the descriptions of birthing, and by the negative assessment of our normal ability to be healthy childbearers.

Further devaluing of women can take place in two ways. First, when our stories, our myths, our descriptions of our bodily and emotional feelings, and our preferences are undermined through ridicule and pathological labeling (for example, as "neurotic," "hysterical" and "masochistic") and disregarded, we feel and are silenced by the power of the patriarchal medical establishment. Secondly, we are not only silenced in the present. We are silenced with respect to the past. We are encouraged to think of the time when maternity and birthing was a woman-centred experience controlled by the birthing mother, her sisters, her woman friends and her midwives as a time of irresponsible, risky and primitive practices much scorned by contemporary technical practitioners. As a consequence our individual reproductive lives, our experiences of our fertility and our collective history are subordinated to the constructions of the dominant patriarchal culture.

Reproduction as Patriarchal Artefact

A second important form of cultural domination takes place when the "natural pathology" assumption regarding women's bodies is used to transform conception, maternity and birthing into a technologized artefact that, optimally, takes place outside women's bodies altogether. While woman's reproductive power is redefined in primitive reductionistic ways, her power to create and give birth to life (which could, in principle, be enhanced by some of the new technologies) is seen as dangerously mediocre when compared with the promises attached to the development of an artificial womb. Gena Corea entitled her influential book *The Mother Machine* to underscore the double meaning of that phrase: on the one hand, the mechanization of conception, maternity and birthing in the actual lives of women so that more and more of what seems to be happening in and to a woman's body and through her agency is controlled, monitored, stimulated and deadened by machines and technicians; and, two, the complete appropriation of human reproduction by men in the form of fertility experts and "fetologists" whose ultimate goal is to breed children outside of the caring bodily presence of women altogether in the artificial "mother machine," that is, the artificial womb. When Grossman says, "Natural pregnancy may become an anachronism ... the uterus would become appendixlike," it is difficult not simply to substitute the word "woman" for "natural pregnancy" since woman is **defined** in heterosexual erotic and reproductive terms under patriarchy.[23] Clearly, then, this is the limiting case of cultural domination: a complete population of sterilized women whose reproductive powers have simultaneously been stolen and destroyed in the same act of political violence.

I believe that what we have in this context is parallel to what happened during the persecution of women as witches. Allegations of insanity, neurosis and bizarre sexual tendencies were made against women by men who tortured them to make "confessions" and who themselves took pleasure both in the narration and in the torture. The judgement of patriarchal history is that the women were largely crazy and their persecutors normal. The judgement of feminist history is just the reverse.[24] Similarly, I hold that with respect to the reproductive technologists, the technologists themselves should be the target of distrust, critique and subordination, and not those women who are fighting to hang on to some goal of reproductive integrity and who are resisting the fragmentation, the reductionism and the messages of pathology.

Coerced Voluntariness

A third form of cultural domination takes place when women struggle to exercise what they are told is "free" choice in a context of coerced voluntariness. In her discussion of Rowland's article, Raymond points out that often the aspects of coercion and control are camouflaged by language and practice that is characterized as benevolent, therapeutic and voluntaristic.[25] She notes that the technologists will either report that their patients want access to technology or insist on some principle of liberal individualism (for example, parents have the right to choose the sex of their child) without examining the social and political context which, as she puts it, "… not only conditions a woman's choices but her motivation to choose as well. This is what one might want to call a voluntaristic means of behaviour control and modification."[26]

What is the importance of focusing on the context? I argue that it is twofold: one, it brings into prominence the extent to which many women continue to live under and are dominated by a situation we might call "obligatory fertility" or "compulsory motherhood"; and, two, it renders visible the extent to which women act in accord with a powerful technological imperative from the moment of conception through birthing itself.[27] If we add to these two coercive aspects of women's lives the struggle to maintain a sense of self in the light of the already discussed aspects of psychological oppression, it is not difficult to make the case that the experience of appearing to make a choice is, at best, only partially real. And in many cases, material, psychological, economic and political forms of coercion are explicit.

The ideology of obligatory fertility and the definition of women in terms of reproductive destiny and fulfilment is one of the most powerfully oppressive psychological forces bearing down on married heterosexual women of childbearing age (particularly if they are white in a white supremacist culture such as Canada).[28] Moreover, as conception, maternity and birthing are brought further and further into the domain of productive activity (as contrasted with natural "happening"), reproduction becomes conceptualized as an area of potential "achievement" for women (and its absence a domain of blameworthy "failure" rather than a sad but natural event).

For those women for whom opportunities for achievement are severely limited, fertility and childbearing continue to be seen as forms of achievement. As more and more achievement is expected from women and broader opportunities for achievement are fought for by women, biological motherhood continues to be seen as obligatory by the liberated or independent woman as well. Under patriarchy, pronatalist maternal ideology makes the conceiving and bearing of children definitional of the "true" woman, the "complete" woman, the "good" woman and, now, the "Superwoman." Like success at heterosexual romantic affiliation, childbearing is bound up with and defined by the culture as the proper form of power, the locus of identity and the guarantee of a woman's womanliness.

For a woman who has internalized that message and whose life manifests the material construction of that ideology so that her childbearing is the key both to her survival and her sense of social identity and place, fighting the pressures of obligatory fertility may lead to her feeling and being desexualized, devalued and identityless in relation to her social world.[29] Often, internalization of the assumption of obligatory fertility expresses itself more clearly in feelings of emptiness, lack of identity and worthlessness associated with not bearing a child than in the desire to have a child, a desire which has many varied and deep roots. In both cases, however, it is clear that the psychological and socioeconomic pressures associated with obligatory fertility are lived out by virtually all women and that whatever choice is made here is affected by these pressures.[30]

A second way in which the voluntary aspect of reproductive choices by women is eroded is through submission to the technological imperatives of the medical establishment.[31] This argument has been convincingly made with respect to the medical technologizing of birthing. It is important to make it in this context as well since the technology is often ordered or recommended in the name of enhanced choice. In one sense, the advance of the technologies is making more choices possible. A woman can now choose the sex of her child, can choose to abort a baby with spina bifida, can choose to have a Caesarean section if indicated by the fetal monitor and so on. The technologies would seem to hold out the promise of greater control, greater options and avoidance of painful, unliveable consequences: in short, greater promise for a genuinely human life of social mothering. In some ways this cannot be denied.

However, as Rothman, Rowland and Hanmer have all argued, much of this freedom is illusory.[32] In reality, actual participation in the patriarchal technologies leads to the consequence that although one's own inner experience feels like that of autonomous choice, the reality of one's world is that one becomes increasingly dependent on a veritable empire of medical experts which may include fetologists, gynecologists, endocrinologists, psychiatrists, anesthesiologists, research scientists and pharmacologists.[33] And it is this group of experts who will create, monitor and bring into existence the desired child, the new life, not the biological mother. Parallel to the medicalizing of birthing as a "crisis event," both informal pressure on women to seek out the reproductive technologies and expert pressure to submit to every invasive procedure of infertility testing, in vitro fertilization experimentation and pregnancy monitoring support the patriarchal cultural domination of the experience. Thus, while women are encouraged to think that this is a choice-maximizing situation, it often turns out to be precisely the reverse. Women are devalued and infantilized, and knowledge and fear are used as coercive levers to bring about the submission of women to the technologies controlled by men.

The upshot of these experiences of devaluation, these allegations of pathology, and these illusory promises of reproductive choice is that women are coming under further psychological oppression as the patriarchal control of women's reproduction takes on more radical and complete forms.

SEXUAL OBJECTIFICATION

Bartky defines sexual objectification as a mode of fragmentation which takes the "...form of an often-coerced and degrading identification of a person with her body".[34] Just as women have to fight against the degrading identification of themselves with parts of their body in the area of sexuality (for example, as "cunt," "piece of ass," etc.) so, too, must women fight against the psychologically oppressive objectifications of themselves in the area of reproduction.

Embodied women have a right to bodily integrity. The first way in which sexual objectification is oppressive to women is through loss of integrity. This integrity is threatened by often repeated procedures such as superovulation, surgical interventions requiring anesthetics, puncturing with needles to search for eggs that are ripening, invasion of the uterus with canulas in the case of chorionic villi sampling and embryo implantations, and other diagnostic tests including amniocentesis and multiple ultrasounds. These processes often culminate in further surgical intervention and anesthetics through Caesarean section births. The experience of women who undergo these dangerous, potentially traumatizing invasions of their bodies is reflected in feelings of manipulation, assault, personal infantilization, physical pain, anxiety and failure. Values of autonomy, bodily integrity, reproductive control and choice are destroyed as the medical conglomerate, family, friends, spouses, and often the woman herself, become increasingly fixated on the achievement of fertility. Humiliation, subordination and sadistic medical practices are often camouflaged as altruistic treatment and therapy.[35]

The second way in which sexual objectification is oppressive is in the personal and collective dissection, dismembering and marketing of women's reproductive powers.[36] An individual woman experiences the fragmentation of the integrated experience of fertility as she, personally, comes to be seen as a "difficult" assemblage of organs and processes, some of which may be malfunctioning.[37] This fragmentation takes place not only at the individual level. At the collective level the new reproductive technologies are conceptualizing conception, maternity and birthing as separable stages of reproduction as they already are in the context of animal husbandry. The process of biological motherhood is literally being dismembered as one woman comes to be valued for her "high quality" ova; a second for her usefulness as a temporary incubator during the early stages of the pregnancy; yet a third for her utility as the long-term incubator subsequent to embryo flushing and transfer. And a fourth woman may be targeted as the appropriate social rearer of the child. The psychological upshot of this is that women, medical researchers and technical practitioners are coming to motherhood in a radically different way: it becomes a collective noun, a collective experience that is intrinsically socially contructed so as to "optimize" the outcome for the child.

As we move more towards this Fragmentation Model of biological motherhood, we can see that the potential for the biological, economic and political exploitation of women and women's bodies is enormous. What is psychologically oppressive about this process is that we are losing any sense of integrity with respect to our own bodies as childbearing bodies; we are simultaneously becoming more reproductively defined at the same time as that definition becomes more dangerously anatomized.[38] We are losing the individual sense of creativity and power that can accompany chosen motherhood, and are being regarded as, at best, fragmentary or partial breeders.

The final scenario of a reductionist nightmare is already with us. I am not speaking here of future scenarios such as ectogenesis and cloning which involve the elimination of biological motherhood altogether. I am speaking of the cases of pregnant brain-dead women who have been kept alive until the fetus was sufficiently mature to be delivered. In one case the woman was kept alive for over two months while the fetus matured.[39] She was kept on support systems until a Caesarean section could be performed, then the life-support systems were removed. In commenting on the case, Dr. Russell Laros of the Department of Obstetrics, Gynecology and Reproductive Sciences at the University of California School of Medicine in San Francisco said, "The experience left me with real confidence that this can be done without any great difficulties.... In the future, I'll suggest to family members that the option is there."[40] Again, whether we consider the prospect of partial ectogenesis through removing mature ovaries from women or through raising female embryos for ova, or whether we consider using the bodies of dead women as (albeit expensive) incubators, the twisted annihilation of the reality of biological motherhood is such that both women who are yet to be born and women who are dead may be politically preferable to women who wish to become independent mothers with a sense of integrity and choice.

This picture is a terrifying one but one we must look at. Otherwise we may fail to see how profoundly these technologies are altering our feelings, our hopes, and the very way we think about motherhood. As conception and maternity move out of the patriarchal categories of the pre-human, the instinctual, the uncontrollable and unpredictable into the domain of technological artefact, patriarchal science is radically reconceptualizing not only the process itself but also the nature of woman and mother in such a way that a patriarchal exclusively male utopia becomes increasingly realizable within the domain of science.

Throughout the world, feminists are calling for the reempowerment of women and the importance of women generating both the knowledge and the political and material control of our own fertility. As I have argued, it is also crucial to fight for psychological control so that we are able, as Adrienne Rich points out, "to recognize the full complexity and political significance *of the woman's body,* the full spectrum of power and powerlessness it represents, of which motherhood is simply one – though a crucial – part."[Emphasis added.][41] Women are central to the fight for choice and the right to reproductive self-determination, women who are dreaming, speaking and creating new visions, perhaps technological in nature, so that we can "… release the creation and sustenance of life into the same realm of decision, struggle, surprise, imagination, and conscious intelligence, as any other difficult but freely chosen work."[42] Without such struggles, we and our daughters may well be the silenced victims of the coming gynocide.[43]

NOTES

1 Adrienne Rich, *Of Woman Born: Motherhood as Experience and Institution* (New York, W.W. Norton and Co., 1976), p. 11.

2 Robyn Rowland, "Motherhood, Patriarchal Power, Alienation, and the Issue of 'Choice' in Sex Pre-Selection" in Gena Corea *et al.,* eds., *Man-Made Women* (Bloomington, Indiana, Indiana University Press, 1987), p. 75.

3 Rona Achilles distinguishes reproductive technologies on the basis of their function in relation to life. She categorizes three kinds: those that inhibit new life, those that monitor new life, and those involved in the creation of new life. See Rona Achilles, "What's New about the New Reproductive Technologies?" Discussion Paper, Ontario Advisory Council on the Status of Women, 1988, p. 1.

4 For a disturbing account of how patriarchal mystification is engineered through the media, see the paper by Ana Regina Gomez Dos Reis, "IVF in Brazil: The Story told by the Newspapers" in P. Spallone, D. Steinberg, eds., *Made to Order: the Myth of Reproductive and Genetic Progress* (New York, Pergamon Press, 1987).

5 This analysis is, of course, only part of a much larger collective feminist critique. Many of the other central moral and political issues are discussed by Susan Sherwin in this volume: the (over-)medicalization of

contraception, conception and childbirth and the medical risks involved; the inequity of access and distribution of reproductive technological benefits; the form of political coercion and economic exploitation of women that are generated by the new technologies; and dangerous eugenicist implications involved along with the correlative social intolerance toward the disabled and those women who choose not to use the technologies.

6 Sandra Bartky, "On Psychological Oppression" in S. Bishop, M. Weinzweig, eds., *Philosophy and Women* (Belmont, California, Wadsworth Publishing Co., 1979), pp. 33-41. I am, of course, not denying that there can be individual, soul-destroying personal forms of psychological oppression sometimes referred to as "mental cruelty."

7 Rich, op. cit., p. 110.

8 Janice Raymond, "Fetalists and Feminists" in *Made To Order,* op. cit., p. 62.

9 Erica Jong, *Ordinary Miracles* (New York, New American Library, 1983). Phrases are taken from the following poems: "The Birth of the Water Baby" and "For Molly."

10 Corea, "The Reproductive Brothel" in *Man-Made Women,* op. cit., pp. 42-43.

11 *Cf.* Ibid.; Gena Corea, *The Mother Machine* (New York, Harper and Row, 1985); and Andrea Dworkin, *Right-Wing Women* (New York, G. P. Putnam's Sons, 1982).

12 Julie Murphy, "Egg Farming and Women's Future" in Rita Arditti, Renate Duelli Klein, Shelley Minden, eds., *Test-Tube Women: What Future for Motherhood?* (London, Pandora Press, 1984).

13 This is the figure cited by Murphy. Ibid.

14 Ibid., p. 70.

15 Ibid., p. 73.

16 Janice Raymond, "Preface" to *Man-Made Women,* op. cit.

17 Tabitha Powledge, "Unnatural Selection: On Choosing Children's Sex" in Helen B. Holmes, Betty B. Hoskins, Michael Gross, eds., *The Custom-Made Child: Woman-Centered Perspectives* (Clifton, New Jersey, The Humana Press, 1981).

18 Robyn Rowland, "Of Woman Born, But For How Long? The Relationship of Women to the New Reproductive Technologies and the Issue of Choice" in *Man-Made Women,* op. cit., p. 75.

19 In her discussion of this issue in *The Mother Machine*, op. cit., Corea entitles her chapter "The Artificial Womb: an Escape from the 'Dark and Dangerous Place.'"

20 Frederick Leboyer, *Birth Without Violence* (New York, Alfred A. Knopf, 1975). This passage is discussed both by Adrienne Rich in "The Theft of Childbirth" in C. Dreifus, ed., *Seizing Our Bodies* (New York, Vintage Books, 1977) and in *OurBodies, OurSelves,* 3rd edition (New York, Simon and Schuster, 1984).

21 Reported by Robyn Rowland in "A Child at ANY Price?" *Women's Studies International Forum,* vol. 8, no. 6 (1985), pp. 542-543.

22 Reported by Connie Clement, "Science Fiction / Science Fact," *Healthsharing,* vol. 6, no. 4 (Fall 1985), p. 18.

23 Rowland, op. cit.

24 See Mary Daly, *Gyn-Ecology: The Metaethics of Radical Feminism* (Boston, Beacon Press, 1978), pp. 211-212.

25 Raymond, op. cit., p. 11.

26 Ibid.

27 I am adopting Achilles' use of the notion of a "technological imperative." See Achilles, op. cit., p. 28.

28 Clearly, reverse forms of coercion, ones forbidding fertility, are often experienced by women whom a racist, heterosexist, patriarchal culture marginalizes and stigmatizes in some way: lesbians, disabled women, unmarried teenage women (and unmarried women in general), women who are "too old," Native women, Women of Colour, and so on. From within their own communities, however, such women may experience equally intense pressures to bear children.

29 This thesis is brilliantly analyzed in a paper by Martha Gimenez, "Feminism, Pronatalism, and Motherhood" in J. Trebilcot, ed., *Mothering: Essays in Feminist Theory* (Totowa, New Jersey, Rowman and Allanheld, 1984). Similar points are made by Sandra Bartky in relation to femininity in Bartky's paper, "Foucault, Femininity, and the Modernization of Patriarchal Power" in I. Diamond, L. Quinby, eds., *Femininity and Foucault* (Boston, Northeastern University Press, 1988); and by Kathryn Morgan in relation to romantic love in "Romantic Love, Altruism, and Self-Respect," *Hypatia,* vol. 1, no. 1 (1986), reprinted in G. Nemiroff, ed., *Women and Men* (Toronto, Fitzhenry and Whiteside, 1986).

30 For a spirited and moving defence by a feminist who lives in a situation of class and race privilege, see Margaret Simons' paper "Motherhood, Feminism, and Identity," *Women's Studies International Forum,* vol.7, no. 5 (1984), pp. 349-360.

31 Achilles, op. cit., p. 28.

32 *Cf.* Jalna Hanmer, "A Womb of One's Own" and Barbara Katz Rothman, "The Meanings of Choice in Reproductive Technology" in *Test-Tube Women,* op. cit., and Robyn Rowland, "Motherhood, Patriarchal Power ..." in *Man-Made Women,* op. cit.

33 I am grateful to Janice Raymond for making this point in relation to the aspirations for transcendence and the undermining conditions of dependence in the context of transsexual surgery. See Raymond, *The Transsexual Empire: The Making of the She-Male* (Boston, Beacon Press, 1979).

34 Bartky, "On Psychological Oppression," op. cit., p. 34.

35 Raymond, "Fetalists and Feminists ..."in *Made to Order,* op. cit., p. 61.

36 Renate Duelli Klein, "What's 'New' about the 'New' Reproductive Technologies?" in *Man-Made Women,* op. cit., p. 65.

37 Of course, this isn't always true. In cases of sex preselection and in vitro fertilization, perfectly healthy women may be involved in submitting to these dangerous procedures.

38 For a terrifying "fictional" account of this see Margaret Atwood's *The Handmaid's Tale* (Toronto, McClelland and Stewart, 1985).

39 This case is described by Rowland in "Motherhood, Patriarchal Power ..." in *Man-Made Women,* op. cit.

40 Russell Laros, *Obstetrics, Gynecology News,* vol. 18, no. 11 (1983).

41 Rich, op. cit., p. 283.

42 Ibid., p. 280.

43 I am adopting this phrase from Andrea Dworkin's essay by that name in *Right-Wing Women* (New York, G.P. Putnam's Sons, 1983).

WHEN IS BIOLOGY DESTINY?

Thelma McCormack

It is no longer adequate for the Women's Liberation Movement to focus primarily on abortion and secondarily on issues around childbirth ... there is a knockout punch coming from another direction.

Jalna Hanmer and Pat Allen,
"Reproductive Engineering: The Final Solution?"
in *Alice Through the Miscroscope,* p. 227.

Five thousand days and twenty million lives later, abortion on demand has buried a nation of children as big as the whole of Canada.

Lewis Lehrman,
"The Right to Life and the Restoration of the Constitution,"
National Review, 29 August 1986, p. 26.

The Vatican's recent document condemning all forms of conception but marital intercourse was ... right about one thing. You don't have the right to a child, any more than you have a right to a spouse. You only have the right to try to have one. Goods can be distributed according to the ability to pay or need. People can't.

It is really simple.

Katha Pollitt,
"The Strange Case of Baby M,"
The Nation, 23 March 1987, p. 688.

I

On 10 March 1987 the Vatican released a text stating the Church's opposition to the new reproductive technologies. *Instruction on Respect for Human Life in its Origin and on the Dignity of Procreation: Replies to Certain Questions of the Day* condemned any form of procreation outside of the "natural" form of sexual intercourse between lawful husband and wife. It acknowledged the problems of sterility and infertility, and approved medical treatment wherever possible, but artificial methods of procreation such as in vitro fertilization (IVF), donor insemination or surrogate parenting were all equally unacceptable. Bearing children and the act of conjugal love must be one.

Governments, according to the Vatican, have an obligation to control the activities of scientists who, for purposes of scientific enquiry, experiment with human embryos.[1] Apart from the observation of embryos, all such activities should be regarded as illegal, an immoral interference with the absolute inviolability of life. Governments which hesitate to control science for fear of politicizing it will ultimately be controlled.[2]

Catholic clergy and lay scholars have varied in their reaction to the Vatican text, ranging from those who approved of it with no reservations, to Professor Daniel Maguire, professor of moral theology at Marquete University, Wisconsin, who described it as "another example of celibate men pronouncing on the reproductive rights of women, when women's voices have not been heard."[3] The Archbishop of Cincinnati defended the document. "There is no right," he said, "to have a child any more than there is a right to destroy a child. The fact that these are loving persons of deep goodwill may make them ideal candidates for God's gift of a child, but it does not give them the right to play God, or to induce others to play God on their behalf."[4] Professor Sidney Callahan, writing in *Commonweal,* disagreed. It is ethically appropriate, she said, for couples to use alternative reproductive technologies: or, at least, for *some* couples: "a normal, socially adequate, heterosexual married couple."[5]

Catholic spokespersons and Catholic scholars, then, are not all in agreement, but their differences should not obscure the common theme among them – the sanctity of the traditional *family*. They differ only on the question of means, not ends. For that reason Catholic hospitals, at least in Europe, indicated that they would continue to operate as they had been operating. In France, the deputy rector of the Catholic University of Lille said, "We accept the Vatican document, except for that part which deals with in vitro fertilization obtained with the sperm and the ova of the parents."[6]

Practising Catholics may also interpret the Vatican text liberally: the pressure to have children is so great and the shortage of babies available for adoption so acute that couples who qualify for IVF will ignore it and find their own rationalizations for doing so. "If God hadn't wanted us to use this technology," one woman said, "he wouldn't have given it to us."[7]

There is, then, an increasing demand for the treatment created by the continuing centrality of the family, the idealization of motherhood, and dearth of babies available for adoption. On the supply side, there are hospitals with large investments, both financial and reputational, in their high-tech infertility clinics. This combination of supply and demand means that in the absence of any very strong countervailing pressures the Vatican's dicta to scientists and its dire warnings to legislators may be disregarded.

The countervailing pressures could come from a feminist discourse which puts the fertility debate in a political context where the sanctity of the nuclear family is itself contested.[8] Until recently, however, feminists, both in theory and action, have concentrated on the problems of fertility, and in particular the right of women to terminate an unwanted pregnancy. Less attention was given to infertility which was sometimes seen as a blessing in disguise and an opportunity to direct a woman's energies elsewhere. Besides, in an already over-crowded planet this was no time for misguided pronatalism. Typical of the attitude was a recent conference on the new reproductive technologies (sponsored by the Quebec Conseil du statut de la femme) where one of the workshops posed the following set of biased questions:

> Does the right to have a child really exist? Can the desire to have a child become unreasonable stubbornness? … Why do we no longer tolerate infertility?[9]

Although the new reproductive technology is sometimes welcomed as permitting single and lesbian women to have children without husbands – clearly a plus for women – feminist literature is overwhelmingly in the other direction. Reproductive technologies are analyzed as further examples of medical abuse, class-gender exploitation and the victimization of women.[10] Reading between the lines, there is often a suspicion of science and a distrust of technology as part of the male hegemony. The result has been the projection of a number of very alarmist scenarios and speculations about what could happen based on technological determinism.

Technological determinism, however, makes for bad sociology and worse feminism. If the question is about reproductive freedom – whether women realize more or less choice, more or less control – the answer lies elsewhere in the social structure. The parameters of reproductive choice are set by the evaluation we put on motherhood and the broader normative system which maintains and keeps it operative, while the parameters of control are determined by institutional access and the gatekeepers who select those who are eligible. In the background, one step removed, is the liberal state with its long-term interests in economic growth based on science and technology, as well as its population policies.

In the comments that follow, I want to look at the construction of reproductive freedom, both choice and control, and suggest two things: first, that as feminists, we need a broader, more inclusive, paradigm which incorporates both abortion and reproductive technology. Second, we need a framework which is consistent, so that we do not say to one group of women, "Biology is not destiny," and to another, "Alas, biology is destiny." In this conceptual scheme, infertility and the desire to have a child is a feminist issue and not a form of foolish intransigence. Second, although the new reproductive technology is not intrinsically anti-woman, there has been very little change with respect to choice and control. It is sexual politics that determines technology, not the other way around. In the concluding section, I want to outline the alternative paradigm and indicate some guidelines for a feminist perspective that would integrate feminist thinking on both abortion and reproductive technology.[11]

II

Our ideal of motherhood is communicated to us through symbolic systems; that is, through images, narratives and homiletic anecdotes based on good mothers and bad, fit and unfit. The former are stable, married, middle-class women who wish to stay at home and raise a family, but are unable to conceive; they are eminently "childworthy."[12] And their involuntary childlessness elicits our sympathy. In every other way, these women conform to the pattern of conventional wives supported by spouses.[13] At the other extreme is the negative image of the pregnant teenager or the pregnant mature woman who puts her child at risk by alcoholism or some form of substance abuse.[14] Because these women are child-unworthy, they are encouraged to abort, or, in the extreme, the state may take a tougher policy by removing the child, once born, from the care of its mother.

Supporting this binary model of motherhood is an evaluative system based on a hierarchy of motives, ranging from sacred to profane. Not all women have the same moral entitlement to either abortion or existing reproductive services. Among those seeking abortion, the most deserving are the tragedies – a woman who has been raped or a pregnancy which has occurred as a result of incest. At the other end of the continuum and engendering the least compassion are cases of expedience; that is, women who for their own private reasons do not wish to carry the pregnancy to term. Cases of fetal damage lie somewhere between the two, and there is a great deal of soul-searching by feminists and others on the ethics of aborting a fetus where there is some evidence of retardation or physical handicap.[15] (Failure of public authorities to provide the necessary support systems for children who need continual care may lead to reluctant abortions and subsequent guilt.) For the large group of women, however, whose reasons for seeking an abortion are economic, there is very little emotional support. At best, there is tolerance and a message that scarce resources are being used by people whose decisions are legal, but hardly edifying.

A similar hierarchy and a similar notion of scarcity (and what they both imply for a system of social control) operate in our thinking about infertility. We differentiate between women whose infertility is medically established and women who have other nonmedical reasons for noncoital procreation. Cutting across this is another division based on whether or not a third party is involved. Both surrogate parenting and donor insemination evoke more negative judgement and are more controversial than in vitro fertilization or artificial insemination by husband. Surrogate parenting, because it involves a legal contract and a payment of money, arouses the strongest sentiments; it is the quintessentially profane, the cynical denial of the sacredness of motherhood. Both parties, the mother who seeks a child and the mother who carries it, are perceived as having broken some unspoken pact about the value of human life.[16] And in both the U.K. and the U.S. there are pressures to make it illegal.

In summary, then, the new technology of reproduction has been accommodated and integrated within the existing system of choice. What appears to some to be liberating, and to others repressive, is neither.

III

In theory, there might be the same degree of *choice* but more *control,* a situation which many women might interpret positively. However, the control over reproduction is itself controlled by a biomedical model of pregnancy and infertility. Both are defined as medical disorders requiring specialized services: medical and psychological counseling, and in some situations, legal assistance. In effect, then, healthy women become sick and dependent on the approval and the authority of others: a hospital therapeutic committee, an IVF screening committee, social workers and judges who serve as the gatekeepers. This lesson was driven home recently when doctors who were on strike in Ontario over "extra billing" threatened to cancel scheduled abortions and delay reviews by therapeutic abortion committees.

A recent case in Alberta illustrates how these various professionals are involved. A sixteen-year-old girl, one of eight children in a Mormon family, became pregnant. Her parents agreed to let her have an abortion if she could find someone who would do it. She did, but after the abortion committee in Medicine Hat passed her application, her parents refused to sign the consent. Shortly after, she attempted to take her own life.[17] When she recovered, she was referred to the Legal Aid Society of Alberta in Calgary where she was assigned a legal guardian. In her sixteenth week of pregnancy the girl was once again booked for the procedure but her parents sought a court injunction to prevent it. Her lawyer argued that the injunction was discrimination against minors, and the injunction was quashed. The parents persisted, and appealed the decision. Three judges who reviewed the case rejected their appeal. So, in the nineteenth week of pregnancy, well into the second trimester, the girl had the abortion.[18]

The outcome of this prolonged, costly and extraordinary struggle between parents on the one hand, and the social workers and legal professionals on the other, could only have taken place in an ideological atmosphere that treats teenage pregnancy as undesirable and preventable.[19] According to the statistics, there is a high probability that a teenage mother will drop out of school and become a long-term public charge, with the child (subsequent children) eventually becoming part of the cycle of poverty and child abuse.[20] Thus, the state which attempts to solve its poverty problem through population policies can limit the options available. These in turn influence the thinking and philosophy of the helping professions. It is useful to remember also that the state, through education and licensing, disciplines and limits the number of professionals.

The dependency of women can be seen, too, in how fertility clinics make decisions. Unlike other branches of medicine, a patient may be turned away for social or psychological reasons. In a study of Ontario physicians who carry out IVF procedures, a third indicated that they would not treat unmarried couples, and almost all said that if there was any indication of ambivalence, they would not treat the persons. However, what the doctors were most concerned about was the consent of husbands; all of them agreed that this was essential even though it is women who endure the tests, take the risks and suffer the trauma of failure.[21]

In summary, the subordinate position of women is sustained, in part, by a focus on conception as an act endowed with social meaning and an elaborate system of norms. A perfect mother conceives through the natural method and, despite her own health and convenience, carries the fetus to term. Women who are unable to handle their pregnancy experiences privately and who seek help come under the

scrutiny of society where they are judged by rules which
ensure that these women understand that such assistance is
scarce and given only in special cases. In effect, both the infertile woman and the pregnant teenager are "social problems."
The gatekeepers who express these values have the penulti-
mate power to control access to the services.

IV

Given the existing images of motherhood and the judgements
made about them, and bearing in mind the medical context of
reproduction, women gain, at most, a few degrees of freedom
through the new reproductive technology. Modern genetics
and its related technology have given us certain benefits. The
woman who postpones a pregnancy until her late thirties can
worry less; the woman who wants children and has been
unable to have them through conventional ways now has a
better chance. But these are weighed against the cost, the risk
of side effects, and the low rates of success.[22]

Eventually, the methods will be improved, the costs
lowered and the rate of success increased so that the test of
this new technology will be whether it reinforces the traditional family and the idealization of motherhood or contributes to a change – a change that would further a more diverse
system of families, greater division of labour between parents,
and more collective responsibility for children by the community. Until these traditional images and values are radically dis-
lodged, women are not likely to have significantly more
choice or control.

Nevertheless, this does not justify the neo-Malthusian
responses of feminists to women who are being, as the Montreal conference suggested, "unreasonably stubborn" in their
desire to have a child. It was not long ago that a woman who
was pregnant and determined to procure an abortion despite
the physical risks was similarly seen as irrational. I want to

conclude then by indicating the propositional basis for a unified theory.

1. *Inferility is a feminist issue.* Reproductive freedom means the right of all women to manage their own fertility. This includes the right to have children, as evidenced by our deep abhorrence towards enforced sterilization of women and coercive infanticide, which are violations of human rights. On the basis of that definition of reproductive freedom, the unwanted pregnancy became a feminist issue; on the same grounds, infertility is a feminist issue, and the women for whom it is most salient are not to be denigrated, patronized or perceived as over-socialized.

2. *All women are both fertile and infertile.* To develop a unified perspective, we need to replace our current discourse based on two separate attitudes towards abortion and assisted reproduction with a single proposition based on fertility and infertility. Implicit in this is a recognition that these are normal stages in the life cycle of all women. There are, then, no longer two classes of women, but women on a fertility-infertility continuum. At different points in her life a woman might require different services such as abortion in her adolescent years. Later, donor insemination, followed possibly by abortion in her later years. In her mind the rationale for these is the same.

3. *Universal access and the myth of scarcity.* The highest rates of infertility in the U.S. are among Blacks and low income groups, while those who use the infertility clinics tend to be white and middle class.[23] But economic and racial discrimination are only part of a larger pattern of discrimination which denies many groups, including unmarried or lesbian women, the services available to others. Whether we call these services social or medical, access to them should not be restricted by male authority, marital status, income, race or sexual identity. By making access universal, we would also

demystify the process and change the role of gatekeepers to facilitators.

4. *Free-standing clinics for both abortion and infertility services.* Finally, although we cannot hope to demedicalize either abortion or reproduction totally – and there may be sound reasons for maintaining the connection – we can insist on removing them from the atmosphere of hospitals and the sick-role relationship.[24] Free-standing clinics should be available for both abortion and infertility services. The free-standing clinic is more likely to provide wider access since hospitals are more apt to be responsive to local political pressures.[25]

These, then, are a minimal set of foundational guidelines and are presented here primarily to indicate the importance of a unified feminist perspective on abortion and reproductive services.

We began this discussion with the Vatican statement. The logical strength of the Vatican's position is its consistency, and no doubt it will continue to oppose both abortion and the use of reproductive technologies. In contrast, the liberal state is flexible; it permits both abortion and reproductive services on a selective basis and preserves both the authority and autonomy of its professional elites. At the same time, in countries like Canada it keeps an eye on health-care costs. But either way – the Vatican's total ban or the liberal state's selective approval – patriarchy remains intact: in one case we have patriarchy based on religious dogma; in the other it is based on the power and privileged status of the guardian gatekeepers. We should never underestimate the historical and intellectual importance of that distinction, but the consequences for the social psychology of women are pretty much the same. Our revolution of rising expectations has followed a different trajectory.

For feminists then the challenge is to confront patriarchy without overreacting to technology and the predictions made on the basis of that technology – which often produce more heat than light. And in our unending battle against sexist stereotypes, it is just as important not to create a new stereotype of women who wish to have children and who voluntarily put themselves through an agonizing procedure. Like their counterparts who seek abortion services, they may indeed be coerced by male partners and influenced by other extraneous considerations. But denying them the services and criminalizing them by prohibitive legislation is a dangerous course. My purpose here, however, was not to argue for or against the wisdom or feasibility of specific legislative proposals, but rather to propose a different paradigm. By adopting a unified perspective, we reject a "we-they" morality and affirm our own solidarity.

NOTES

1 Since the 1970s, there has been a ban on federal support for fetal research in the U.S.

2 *Origins,* 19 March 1987, pp. 708-709.

3 *The New York Times,* 11 March 1987, p. 13.

4 The most Reverend Daniel E. Pilarczyk, "Taking It on the Chin – for Life: Reflections on a Vatican Instruction," *America,* 11 April 1987, p. 296.

5 Sidney Callahan, "Lovemaking and Babymaking," *Commonweal,* vol. CXIV, no. 8, 24 April 1987.

6 "In Sight," *America,* 11 April 1987. The Catholic University of Louvain (Belgium) and the Catholic University of Nijmegen (Netherlands) have indicated that they will continue to offer in vitro services, and it is expected that Catholic hospitals in Canada will too.

7 *The Globe and Mail,* 14 March 1987, sec. A, p.9. This was a Catholic woman from Newfoundland who had no fallopian tubes and spent several weeks at the Toronto General Hospital.

8 Margrit Eichler in a forthcoming paper makes the point that the intervention by the medical profession is to protect the family since women with infertile husbands could easily conceive through adultery. It is to restrict adultery that we have artificial insemination by unknown

donor. Margrit Eichler, (forthcoming) "New Reproductive Technologies," *Families in Canada Today. Recent Changes and their Policy Consequences* (Toronto, Gage), second enlarged and revised edition.

9 *Maternity in the Laboratory,* International Forum on New Reproductive Technologies (Concordia University), 29, 30, 31 Oct. 1987, p. 7.

10 Susan Robinson M.D. and H.F. Pizer, *Having a Baby without a Man,* (New York, Fireside, 1985). For the critics of reproductive technology the following articles and collections are representative: Rita Arditti, Renate Duelli Klein and Shelley Minden, eds., *Test-Tube Women: What Future for Motherhood?* (London, Pandora 1984); Linda Birk *et al., Alice Through the Microscope,* (London, Virago, 1980); Gena Corea, *The Mother Machine,* (New York, Harper & Row, 1985); Margrit Eichler, "New Reproductive Technologies," *Families in Canada*; Jalna Hanmer, "Reproductive Technology: The Future for Women?" in Joan Rothschild, ed., *Machina ex Dea* (New York, Pergamon, 1983); Helen B. Holmes, Betty B. Hoskins and Michael Gross, eds., *The Custom-Made Child. Woman-Centered Perspectives* (Clifton, New Jersey, The Humana Press, 1981); Robyn Rowland "Technology and Motherhood: Reproductive Choice Reconsidered," *Signs,* vol. 12, no. 3 (1987).

11 Like many people doing research in this field, I have been interested in the questions of ethics raised by bioethicists and by feminist philosophers. Although I am unable – for reasons of space – to comment on the questions they raise, I want to acknowledge my debt to Sue Sherwin and Eileen Manion.

12 R. Snowden and G.D. Mitchell, *The Artificial Family* (London, George Allen & Unwin, 1981).

13 It is ironic that among couples who apply for IVF, the husband may have been divorced; childlessness is a stigma, especially for men for whom it is often confused with lack of virility. In a British study of couples who had participated in DI, about ten percent had been married before, and "it was three times as likely for husbands to be in second marriages than wives." R. Snowden, G.D. Mitchell and E.M. Snowden, *Artificial Reproduction: A Social Investigation* (London, George Allen & Unwin, 1983), p. 71.

14 Coffee consumption, smoking and over-the-counter pain killers have been found to carry a risk to the fetus. In Canada, the courts have begun to treat this as "child abuse." In the U.S.S.R., there is a policy of requiring women who are alcoholic or drug addicted to have abortions. Very often, the damage to a child's health through substance abuse is not permanent; with

proper neonatal care and nourishment, the baby can live a full and healthy life.

5 Anne Finger, "Claiming All of our Bodies: Reproductive Rights and Disabilities," in Arditti, Duelli Klein and Minden, eds., *Test-Tube Women*; E. Lapham and Virginia Sheppard, "Living with an Impaired Neonate and Child. A Feminist Issue," in Holmes, Hoskins and Gross, eds., *The Custom-Made Child*; Janice J. Tait, "Reproductive Technology and the Rights of Disabled Persons," *Canadian Journal of Women and the Law,* vol. 1, no. 2 (1986).

16 One of the few studies done of women who volunteer to be surrogate mothers suggests a variety of motives for their action – ranging from an altruistic desire to help someone, to personal guilt about an earlier abortion. Philip J. Parker, "Motivation of Surrogate Mothers: Initial Findings," *American Journal of Psychiatry,* vol. 140, p. 1. The legal discussions tend to be less judgemental. Theodore Benditt, "Surrogate Gestation. Law and Morality," in James M. Humber and Robert F. Almeder, eds., *Biomedical Ethics Reviews* (Clifton, New Jersey, Humana, 1983); Robert C. Black, "Legal Problems of Surrogate Motherhood," *New England Law Review,* vol. 16 (1981), p. 3; Theresa Mady, "Surrogate Mothers: The Legal Issues," *American Journal of Law and Medicine,* vol. 7 (1981), p. 3; Ralph D. Mawdsley, "Surrogate Parenthood: A Need for Legislative Direction," *Illinois Bar Journal* (1983) 412; Andrea E. Stumpf, "Redefining Mother: A Legal Matrix for New Reproductive Technologies," *The Yale Law Journal,* vol. 96 (1986), p. 1. See also Martha Hall, "Rights and the Problem of Surrogate Parenting," *The Philosophical Quarterly,* vol. 35 (1985), p. 141. This was written in response to an article by Dame Mary Warnock opposing surrogate parenting.

17 It turned out that there was no legal reason why she needed them to sign the consent, but hospitals often have their own policies for minors.

18 The details of the case were provided by a physician closely involved in the case. Information about it is also found in *Pro-Choice News* (Winter 1987). Published by Canadian Abortion Rights Action League, (CARAL), Toronto.

19 Frank Furstenberg Jr., *Unplanned Parenthood: The Social Consequences of Teenage Childbearing* (New York, The Free Press, 1976).

20 This is not, of course, irreversible, but the social costs may be high and politically unpopular. See Alan Guttmacher Institute, *Eleven Million Teenagers: What can be done about the Epidemic of Adolescent Pregnancies in the United States?* (New York, 1976); Frank F. Furstenberg

Jr., *Unplanned Parenthood: The Social Consequences of Teenage Childbearing* (New York, The Free Press, 1976); Catherine S. Chillman, ed., *Adolescent Pregnancy and Childrearing: Findings from Research,* (Washington, D.C., U.S. Department of Health, 1980). For a dissenting view see Ester Schuler Buchholz and Barbara Gol, "More than Playing House," *American Journal of Orthopsychiatry,* vol. 56, no. 3 (1986), pp. 347-349.

21 Ontario Law Reform Commission, *Report on Human Artificial Reproduction and Related Matters,* vol. I (1985) p. 23.

22 Ruth Hubbard, "The Case Against In Vitro Fertilization and Implantation" in Holmes, Hoskins and Gross, eds.' *The Custom-Made Child;* Barbara Katz Rothman, "The Meanings of Choice in Reproductive Technology," in Arditti, Duelli Klein and Minden, eds., *Test-Tube Women.*

23 Judith Lorber, "Test-Tube Babies and Sick Roles," Paper given at 82nd Annual Meeting of American Sociological Association, Chicago, Illinois (1987).

24 Monica Boyd, "How the People Feel: Canadian Attitudes on Abortion." Paper presented in the "Fertility, Fertility Regulation and Abortion," section of the 1985 annual meeting of the Canadian Population Society, Montreal (1985).

25 Susan A. McDaniel, "Implementation of Abortion Policy in Canada as a Women's Issue, *Atlantis,* vol. 10, no. 2 (1984). See also Marion Powell, *Report on Therapeutic Abortion Services in Ontario* (1987). Study commissioned by the Ministry of Health. Just recently, Grace Maternity Hospital in Nova Scotia announced it would restrict access to donor insemination to married women only. *Feminist Action* (Nov. 1987).

1938-1988: FIFTY YEARS OF DES – FIFTY YEARS TOO MANY

Harriet Simand

THE YEAR 1988 MARKED the fiftieth anniversary of the creation of the synthetic hormone diethylstilbestrol (DES). During its heyday, millions of women were prescribed this "miracle drug" for a wide variety of purposes, most commonly to prevent miscarriage. Today, the children of these women, as well as the mothers themselves, continue to suffer from a variety of medical problems, ranging from cancer to infertility to pregnancy problems.[1] The story of DES should not be viewed as an historical aberration. Its history, marketing and effects raise many troubling issues that are still applicable concerning the testing of drugs, the long-term health implications of prescribing drugs to healthy women, the medical profession's capability and willingness to deal with iatrogenic problems and the legal implications of new reproductive technology.

HISTORY OF DES

DES is a synthetic estrogen that was first synthesized in a British laboratory by Sir Charles Dodds in 1938.[2] DES was considered a preferable alternative to natural estrogen because it could be administered orally and produced inexpensively. DES was never patented. Consequently, more than three hundred pharmaceutical companies produced DES over a thirty-year period.[3]

In 1939, Eli Lilly & Company (Lilly) and other pharmaceutical companies filed an application with the U.S. Food and

Drug Administration (FDA) to have DES approved. The initial request was refused, but the FDA encouraged Lilly and twelve other manufacturers to pool their resources and submit new studies. Lilly chaired this committee and, in 1941, the FDA approved DES for use in menopausal women, to prevent lactation and to treat breast and prostate cancer. Animal research at this time, however, indicated that mice exposed to DES could develop tumours.[4]

The approval of DES in 1947 to prevent miscarriage was based largely on a study performed by researchers at Harvard University involving women who were prescribed DES.[5] Unfortunately, there was no control group consisting of pregnant women who were not prescribed DES, so the results of this study were scientifically questionable. A double-blind controlled study[6] on the effectiveness of DES by Dr. Dieckmann in 1953 indicated that not only was DES totally ineffective in preventing miscarriage, but that bed rest alone was more effective.[7] Four years after the Dieckmann study was published in the *American Journal of Obstetrics and Gynecology,* an advertisement for DES appeared in the same journal which stated that DES was "recommended for routine use in ALL pregnancies … bigger and stronger babies too." DES was only contraindicated during pregnancy by the FDA in 1971 when it was linked to a rare form of cancer in some of the daughters of women who were prescribed DES.[8]

LEGAL LIABILITY

What protection can the legal system offer to people who have been injured by new technological products or devices? Who is legally liable for the damages suffered by the DES-exposed? The legal difficulties facing DES daughters provide insight into the type of future legal problems that will arise as sophisticated technology becomes more and more involved in the process of reproduction.

As yet, there have been no DES lawsuits launched in

Canada. In order to successfully sue a pharmaceutical company, it is necessary to establish negligence. The plaintiff (the individual launching the suit) must prove on the balance of probabilities that the company inadequately tested the drug, that the DES caused her injury and that the DES was produced by the particular manufacturer being sued.

The plaintiff's difficulty has been in attempting to establish the causal link between the manufacturer and the damage. There is a latency of twenty years between in utero exposure to DES and the appearance of cancer. It is unlikely that many mothers will be able to recall the name of the manufacturer of pills taken decades earlier. Legally, medical records must be retained by physicians for only five to ten years, depending on the province.[9] Records are often lost or destroyed. There have also been an alarming number of reported fires and floods occurring in doctors' offices as soon as there is publicity advising women to verify if they are DES-exposed. Consequently, the vast majority of plaintiffs are unable to name the specific pharmaceutical company which manufactured the DES.

THE AMERICAN SITUATION

Some American courts have dismissed cases in which the defendant could not be identified. Other courts have tried to expand existing theories to accommodate DES-injured plaintiffs or have fashioned remedies of their own. These theories will be briefly examined to understand how the courts can adequately deal with the DES question and the applicability of the American solutions to the Canadian judicial system.

"CONCERT OF ACTION"

Joyce Bichler was a young New York woman who developed clear-cell adenocarcinoma, the vaginal cancer associated with DES. She could not identify the specific manufacturer who produced her mother's pills. She successfully argued in court[10] that the twelve companies who originally applied for the approval of DES acted in concert by inadequately testing the drug. Therefore, they should all be held liable regardless of who actually produced her mother's pills.

This was a novel use of the legal theory of "concert of action." This theory is usually applied in cases, for example, where two cars are drag racing down a street and one car hits a pedestrian. Both drivers can be held jointly liable – even though only one car was responsible for the damage – because they both either expressly or tacitly agreed to participate in a reckless act. "Concert of action" is usually advanced when the identity of the wrongdoer is known and the plaintiff seeks to extend liability to others who participated in the activity, but who may not have caused the harm. In the DES case, it was used to overcome the identification burden altogether.

Many other courts have refused to allow a DES plaintiff to argue "concert of action." The sharing of information and test results is a common industry practice. Some judges fear that manufacturers could be held liable for all defective products manufactured by another industry company, even if that manufacturer could prove definitively that it did not produce the product.[11]

MARKET SHARE LIABILITY

One of the more innovative approaches adopted by the California courts to overcome the DES causation problem was the development of the theory of market share liability. If a DES daughter could not identify the specific manufacturer, she could sue a substantial share of the industry who produced DES. The companies would each be responsible for the percentage of the DES market they occupied at the time the plaintiff's mother took the pills. A company could only escape liability by providing conclusive evidence that it could not have produced the mother's pills. A company that produced sixty percent of the DES on the market would have to pay sixty percent of the damage award. Judges have justified this solution on policy grounds.

> We are faced with a choice of either fashioning a method of recovery for the DES case which will deviate from traditional notions of tort law, or permitting possibly negligent defendants to escape liability to an injured, innocent plaintiff. In the interest of justice and fundamental fairness, we choose to follow the former alternative.[12]

THE CANADIAN SITUATION

There have been no DES lawsuits in Canada even though there are an estimated 200,000 to 400,000 exposed persons.[13] The first issue is whether a DES lawsuit would likely succeed in Canada. The second issue is whether the Canadian court system is the best way to address DES compensation.

The American states as well as every Canadian province, except Quebec, are based on the "common law" system. The American decisions may be relevant to Canadian cases, although Canadian judges are not bound to follow American decisions. Canadian courts have not yet adopted the theory of market share liability. The Supreme Court of Canada, however, has decided a case based on a similar line of reasoning as the California DES cases. In the case of *Cook v. Lewis*,[14] two hunters negligently shot in the direction of a plaintiff who was injured by one of the shots. The plaintiff was unable to determine which hunter was liable for his injuries. The Supreme Court held that as with an innocent plaintiff and two wrongdoers, the hunters should have the burden of proving they were not responsible. If they could not do so, both would be held liable for the plaintiff's injuries. It remains to be seen if Canadian courts would be willing to go one step further and allow the entire pharmaceutical industry to be sued based on each company's respective market share.

There are other reasons why women may be unable to sue

in Canada. Launching such a lawsuit can be extremely expensive. Aside from lawyers' fees, there are the costs of providing expert witnesses to establish the standards of drug testing in the 1940s, and that the DES was the cause of any subsequent injuries. Furthermore, most provinces are based on a winner-take-all system. If the case is unsuccessful, not only is the plaintiff liable for her expenses, but she may also be ordered to cover some or all of her opponent's costs. In a 1984 environmental case in Nova Scotia, several plaintiffs sought to stop the spraying of the herbicide 2,4D (commonly known as "Agent Orange"). Not only was their request for an injunction refused, but they were ordered to pay the defendant's costs of approximately $200,000.[15] Many American lawyers will accept cases on a contingency fee basis. If the case is successful, the lawyer will receive a percentage of the damage award. More importantly, if the case is unsuccessful, the plaintiff is not required to pay costs because the lawyer will absorb the expenses. In some Canadian provinces such as Ontario, this arrangement is not permitted.[16]

Canadian courts are generally more conservative regarding damage amounts awarded. Firstly, most of the medical expenses incurred are covered by Medicare. A DES daughter may claim for emotional damages, but this award is likely to be much lower than in the United States. The Supreme Court has placed a limit on the amount that can be claimed for emotional damages. The possibility exists that the amount that may be received – if the case is successful – will not be substantially more than the cost of launching the lawsuit.

THE CLASS ACTION

A possible solution to overcome these economic barriers is the class action. A "class action" involves one person (the representative plaintiff) suing on behalf of all people who have suffered similar damages. This would minimize costs since there would be only one lawsuit instead of many. Injured

individuals who may not have the resources to sue individually or who were unaware of their right to sue would also be
entitled to claim compensation. Unfortunately, the consumer
class action is virtually impossible in all Canadian provinces
except Quebec.[17] In order to launch a successful "class
action," all DES daughters in the class would have to claim the
same amount of damages. This is unlikely because DES causes
many different medical problems. The severity of the injury
might vary from person to person.

A further solution would be for the government to organize
a fund to compensate DES children. This would occur only
after a massive lobbying campaign which would involve tremendous time and energy, and which might be beyond the
capabilities of an individual victim. This would also entail that
for every new drug or technological problem, the individual,
instead of having recourse to the courts, would have to organize publicity campaigns in an attempt to receive government
compensation. The government is unlikely to act of its own
initiative. Since 1971, when the link between DES and cancer
was established, the Department of Health and Welfare has
issued only one press release advising the public to be
screened if they were DES-exposed. Federal funding became
available only once DES Action, a non-profit women's health
group comprising individuals exposed to DES, was organized
in 1982.

CURRENT IMPLICATIONS

Infertility is becoming a growing issue in today's society. As a
result, medical research is developing a variety of techniques
such as in vitro fertilization (IVF) to overcome the problem.
These discoveries are being hailed as medical breakthroughs.
In the light of the DES experience, several issues should be
considered.

Firstly, what are the long term effects of these treatments?
Will any of the hormones presently being used to induce

ovulation or to assist in embryo transfer, for example, have any long-term effects on the child? The effects of DES appeared only twenty years after exposure in utero to the drug. If there are any ill effects from these new treatments, they are unlikely to appear for decades. Yet, little caution is being expressed about these possibilities. News reports of healthy children being born as a result of new reproductive technology may be misleading – DES children too appeared normal at birth.[18]

Secondly, while tremendous energy and resources are being channelled into organizing IVF clinics, little time or money is being spent to set up DES screening clinics or to publicize the issue.

The priorities of medical research need to be examined. A greater focus should be placed on identifying and eliminating the causes of infertility, rather than simply developing new technological procedures to deal with the problem once it arises. It is ironic that many DES daughters, who are suffering from infertility or pregnancy problems *because* of DES, are now the ones undergoing new infertility treatments. New technology is being touted as the solution to problems created by previous technological mistakes.

Finally, the DES issue has demonstrated that compensation for the DES-exposed has proved difficult, if not impossible, to obtain in Canada. Therefore, we should not be concerned solely with future compensation for victims of other technological errors. Rather, we are faced with rethinking our approach to issues like DES – a wonder drug gone horribly wrong – remembering that caution and prevention are always our first and best options. We should be focusing more on preventing these tragedies from arising instead of expecting legal or medical solutions once the damage has occurred. Among the best vehicles for public education on this issue are grass-roots organization such as *D.E.S. Action Canada*. When people educate and organize themselves, they become best able to identify and confront issues that would otherwise become lost in the workings of larger institutions.

NOTES

Note: Part of this paper was published in the DES Newsletter and is reprinted here with the permission of the Newsletter.

1 R.J. Stillman, "In Utero Exposure to Diethylstilbestrol: Adverse Effects on the Reproductive Tract and Reproductive Performance in Male and Female Offspring," *American Journal of Obstetrics and Gynecology* 142 (1982), pp. 905-921.

2 Joyce Bichler, *DES Daughter* (New York, Avon Books, 1981), p.187.

3 Abel v. Eli Lilly & Co., 289 N.W. 2d 20 (Mich. CT. App. 1979).

4 A. Lacassagne, "Apparition d'adenocarcinomes mammaires chez des souris mailes traitées par un substance oestrogene synthetique," Compte Rendus Biologiques 129 (1938), p.641.

5 O.W. Smith, "Diethylstilbestrol in the Prevention and Treatment of Complications of Pregnancy," *American Journal of Obstetrics and Gynecology* 56 (1948), pp. 821-834.

6 This is a study where neither the subjects nor the researchers know who is receiving the experimental drug or the placebo.

7 W.J. Dieckmann *et al.,* "Does the Administration of Diethylstilbestrol during Pregnancy have Therapeutic Value?" *American Journal of Obstetrics and Gynecology* 66 (1953), pp. 1062-1081.

8 A. Herbst *et al.,* "Adenocarcinoma of the Vagina: Association of Maternal Stilbestrol Therapy with Tumor Appearance in Young Women," *New England Journal of Medicine* 284 (1971), pp. 878-881.

9 Physicians in Quebec, for example, are required to keep their medical records for five years since the date of the last entry. Regulation Respecting the Keeping of Records by Physicians, R.R.Q. 1981, c. M-9, r. 20, s. 3.02.

10 Bichler v. Eli Lilly & Co., 436 N.Y.S. 2d 625 (App. Div. 1981).

11 Sindell v. Abbott Laboratories, 163 Cal. Reptr. 132 (S. C. CAL. 1980).

12 Collins v. Eli Lilly & Co., 342 N.W. 2d 37.

13 L. Martin, "The DES issue," *Protect Yourself* (Sept. 1983), pp. 42-44.

14 1951, S.C.R. 830 (1951).

15 "Ruling shakes spray plaintiffs," *The Halifax Mail Star* (16 Sept. 1983).

16 Solicitor's Act, R.S.O. 1980, ch. 478, s. 18(2).

17 Naken v. General Motors of Canada Ltd. (1978), 92 D.L.R. 3d 100 (1978).

18 Anita Direcks, "Has the DES Lesson Been Learned?" *DES Action Voice* 28 (Spring 1986) pp.1-2.

Donor Insemination: The Future of a Public Secret

Rona Achilles

> I spend a good deal of time wondering how we will seem to the people who come after us.... What we live through, in any age, is the effect on us of mass emotions and of social conditions from which it is almost impossible to detach ourselves. Often the mass emotions are those which seem the noblest, best and most beautiful. And yet, inside a year, five years, a decade, five decades, people will be asking, "How *could* they have believed that?" because events will have taken place that will have banished the said mass emotions to the dustbin of history. To coin a phrase.

Doris Lessing,
"When in the Future They Look Back on Us,"
Prisons We Choose to Live Inside
CBC Massey Lectures,
Toronto, CBC Enterprises, 1986

Among the innumerable social tasks we face in the last decade of the twentieth century is understanding and regulating the social consequences of an explosion in new reproductive technologies (NRTs). This chapter will focus on one procedure – donor insemination (DI) – which is generally included in discussions of NRTs. Although it is neither new nor, strictly speaking, a technology, donor insemination embodies several of the issues surrounding more sophisticated artificial reproduction procedures. It also reveals the social meanings we attach to biological reproduction and our cultural notions about what constitutes family.

The fact that it is no longer necessary to have sexual intercourse to biologically reproduce oneself has inalterably changed the potential social relationships surrounding human reproduction. "Non-coital" reproduction is one of the many terms used to describe these procedures; "artificial reproduction," "assisted conception" and / or " asexual reproduction" are all terms used to describe a variety of techniques. None is entirely adequate to describe the features of individual technologies. The development of a more appropriate language is an important part of understanding the technical and social processes involved in these developments.

Artificial insemination, in its most elementary form, is an extremely simple procedure. Semen, usually obtained through masturbation, is inserted into a woman's vaginal tract around the time of ovulation with "technology" as simple as a syringe. In other words, insemination occurs without sexual intercourse. Since conception and gestation occur as in any other pregnancy, the use of the word "artificial" is misleading. It tends to imply that something is "not natural" or "not real" – as in "artificial" flowers rather than "real" flowers, or that events are humanly constructed rather than naturally given. But artificial insemination, in its simplest form, is no more humanly constructed than is sexual intercourse to achieve pregnancy. Donor insemination is a version of artificial insemination in which the semen is obtained from a man who is neither the spouse nor the partner of the recipient. Paradoxically, this simple procedure is accompanied by complex and volatile "mass emotions" (to use Lessing's term).

Donor insemination is most commonly used when (1) a woman's male partner is infertile, (2) when a heterosexual couple wishes to avoid the possibility of transmitting a genetically inherited disease to their offspring or (3) when a single woman or lesbian couple wants to have a child without physical contact and / or social involvement with a male. Since all three trends appear to be on the increase, donor insemination will likely remain a reproductive option for some time. It may, however, eventually be replaced by more sophisticated technical procedures. For example, in vitro fertilization (IVF), originally used for women with blocked fallopian tubes, is currently being used for couples where the woman is fertile and her partner has a low sperm count. Replacing donor insemination is unnecessary since it is potentially a low-tech, non-invasive reproductive alternative. DI does, however, present several social dilemmas which become apparent in an examination of the current practice.

It is useful to detach ourselves as much as possible from what Doris Lessing refers to as the "mass emotions" which surround the procedure of donor insemination. The "facts" of the procedure are grounded in a social and political context. The following are some of the barest social facts concerning donor insemination.

DI is simple and can be performed without medical expertise. Nevertheless, the majority of interested recipients will use a medical setting to acquire donor sperm. Within the medical setting, a number of ancillary medical steps may be taken to increase the *efficiency* of the procedure. These may include the use of fertility drugs and a standard infertility work-up on the recipient (which is, in parts, painful, invasive and costly). If the recipient is fertile, pregnancy can be achieved without sophisticated technology, and there is no technical reason for the procedure to be medicalized.

Another striking social fact is the importance of anonymity. The current practice of donor insemination involves a complex of social interactions to ensure that the sperm donor and the recipient(s) never meet. This is generally true in non-medical as well as medical settings. (For an exception to this, see Elizabeth Noble's description of her relationship with her donor, a trusted friend, in *Having Your Baby by Donor Insemi-*

nation (Boston, Houghton Mifflin Co., 1987). The use of frozen sperm alleviates the dilemma posed by fresh sperm (a donor must drop off his fresh sample at the physician's office or at a "drop-off point" in a hospital without bumping into the woman who will receive it).

As well as remaining anonymous, donors and recipients are generally encouraged to keep the DI procedure secret. The widespread ignorance of the fact that donor insemination has been practised in humans for more than one hundred years demonstrates the effectiveness of this code of secrecy. The secrecy surrounding DI is reminiscent of adoption practice thirty to forty years ago – a practice which has been replaced with a philosophy that openness and honesty about the adoptee's origins, although not uncomplicated, is healthier for everyone involved.

These social facts – a simple exchange medicalized, the importance of anonymity between participants and secrecy about the procedure – add up to a process that is more complex socially than it is technically or medically. In addition, a number of legal issues are involved. These include donor and / or physician liability; issues of access – that is, the question of whether individuals have a fundamental right to procreate; the rights and responsibilities of the mother's partner (if present) in relation to the child; and the question of record-keeping.[1] In Canada, donor insemination has been practised by a number of physicians since (at the very latest) the 1940s and by many more since the 1960s. As serious legal issues are involved, it is astonishing that, with the recent exceptions of Quebec and the Yukon, the very simple legislation required to clarify the rights and responsibilities of participants has not been enacted. At the most basic level, this would include ensuring that the donor has no legal rights to the child, that the rights and responsibilities of the mother's partner in relation to the child are protected and that records are kept that could link donors, recipients and offspring.[2]

In our current social context, most mothers are the *primary* caretakers, the primary parents of their children – a role which is extremely undervalued. At the same time, fathers' rights activists are increasingly asserting custody rights over disadvantaged and undervalued mothers. Amidst this power struggle over parental rights, children become vehicles for spousal warring. Therefore, it is crucial that any legal rights of the sperm donor, the biological father, be removed at the outset and not left to be battled out in a courtroom.

In an exploratory study of participants in donor insemination, current practice emerges as an attempt to conform to a particular image of the family. This image is an increasingly mythological one – a heterosexual married couple who rear their biologically linked children to adulthood.[3] For heterosexual couples, secrecy about the use of DI was an important component of conforming to this image of the family. The secrecy serves to disguise some of the more difficult social questions and dilemmas posed by donor insemination. It avoids, for example, (1) the social stigma associated with infertility, in this case male infertility, (2) the potentially painful psychological process which may be required to resolve feelings about infertility, (3) the difficult questions about whom to tell, and (4) if, when and how to tell the child(ren) about their origins. Secrecy also serves to deny the difficult and possibly powerful emotions of a woman bearing the child of a man who is unknown to her, her feelings about the experience, her partner's feelings, and the child or children's feelings about an unknown and potentially unknowable biological father.

For single women and lesbian couples secrecy was not an option. Family members were told, the child was told or was going to be told and the innovative family form created through donor insemination was acknowledged.[4] Due to the socially invisible nature of paternity, heterosexual couples using donor insemination are offered the opportunity to "pass" as fertile, as a biologically linked family. The fact that so many heterosexual couples choose to keep the donor insemination secret even from their DI offspring is, at least partially, an indication of the persistence and strength of mythologies and norms about what constitutes a family and what constitutes a "real" parent. In choosing to "pass" as the norm, they also reinforce its strength and mythological status in our culture.

Among the participants from whom data were collected, however, the secrecy about DI posed some difficulties. DI mothers expressed isolation and a need to talk to others in their situation about their children's origins – "a liveable cost" as one mother expressed it. In other cases, secrecy proved to be neither feasible nor beneficial and "the story came out" during family arguments. The adult offspring who were contacted said that they had been told about their origins during crises which exacerbated already existing problems. If, for example, something happened to the offspring's father which had, or was perceived to have, a genetic link (such as mental illness), the DI offspring was confronted with a number of things at once – the familial crisis which acted as a catalyst for "telling" (in more than one instance this involved the father's suicide), the fact that she had been "deceived" for a number of years, and the fact that she had another "father" biologically linked to her somewhere "out there." Since the sample is small, it is impossible to know what the spectrum of responses of DI offspring to their origins is, or will be. One thing, however, is clear – that substantial cultural meaning is attributed to the biological link in our social context. The "secret," in other words, is not a trivial one; otherwise so much energy would not be required to keep it.

There are a number of social policy issues which arise out of current practice in DI. In relation to the donor alone, for example, guidelines on issues such as selection, screening, payment, record-keeping, the number of children (biologically) fathered by one donor, and informed consent are vital to a healthy practice for participants and for society.

If donors in DI and other procedures which employ donor gametes were to be selected for certain more socially valued traits, such as a particular kind of intelligence, skill or physical features, then the procedure would have potential eugenic (selective breeding) implications. Although a preference for certain traits (other than matching to physical features of the recipients) did not appear in exploratory data, there are reports of recipients choosing donors for high I.Q.s or particular skills. (The emphasis on "perfect" children means that, for example, hockey player Wayne Gretzky's sperm would be more valued than the sperm of a postal worker.)

The importance of screening sperm donors became particularly apparent with the advent of acquired immuno-deficiency syndrome (AIDS). Several guidelines for screening of donors have been issued by medical associations. However, my own exploratory study, as well as a broader survey of U.S. physicians, indicated that most physicians did not follow the guidelines – only forty-four percent report testing for human immunodeficiency virus (HIV) antibodies.[5] The use of frozen sperm will facilitate more rigorous screening of sperm donors. It is not, however, clear yet whether the use of frozen sperm has any long-term consequences.

Payment to donors generally ranges from fifteen to fifty dollars per sperm sample – a seemingly minimal sum. However, depending on how frequently a donor "donates"[6] and his own financial circumstances, it could constitute a motive for "donation." Payment to donors also sets a precedent for gamete "donation," and is used as a rationale for commercialization in other arrangements such as contract mothers (popularly referred to as surrogate mothers) and more recently with egg donations.[7]

The issue of keeping records which would link the recipient, offspring and sperm donor (that is, the two biological parents and their offspring), also has important social ramifications. These include: (1) access to medical information about the offspring's genetic heritage – this may be desired by the recipients (to obtain optimal health care) or by the child at the age of majority, or both; (2) a method of monitoring the number of children biologically fathered by one donor (one donor in my study had donated approximately 240 times); (3) the possibility that a donor might want to update his file regarding medical information (he could, for example, develop diabetes later in life; and (4) the potential desire of DI offspring to have more information about their biological father for reasons of identity or self-concept.[8]

Current practice regarding record-keeping in Canada is ad hoc and dependent on the discretion of individual physicians.[9] Key to the issue of record-keeping is the fact that sperm donors are defined as patients (as recommended by the Ontario Law Reform Commission report).[10] Physicians are required to keep records on donors (as patients) for varying amounts of time depending upon the province and the healthcare setting. Adequate record-keeping would require that records be kept for approximately a lifetime (of the offspring) and that a centralized registry be devised to facilitate linkages and monitor the number of children (biologically) fathered by one donor. A system such as this is increasingly possible, given advances in computer technology. As several commentators have pointed out, if we can do it for cattle, surely we can do it for humans!

Finally, as with all participants in all the new reproductive technologies, the issue of informed consent is a vital and complex problem. In relation to sperm donors, informed consent and / or decision making requires that sperm donors be encouraged to reflect upon the consequences of their donation. In exploratory data collected, donors frequently expressed concern that they had not adequately understood that they (potentially) had biologically fathered several children "out there" whom they would never meet or know about. This reaction was more likely to occur with younger donors and donors whose reasons for donating were adventuresome rather than altruistic and additionally tended to change with time and circumstance.[11]

Issues for recipients include questions of access, choice regarding the donor, and problems concerning informed consent and decision making. The movement of conception from the private to the public realm (a shift which occurs not just with DI in clinical settings but with all artificial reproduction technologies) engenders a number of changes in decision making regarding reproduction. Increasingly, for example, conception, gestation and birth are negotiated with physicians and lawyers and involve commercial transactions and contracts. Different social values and influences, including market influences, are therefore brought to bear on reproductive decisions which were previously private, face-to-face and between two people. In addition, what was previously surrendered to the random realm of nature is increasingly subjected to attempts to control quality and design of the so-called "product."[12]

The movement to the public realm, in the case of donor insemination to a clinical setting, means that physicians will decide who will become parents (through control of access to their services) and who will conceive with whom. In most cases, traditional norms about what and who constitutes a family or a good parent can be expected to be upheld. Lesbians, single women and / or those with lower incomes, for example, will not likely be considered good parents.

In addition, DI recipients in clinical settings generally have no choice about their donor (the biological father of their child) and in most cases cannot obtain even minimal information about him (for example, a non-identifying medical profile). Physicians, therefore, choose not only who will become parents, but who will "mate" with whom. This practice is somewhat reminiscent of arranged marriages, yet it is historically unprecedented because, in some cases, the biological father is unknowable.

Informed decision making regarding DI would require some alterations in current practice. Respect for the life crisis and deep psycho-social processes that are frequently triggered by a diagnosis of infertility (among individuals who *want* pregnancy and children) requires participants to engage in a two-stage process. The first stage would involve dealing with the crisis of infertility, and the second would involve decision making regarding DI (or other reproductive options or childlessness). Exploratory studies found that heterosexual couples were frequently presented with the diagnosis of infertility in one breath and the solution of DI in the next.

There were some indications that male physicians (and most fertility specialists are male) had some difficulty telling their male patients about the diagnosis of infertility. Donor insemination participants were frequently given the diagnosis over the phone in a perfunctory manner. In some cases the physician told the female partner and stated his preference that she do the emotional work of telling her male partner about his infertility.

Culturally, we associate fertility and infertility with, among other things, gender identity and self-esteem. It would appear that, for males, fertility is associated with masculinity, sexual power and virility, whereas infertility is associated with impotence and a loss of manhood. One donor referred to infertile husbands as "the third sex."[13]

When DI is understood as a social as well as a technical procedure, its social ramifications become apparent. This has occurred in some other countries, and it is useful to look at their models of DI practice. In 1973, France re-organized its practice of DI and created Centre D'Etude et de Conservation de Sperme (CECOS). CECOS has rigorous technical standards regarding the screening of donors and employs a service model which encompasses the Centre's social and technical objectives. The model referred to as "a gift from one couple to another" is a conservative one, but suggests possibilities in this new realm of reproductive relationships. The donor must be married and have a least one child. (Israel takes the opposite stance on this issue and insists that the donor not be married.) He must have his wife's consent, he is not paid or reimbursed financially in any way, and there is a limit of five pregnancies per donor. Two things resulted from these changes – first, an increase in the demand for DI and second, an increase in the public debate on DI – both of which transformed DI into a more visible social practice.[14]

In March 1985 Sweden passed legislation which guarantees that when a child has reached "enough maturity," she has the right to learn who her biological father through donor insemination is. What constitutes "enough maturity" is decided by the hospital and a social worker. At this point, it is possible for the child / offspring to have contact with the donor. No one else has the right to search for the donor's name – not even the recipients. It was feared that no one would volunteer as a donor if donors were required to file information about themselves which offspring could have access to at some later date. What is interesting about the Swedish legislation is that this fear has not been realized. The initial response was exactly as predicted: current donors stopped donating. But within months the number of donors had risen again to previous levels, and reports indicate that a different kind of donor is becoming involved in programs.[15]

In the Netherlands, secrecy about the DI child's origins has recently become unpopular. However, information provided to the offspring has been limited to non-identifying features.[16] Similarly, Britain's Warnock report states, "On reaching the age of eighteen the child should have access to the basic information about the donor's ethnic origin and genetic health and that legislation be enacted – to provide the right of access to this" (p. 82).[17] In Australia, a precedent-setting Act – the Infertility (Medical Procedures) Act – was passed in 1984 in Victoria. Its regulations include the establishment of a Central Register "containing complete information on those gamete donors where successful pregnancies ensue, including DI as well as IVF procedures" (p. 22).[18]

Practices vary historically as well as internationally. In 1921 an Ontario Supreme Court decision (Orford v. Orford) declared DI adulterous – a decision unlikely to hold court in the late 1980s except in the Vatican.[19] Britain, in particular, has undertaken a series of governmental commissions and reports on donor insemination. In 1948 a British report declared DI "a criminal offense,"[20] in 1960 it was declared "undesirable" but not illegal,[21] and in 1973 it was recommended that it be covered by the National Health Service.[22]

An old friend of mine, Brian,[23] recently mentioned that he had been approached by "a friend of a friend" to donate sperm for a single woman, Leslie, who wants to become a mother. She is in her mid-thirties, unhappy with prospective partners, and able and willing to rear a child on her own. If Brian's partner agrees, Leslie and Brian will begin negotiating the process and terms of this new family form.

Another friend, Tania, decided that her daughter conceived through DI should know about her origins. Over the past few years she has been repeating the following story to her daughter: "Your dad and I really wanted to have a baby. We had a hard time because when your dad was a teenager he had an operation which meant that he no longer had any seeds. So we went to the doctor and the doctor said he knew a man who had lots of seeds and would be able to help us. So that man gave the seeds to the doctor and the doctor put them into Mommy and that's how we got you." So far, this DI offspring's only concern is that her dad's operation didn't hurt him. Cognitively (as with adoptees), she will not fully comprehend the implications of her origins till early adolescence or even later. However, she will have no surprises bursting out amidst family stress.

These are just two scenarios indicating the extent of innovation currently occurring in family forms. The variety of forms created through step-parenting, adoption, foster-parenting, donor insemination and, increasingly, by other reproductive technologies challenges us to redefine our obsolete notions of what constitutes a parent and what constitutes a family.

NOTES

1 This is a minimal listing of what are potentially complex legal problems. For a more complete detailing of the legal problems surrounding donor insemination, see Ontario Law Reform Commission, *Report on Artificial Reproduction and Related Matters* (Ministry of the Attorney General, 1985).

2 In the last decade in Canada, there have been several provincial reports and at least one federal report on donor insemination. It is unfortunate that the most recent and comprehensive provincial report from the Ontario Law Reform Commission includes donor insemination among much more complex and sophisticated technologies; this is likely to slow down the legislative process.

3 Rona Achilles, *The Social Meanings of Biological Ties: A Study of Participants in Artificial Insemination by Donor* (Doctoral Thesis, University of Toronto, 1986). Forthcoming from Temple University Press, Philadelphia.

4 Ibid.

5 Achilles, op. cit.; and Martin Curie-Cohen, Lesleigh Luttrell, and Sander Shapiro, "Current Practice of Artificial Insemination by Donor in the United States," *New England Journal of Medicine* 300 (15 March 1979), pp. 585-590; Office of Technology Assessment, "Artificial Insemination Practice in the U.S. Summary of a Survey," August 1988.

6 Sperm "donors" may more accurately be termed sperm "vendors" since they are paid for their sperm donations. See George Annas, "Father's Anonymous: Beyond the Best Interests of the Sperm Donor," *Child Welfare* vol. 60, no. 3, pp. 161-174.

7 Nadine Brozan, "Rising Use of Donated Eggs for Pregnancy Stirs Concern," *The New York Times,* 18 January 1988, p. A.

8 This issue is similar to that of adoptees seeking information about their biological parents. See Ralph Garber, *Disclosure of Adoption Information* (Toronto, Ministry of Community and Social Services, Government of Ontario, 1985).

9 Most guidelines, including the latest report by The Ethics Committee of The American Fertility Society, "Ethical Considerations of the New Reproductive Technologies," *Fertility and Sterility,* vol. 46, no. 3, Supplement 1 (September 1986), and *Reproduction and Related Matters* (Toronto, Ministry of the Attorney General, 1985), recommend that physicians devise a record-keeping and linkage system. However, practice seems to coincide more with a report by Health and Welfare Canada, Report on the Advisory Committee on the Storage and Utilization of Human Sperm (Ottawa, 1981), p. 25. In this the authors state, "When protective legislation exists [to protect the donor from legal suits], the committee recommends that links be kept between the records of the donor and those of the recipient."

10 Ontario Law Reform Commission proposed recommendation, vol. 22, no. 2, p. 278.

11 Achilles, op. cit. 1986.

12 As Barbara Katz Rothman comments in her book *The Tentative Pregnancy* (New York, Penguin Books, 1986), p. 2, "Even in a more usual, 'naturally' occurring pregnancy, the technology of reproduction encourages and reinforces the commodification process: genetic counselling serves the function of quality control, and the wrongful life suits are a form of product liability litigation." This book is an excellent study of women using amniocentesis.

13 Education and support services, therefore, should be provided (but generally are not) to facilitate this two-stage process. There are a number of potentially difficult issues a heterosexual couple must face. These include: (1) the issue of bearing a child biologically linked to a man the DI mother has never met and probably will never meet, (2) the feelings of her partner about her carrying "another man's child," (3) the issue of imbalance in biological ties – the child will be biologically tied to the mother who will rear her or him, but not to the father, and (4) that one-half of the child's biological heritage is potentially unknowable, etc.

4 The actual practice of DI became more socially visible, but the issue of secrecy remains important to individual recipients. All this information has been culled from Simone Novaes' paper, "Social Integration of Technical Innovation: Sperm Banking and AI-D in France and the United States." Paper presented at the Feminist International Network on New Reproductive Technologies, Ostra Grevie, Sweden (July 1985).

5 G. Ewerlof, "Artificial Insemination – Legislation and Debate," *Current Sweden,* 329, pp. 1-9, and Lena Jonsson, "Artificial Insemination in Sweden," in *Sortir la maternité du laboratoire* (Gouvernement du Québec: Conseil du statut de la femme, 1988), pp. 148-155.

6 Maurice de Wachter and Guido de Wert, "In the Netherlands, Tolerance and Debate," *Hastings Centre Report,* Special Supplement, vol.17, no. 3 (June 1987), pp. 15-16.

7 Mary Warnock, *A Question of Life* (New York, Basil Blackwell, 1985).

8 Cited in Louis Waller, "In Australia, the Debate Moves to Embryo Experimentation," *Hastings Centre Report,* Special Supplement, vol. 17, no. 3. (June 1987).

9 See Bernard M. Dickens, *Medico-Legal Aspects of Family Law* (Toronto, Butterworths, 1979).

10 *Artificial Human Insemination: The Report of a Commission Appointed by His Grace the Archbishop of Canterbury* (London, SPCK, 1948).

11 Lord Feversham, *Report of the Departmental Committee on Human Artificial Insemination* (Cmnd 1105, London; HMSO, 1960).

12 Sir John Peel, "Report of the Panel on Human Artificial Insemination ," *British Medical Journal,* vol. 2, Supplementary Appendix V, 3.

13 Pseudonyms are used in these references for the purposes of privacy.

No Relief Until the End: The Physical and Emotional Costs of In Vitro Fertilization

Linda S. Williams

In 1978, the first so-called "test-tube baby" was born in England. Since then, it is estimated, approximately three thousand babies have been born worldwide by in vitro fertilization (IVF) procedures, and IVF clinics currently exist in almost every country.[1]

Most women who undergo IVF do *not* give birth to the baby they so desperately want. It is estimated that in the U.S. only four to five percent of all IVF attempts resulted in a live birth in 1985.[2] In spite of this very low success rate, newspapers, magazines and the electronic media tend to focus on these few successes, and regularly print pictures of, or conduct interviews with, ecstatic IVF parents. These accounts usually include a brief description of the IVF procedure, and sometimes even a limited account of its stresses and strains. However, the harsh reality of the IVF experience is never completely portrayed, and the limited accounts which are available are overshadowed by the "happy endings" being reported.

This article is an attempt to present the reality of in vitro fertilization as it was experienced by twenty Canadian women who participated in my Ph.D. research on the parenthood motivation of couples seeking IVF.[3]

The following is a basic outline of the IVF procedure which

these women underwent and which is still used today, with slight variations, in all hospital-based IVF clinics in Ontario.

THE PROCEDURE

An IVF procedure usually begins around the fifth day of a woman's menstrual cycle when she begins taking one or two tablets of Clomid daily for approximately four days. Clomid is a fertility drug that stimulates the development of egg follicles in the ovaries. Two days after she begins taking Clomid she will also begin receiving a daily injection of Pergonal, an extremely powerful fertility drug that induces ovulation. This treatment continues for approximately one week. Initially, only one vial of Pergonal per day is given; if the woman's ovaries do not respond to this amount, it will be increased to two vials daily, which usually becomes the standard dosage. Occasionally, it is necessary to administer three vials daily to achieve the desired effect.

Around the time that Pergonal injections begin, daily blood tests will also commence. A daily, or every-second-day ultrasound scan will be required to assess the development of the egg follicles as well as to make sure that the ovaries are not being dangerously overstimulated by the Pergonal. In two of the three hospitals surveyed in this study, blood tests and ultrasound scans were done at approximately 7:00 a.m. and the patient had to return to the hospital in the afternoon for her Pergonal injection. One hospital did all these procedures together in the afternoon.

If the blood tests and ultrasound scans show that the woman's hormone levels are rising sufficiently and that her ovaries are developing a sufficient number of egg follicles, she will be admitted to the hospital for egg collection between the eleventh and the fourteenth day of her menstrual cycle. However, if the results of these tests show that the ovaries are not responding to the drug regimen, the IVF attempt will be "canceled." This can occur at any point in the procedure up to the time of hospital admission.

Women who are admitted to the hospital will usually have at least one more ultrasound. Daily blood tests will continue, and may even be done every few hours around the clock. Once the woman's hormone levels have risen sufficiently and the time of ovulation is near, an injection of human chorionic gonadotropin (HCG) is given to induce ovulation. Timing becomes especially crucial at this point because HCG is known to induce ovulation in approximately thirty-six hours. Consequently, a surgical laparoscopy to collect the eggs is scheduled for thirty-four hours after the injection. However, ovulation may occur before the eggs can be surgically removed, and if a woman's hormone levels show that she has, in fact, ovulated before egg collection can be performed, her attempt will be "canceled" and she will be discharged from the hospital.

Most programs schedule the HCG injection for the evening so that the laparoscopy can take place in the morning two days later, since having all IVF patients ready for surgery at the same time and also in the morning (which is when most hospital surgery is scheduled) is more convenient for the doctors and staff. As a general anesthetic is required for this surgery, the woman must begin fasting the night before it is scheduled.[4]

The actual laparoscopy procedure is relatively straightforward. The ovaries are visualized and the egg follicles are aspirated (drawn by suction) to remove the eggs. Sometimes, egg collection is difficult due to the inaccessibility of the ovaries and only a few eggs will be retrieved, which severely reduces the chances of eventual pregnancy. Following the egg collection, the woman will go to the recovery area and later return to her hospital room. The collected eggs are placed in a culture medium and closely observed to make sure that they are healthy. Defective eggs are discarded; the rest are incubated for five to six hours and then combined with the prospective father's sperm sample which has been specially treated to increase the chance of fertilization. This stage is also crucial to the success of the procedure since some eggs may not fertilize, and even eggs that do fertilize may not undergo cell division, that is, they may stop developing and cease to be living organisms.

Approximately forty-eight hours after the laparoscopy, all eggs which have fertilized and are developing properly (which are now human embryos) are returned to the woman's uterus by means of a thin catheter inserted through the cervix. This procedure is called embryo transfer and it does not require any anesthetic, although it can be painful for some women. The woman remains in the hospital for a few hours, lying on her back with the bed tilted so that her feet are elevated, and then she returns home. Twelve days after embryo transfer, a blood test is done to see if the embryos have implanted in the uterine wall and a pregnancy has begun. Since implantation does not usually occur, most women will have a negative pregnancy test and begin their menstrual period either shortly before, or shortly after, the pregnancy test. The few women who have become pregnant will go on to bear a child (or children) in nine months or miscarry.[5]

THE PHYSICAL AND EMOTIONAL COSTS OF IVF

The table shows the total number of attempts that each woman in the study underwent and the outcome of those attempts.

While the table tells us the physical outcomes of the IVF attempts of these women, it does not begin to convey the immense emotional and physical stress of IVF. The following description of these women's IVF experiences is divided into three parts: the period prior to hospital admission, the period

Results of All IVF Attempts
(Number of Women = 20, Number of Attempts = 50)

SUBJECT NUMBER	1	2	3	4	5	6	7	8	9	10	11	12	13	14	15	16	17	18	19	20
TOTAL NUMBER OF ATTEMPTS/WOMAN	1	1	1	5	2	2	3	3	3	1	1	1	1	6	1	1	6	6	4	1
OUTCOME OF EACH WOMAN'S ATTEMPTS																				
Cancellation		1	1	2			2	1	3					2			1	1	2	
Egg collection, but no fertilization											1						1			
Embryo transfer completed but no pregnancy	1			3	2	2	1	2					1	4		1	3	3	2	1
Miscarriage following diagnosed pregnancy																		2		
Pregnancy, expressed in number of live births/pregnancy										1		3*			1		1			

* This woman had triplets

in the hospital, and the approximately two-week long period following hospital discharge when a woman waits to see if she is pregnant.[6]

1) The Period Prior to Hospital Admission

The first phase of the IVF procedure lasts from seven to ten days, and consists of taking Clomid tablets and having blood tests, Pergonal injections and ultrasound scans according to a precise schedule as described above. Most women found the daily routine of having to be at the hospital or clinic very early in the morning for their blood test and ultrasound, and having to return in the afternoon for their Pergonal injection, very tiring and stressful. Women who continued their paid work during this period had to deal with the added anxiety of being away from their jobs for a large part of the day during this initial phase of the IVF program.

> ANNE – You get up so early and you have to be downtown at 7:30 and then you're rushing from the lab to the hospital to have your ultrasound done, and you seem to be waiting there forever and all you can think of is getting back to your job, onto the desk 'cause no one's covering you while you're gone for most of the morning. Most times I didn't get back until 11:30. The morning is shot and then you had to leave work at 3:30 or so to get downtown just to wait for the doctor to get in there to let you know if you needed Pergonal or whether you were kicked off the program (canceled). Then you come home and have supper and kind of hop into bed. You're like a zombie those days. You're tired and you know you have to get up so early again the next morning. And depending on what time of year you're going you're not only fighting the traffic but you could be into winter weather on top of it.

While the timing of these procedures produced a great deal of stress and fatigue for most women, the procedures them-selves were often very difficult. For technical reasons, an ultrasound scan must be done with a full bladder, and a few women related harrowing tales of having to "hold it" while they traveled to the hospital or clinic for the procedure, or while they waited their turn to have it done once they arrived.

FRANCES – You have to have a full bladder through the whole thing, for the ultrasound to work. That's very, very uncomfortable too … You're supposed to drink four glasses of water before you leave the house. I'd leave here at 6:00 to be there for 7:30. The first few times I'd drink four glasses of water here and by the time I got off the train at Union Station I'm just about dead. And then you get there and they've got to do your blood and then you wait around and the doctor comes waltzing in about 8:30 and there are fifteen of you sitting there with your legs crossed. Like it's awful! But then I got it down to a fine art. I knew just exactly how much water I could drink here and how much I'd drink at Union Station. I had it all timed so I could get there with just the right amount (she laughs). I still have problems with my blad-der right now and I swear it's because it was stretched to oblivion going through that. There has to be a better way, I think.

Two women in the sample experienced so much difficulty with the blood drawing which is an essential part of IVF that they both described this part of the process as "torture." Another woman mentioned that she sometimes fainted.

DEBRA – I have very bad veins, very bad veins, and that was tortuous. On two occasions in the first two days they couldn't get blood after about six needles. So I was pretty pockmarked from that. I was also very depressed about that. I felt that that was a bad omen. That it wasn't going well and I got sort of dejected.

Almost all twenty women experienced at least one side effect from the Clomid and Pergonal used in IVF, and most women experienced more than one. The most upsetting side effects were excruciating headaches and extreme mood swings that would leave some women – quite literally – laughing one minute and crying the next. Other side effects included hyperactivity, drowsiness, nausea, weight gain, dizziness, hot and cold flashes, and inability to concentrate. One woman reported that her ovaries had become hyperstimulated, which is one of the most dangerous side effects of Pergonal.[7] These side effects began with the administration of the fertility drugs but often continued into the waiting period following hospital discharge since the drugs would still be present in the women's bodies.

DEBRA – I had unbelievable, unbelievable headaches. Like nothing I'd ever had in my life. I could not work, I could barely keep my head up. They were pounding, pounding. And I was petrified to take anything. And I didn't say anything for about two days, and they wouldn't go away, and I finally asked the doctor whether I could take something and he said I could and it would take like three or four aspirins until I could get some relief. I was upset about that.

CONNIE – In the afternoon I could practically sleep the whole afternoon and night away, if Frank hadn't come in and woken me up, or I would force myself not to lay down. I would force myself to keep working or do something around the house because the simple reason is I was sleeping all the time. That was my first reaction to the drugs. And maybe a little hyper too.

During a later attempt Connie experienced an additional side effect.

CONNIE – I was getting a little nauseated this time with the drugs. There were a lot of girls there who were having the same side effect. I was a little drowsy, but the nausea was bad.

INGRID – It's hard on you. And you get overweight. Oohh. Twenty-five pounds ... The second time I added fifteen pounds in one month. That's a lot to add, especially me, because I never put an ounce on, and I eat a lot ... I am starting to lose now again. But it takes a long time. And it doesn't matter if you go on a diet and exercise because it just sits there until it goes out of your system, I guess. I guess it's water retention basically. It's a lot of weight. That's a side effect.

JANICE – I could hardly concentrate on my studies with the Pergonal. I could hardly keep up with my school work but was maintaining it. I was managing to keep up with it, barely. And I had a term paper to hand in and I couldn't sit down to do it. I knew it had to be done, and I was trying to do it ahead so that if I had to be admitted it would be done, and I just couldn't do it. And the prof was not going to take it in late and I was going to get docked a mark for every day late.

A pervasive theme in almost all the women's accounts of the period prior to hospital admittance was a profound fear of being "canceled" because their hormone levels were not rising, or their egg follicles were not developing properly. Each day's blood test and ultrasound scan were perceived as "hurdles" which they had to overcome, or "tests" which they had to pass in order to be allowed to continue in the program.

JANICE – It was a waiting game. There were four of us who would meet and have breakfast together and things like that. When Amy got canceled that's when I first realized the hurt of being canceled. All of us lived in the fear all week of being the ones that would be canceled at any time. And I would ask about my levels of estrogen and you compare. And you compare sizes of follicles.

2) In the Hospital

Being admitted to hospital was an extremely important step for the women in this study, for it meant that they had successfully completed the first stage in the IVF process and were likely candidates for egg retrieval surgery. Women were generally not admitted to the hospital unless their hormone levels and the number and size of their egg follicles indicated that a laparoscopy to retrieve eggs would probably be successful.

Most of these women described their time in hospital prior to surgery as tense and emotionally charged, but spoke warmly of the camaraderie and support that they received from the other women who were also going through the program. They firmly believed that this mutual support made the extreme stress of this period somewhat more bearable. Although women at this stage of the process are hospitalized, they are generally free to wander in and out of the hospital whenever they are not needed for a medical procedure. So this mutual support sometimes took the form of restaurant or shopping expeditions as well as meetings in each other's rooms.

ANNE – There were five of us girls who made it all the way through the program. We used to get together. We had lunches and dinners together. We did a lot together ... And I think for us we made it for each other. Most people might find it a little bit hard if you're not outgoing to be able to live with that situation. Because each day you might be meeting someone different and losing someone you're just getting to know who's in the same situation as you. So I think the team spirit was really great for us.

Worry about possibly being "canceled" did not end once a woman was admitted to hospital. If she should happen to ovulate before her egg collection surgery could be performed, she would be "canceled" and discharged from the hospital shortly thereafter. The experience of being "canceled" at this stage was perhaps even more devastating than being "canceled" prior to hospital admission, since it occurred further along in the program when the women were even more emotionally invested in the whole procedure.

MARILYN – I was really disappointed. I was really upset. Andrew took me out for dinner, and I don't drink, but I had a drink because I was really upset. And he didn't know what to do for me. So it was very frustrating at that point. And again, I felt like I'd let him down, I'd let myself down. I think it was more of a rude awakening, because it had gone so well in July and I went through the whole program, how the hell did I get canceled? So you go through a lot of what did I do wrong? I didn't do anything. Every period is different and your body reacts differently each time.

LOIS – … I remember getting in the car and crying all the way home. I'm never going back there! They've had enough! I'm not a guinea pig any more! (she laughs nervously) And I was just … I'd had it. I thought – this is it. I'm not doing this again. But about two days afterwards it was, okay, let's go back in (she laughs).

For women who are not "canceled," the next stage in the IVF procedure is the surgical laparoscopy to collect the ripening eggs in the woman's ovaries. Interestingly, only one of the women in this sample made any comment at all about the laparoscopy itself. This surgery seemed to be much less stressful than the periods leading up to it and immediately following this crucial procedure.

The period following laparoscopy brought a shift in the focus of the women's attention from their own bodies to the fragile eggs which had been surgically removed, and new questions now occupied them. How many eggs were collected? Are they "good" eggs? Once the eggs and sperm had been combined in the laboratory, the women then became concerned about whether the eggs had fertilized and were undergoing proper cell division. Several women spoke of the stress of trying to get information from the hospital staff and constantly wondering about what was happening to their eggs which, they fervently hoped, were fertilizing and becoming human embryos. Unless these eggs fertilized and developed properly, they would not be returned to the uterus and their attempts at IVF would fail at this point.

One woman who had five eggs removed from her ovaries, none of which fertilized, described her feelings in this way:

> LOIS – That was horrible, horrible to go through. There were other girls in the room with me, and when the doctor came down and he looked at me I could tell by his face. His whole face shows his emotions and he just looked at me and he goes, "Not good news." And he came over and he sat down beside me and he put his arm around me. And I said, "Don't say anything, give me a few seconds." I took a couple of deep breaths, and I said, "Okay. I'm fine. Now you tell me what's going on." He said, "They're no good. They're not going to fertilize. You can go home." And I just burst into tears in front of everybody, and I'm not like that. I couldn't help myself.

3) The Waiting Period
The sixteen women who reached this stage in the IVF process

experienced a complex and shifting mixture of emotions which made this period the most stressful part of the procedure for most of them. The primary cause of their extreme anxiety was the fact that each of these women went home knowing that she had a number of embryos in her uterus which might, or might not, implant to produce an ongoing pregnancy. One woman described her feelings on returning home with three embryos in her uterus in the following way:

> JUDY – I was excited. I was very optimistic. I had been kind of up and down during all the drugs, and whether that was just my emotions or the drugs having an effect on my emotions or whatever. I was also tired, it was a lot of running around. It was stressful. But I was very optimistic. I was very excited. I mean there were these little possible Schwartz-Lipmans in there. There were three of those.

The anxiety that some of these women experienced could also be traced to the fact that they had been given conflicting instructions from their doctors about how they should conduct themselves during this period to maximize their chances of pregnancy, or they had not been given any instructions at all.

> JILL – All the doctors have different things. Some of them were saying, oh, you can go right back to work, skydive, you name it. One of the other doctors said he would have everyone lying on their backs for nine months with their legs in the air.

Most women, however, seem to have been told to rest and "take it easy" during the waiting period in order to increase their chances of conception.[8]

> ANNE – They wanted you to keep your feet up and if your employment would let you stay home they felt it

was better because you weren't getting tired and overworked and the stress wasn't on you. So they wanted you to be totally relaxed. Which is fine, but it's not very good for you. How are you going to take your mind off it? That was the hardest, because in the hospital you had your friends there all the time (other patients in the IVF program). You visited. We even went out shopping in between our surgery and the implant. So you had those extra things to do, and now all of a sudden you were told not to do all these kind of things. I think that was very hard. So we spent a lot of time on the phone talking to each other saying the same things over and over I'm sure.

Most of the women who made it to this stage of the procedure reported that they became intensely preoccupied by their bodies and severely limited their movements so as not to dislodge the minute human life that might be developing within them, even though some of them recognized that such restricted behaviour probably had little effect on their pregnancy.

MARILYN – The weird part of it is that you could have discharged the embryo hours after coming home, or a day after coming home. And it's microscopic and you can't see it, but every woman you ever talk to, no doctor can understand it, will get up from peeing and look in the toilet to see something wave at you, because you're sure you've lost it (the embryo). So every time you go to the bathroom you don't push and you just walk like you're walking on eggs … You don't move. You get up slowly. You don't want to lift anything. You rub your stomach. You just do these things naturally. I think it's also the reaction to still having Pergonal and Clomid in your body, because your body thinks it's pregnant. Your mind's going, what the hell are you doing? And that's where you're playing basketball with your emotions, you're up and down like a yo-yo. So it's incredibly hard on you, it's incredibly hard on your spouse, because he doesn't know what to make of you because one minute you're laughing and the next minute you're crying. Two weeks become virtually two years. It could be the same thing. It's the longest time.

Many of the women in this study experienced intense psychological conflict between being optimistic that they would become pregnant through IVF while, at the same time, being realistic about their chances of pregnancy, which they all understood to be very small. Over and over again, these women related how they were told by the medical staff and other IVF patients that their mental attitude played an important – but never clearly defined – role in the possible success of the procedure, and that if they did not "think positive" it would not work. In fact, the idea that a positive mental attitude was essential in order to become pregnant through IVF, or conversely, that a lack of confidence could somehow prevent a pregnancy from occurring, was one of the strongest and most pervasive themes uncovered in this research.

This way of thinking about IVF created a psychological "no win" situation for some of these women, who strove to remain hopeful while, at the same time, trying to protect themselves from being *too* hopeful, as that would make failing to become pregnant even more devastating. The themes of the necessity of being confident that the procedure will work and psychological conflict between hopefulness and realism emerged in the women's accounts of all phases of the procedure, but they seemed to be experienced most acutely during the waiting period.

MARILYN – This is where it's the hardest thing psychologically. You've got to be optimistic. And at the same time you have to be realistic, and realistically speaking the chances of it being successful are not that great. So on the one hand you're going, "This is working and I'm pregnant." On the other hand I'm going, "Why am I doing this? I could be back at the office doing something instead of sitting here with my legs propped up."

ANNE – I told myself that I didn't want to really think that I was pregnant, because I think the fall would have been harder if you psyche yourself up for being pregnant only to find out you're not. But then you can look at it the other way. You can psyche yourself up and if you are, you're already there, right?

The final phase of the IVF procedure is a blood test to see if a pregnancy has occurred, and this is done approximately twelve days after embryo transfer. Some women knew that they had not become pregnant because their menstrual period began before the test was scheduled. However, women were generally instructed by the medical staff to come for this test even if they had already begun to menstruate. Having to do this, knowing that their IVF attempt had failed, was emotionally upsetting.

ANNE – I always got my period on the day I was going down for the blood test … You think to yourself, why couldn't it happen after you had your blood test and you got home but this way you have to go back out and face the world again. It was a little touching, yeah (this last comment delivered in a very soft voice).

For some women, however, the blood test was their first confirmation that they were not pregnant, and this news came by phone after the test was completed. This situation was also extremely difficult, especially if the woman received the news when she was at work, or in a situation where she could not immediately express her grief and disappointment. One woman had not told her family that she was going through

IVF, and she got the news that she was not pregnant on a day when they were visiting.

> LOIS – The doctor called and said, "I'm sorry, it's not positive." I got off the phone and I wanted to bawl. I was just shaking. And I had to wait until everyone left the house until I finally (broke down) … I went to bed for two days.

As the above account clearly demonstrates, the experience of IVF was extremely stressful both physically and emotionally for most of the women in this sample. Although each phase of the procedure has its unique aspects and stresses, the overall theme that emerged from the women's accounts of their experiences was the idea that the stress was unrelenting. One woman expressed this very clearly when I asked her what the most stressful aspect of the IVF experience was for her:

> JOANNE – Getting through it. Day by day. A friend had been through it and we talked about it and she said, "It's going to be really hard on you." And I, Miss Naivete then too said, "Oh no, after all I've been through, I don't think that will be too bad." Wrongo, that was really stressful. It was so bad, so stressful. And I consider myself pretty good at coping with things usually. But at one point, and it was on into the thing too, I think it was even past the laparoscopy, anyways, at one point honest to God I almost packed up and left. I thought, "I cannot stand this another second." It was like a time capsule of all of your expectations and all of your stress just jam packed into five days or six days or whatever it was. And you never got any relief from it. You made it through one day and then you couldn't celebrate because you may not make it through the next day. And so you were just constantly so upset. And those around you were dropping off like flies perhaps. There were girls in the program who would leave in tears who didn't get as far as you were. That was

terrible. The day by day pain of trying to make it through each hurdle with no relief until the end.

CONCLUSIONS

The above account of the IVF experiences of twenty Canadian women reveals in a dramatic way the unrelenting physical and emotional stress of in vitro fertilization which, because of its low success rate, actually allows only a very few infertile women to bear children while using vast amounts of scarce health care resources. Since this research has provided information on women's IVF experience which has not previously been available, it may help some infertile women to decide if they really want to undertake IVF. However, it also raises some important questions.

Is in vitro fertilization a safe technology for women? Given the wide array of drug side effects and the depth of emotional stress reported by most women in this study, I strongly believe that the physical and emotional safety of IVF should be thoroughly investigated by medical researchers who do not stand to benefit from its continued use. This research also makes obvious the need for IVF clinics to provide counseling for those women who do undertake IVF, both during and after their attempt(s).

Although IVF doctors and scientists present IVF to the public as an established technology, it still remains controversial for many Canadians. Most of the ethical, legal and financial issues surrounding its use still remain unresolved. Before we, as a society, can thoroughly evaluate this technology, we must understand what it really entails, especially for those whom it affects most directly. Our understanding will not be complete unless we listen closely to the women who have actually used this demanding and often dangerous technology.

NOTES

1 Chris Anne Raymond, "In Vitro Fertilization Enters Stormy Adolescence As Experts Debate the Odds," *Journal of the American Medical Association,* vol. 259, no. 4, 22-29 Jan 1988, pp. 464-465, 469.

2 Ibid.

3 I interviewed these women and their husbands individually between January and July of 1986. Each woman had undergone at least one IVF attempt in Ontario. All attempts except one took place prior to, or during the data collection period beginning in 1983. The last attempt took place in the first half of 1987.

4 Some hospitals have started to use ultrasound-guided egg selection for some patients. This does not require a general anesthetic.

5 The miscarriage rate for IVF pregnancies is twenty to thirty-five percent, which is approximately equal to the miscarriage rate for normal pregnancy. Raymond, op. cit.

6 All the names used in this article are pseudonyms.

7 Ovarian hyperstimulation can lead to the development of ovarian cysts with accompanying abdominal discomfort or severe pain. Ovarian cysts may rupture, resulting in bleeding into the abdominal cavity which may require surgery and the removal of part or all of the affected ovary. Ovarian hyperstimulation can also lead to temporary or permanent ovarian dysfunction.

8 Currently, this advice seems to be changing towards a "carry on as usual" approach.

Delivering Babies: Contracts and Contradictions [1]

Somer Brodribb

THE RECENT AMERICAN decision to "terminate" Mary Beth Whitehead's right to her child, and to grant custody to the alleged father, William Stern, signals a victory for the surrogacy industry and liberal democratic patriarchy. In awarding custody to the biochemist and not the "former gogo girl," as Whitehead was caricatured,[2] the courts upheld contract law and a regulation of the relations of reproduction by the marketplace. Clearly class biased, New Jersey Judge Harvey Sorkow's decision was also based on a genetic and masculine model of the relationship to a child.

In contrast, two weeks earlier, a British court had upheld the woman's right to her child in another "surrogacy" dispute, in spite of the more economically privileged character of the biological father's home.[3] In February 1988 Chief Justice Robert Wilentz of the New Jersey Supreme Court overturned Sorkow's decision and restored Whitehead as the mother of "Baby M." While a blow to the surrogacy industry, Wilentz's decision has not defeated the thinking of Judge Sorkow in other jurisdictions or countries. The Ontario Law Reform Commission (OLRC), for example, issued the only government report in the world which recommends that surrogacy be legalized. "Surrogate mother contracts" are arrangements which have developed with the purpose of enabling a man to claim custody of a child born through artificial insemination of a contracting woman.

Margaret Atwood's terrifying novel, *The Handmaid's Tale*,[4] presents us with an interesting social theory of the position of breeder women, and the interaction among women and with men. Her futuristic vision is set in the Republic of Gilead, a monolithic theocracy that resembles what once was Cambridge, Massachussetts. In a society weakened by nuclear war, a religious totalitarian government has successfully seized power and, by freezing assets with the push of a button, abolished cash and curtailed freedom of movement. Radiation has caused widespread infertility and severe genetic damage: many babies are "shredders" and live only a few hours. The Republic of Gilead takes the Book of Genesis at its word. The regime controls sexuality and reproduction by categorizing women as Marthas, Marys and Handmaids. Marthas are the domestic workers, Marys the Wives, and the Handmaids are the breeders, in a hierarchy of women controlled by, and subordinate to, men. A Handmaid exists to be bred by the Commander, and her child is appropriated in a ritual where the Wife of the Commander imitates the birth. As a futuristic image of "surrogate motherhood," Atwood's work is already out of date, as the following discussion of medical and legal techniques of control illustrates.

"Surrogate" motherhood is a completely inaccurate term. It is an ideological device reflecting patriarchal interests and is based on a male consciousness of the birth process. Any woman who labours to give birth with her own ova and from her own womb is a real mother. We should not be persuaded, even in the case of embryo transfer (placing the fertilized egg of one woman in the uterus of another), which attempts to divide maternity among uterine, genetic and social mothers, that women relate to pregnancy as Aristotle's passive receptacle. Indeed, women's genetic contribution to the child is a relatively recent challenge to Aristotle's dictum: "The female always provides the material, the male that which fashions it ... while the body is from the female, it is the soul that is from the male."[5] The classical ideologies of woman as empty vessel for the male seed did not succeed in negating women's relationship to pregnancy and children, as the history of female birth ritual indicates. To emphasize the genetic is to adopt a masculine consciousness of birth.[6] "Surrogate" mothers are really surrogate wives to men whose legal wives are infertile. The current legal controversy reflected in the Whitehead baby case has come about because there is currently no way to appropriate the children of women who have been artificially inseminated.

In the legal and media discourse surrounding these technologies, questions of legitimacy and paternity emerge as central. However, biological paternity has always been uncertain. Mary O'Brien in *The Politics of Reproduction* argues that it is for this reason that men elaborate the legal fiction of social paternity and legitimacy in order to establish rights to children. "Paternity, then, is not a natural relationship to a child, but a right to a child ... the assertion of one man's right to a child."[7] The legal assumption that the husband is the father is a central concept in the Western legal tradition: *pater is est quem nuptiae demonstrant* (the father is he whom the marriage points out). This contrasts with the historical certainty of maternity: *mater semper certa est* (the mother is always certain).

It is not irrelevant that these biomedical techniques emerge at a time when, for a variety of reasons, including women's increased economic and social independence, fewer women are relinquishing their children to adoption, and self-insemination is a growing practice. Human artificial insemination was practised in the 1800s. Western society has long glorified that pre-eminent surrogate mother: the Virgin Mary. But now, men as husbands, scientific rationalists, bioethicists, state paternalists and religious sperm freaks are renegotiating the patriarchal alliance and respecifying the terms of rights to paternity in the light of women's increasing reproductive autonomy. Unmarried women and lesbians are acting to inform themselves and other women of the self-insemination procedure, and these informal and almost underground, anonymous networks are a clear political challenge to the patriarchal state and family. It is because this movement for female reproductive autonomy is already in progress that paternity is being redefined and reasserted. And the increasing number of "surrogate" mothers who default on their contract and keep their babies indicates women's resistance to the commodification of their children.

It is regrettable that it takes an American case and a statement by the Pope to bring our attention to the Canadian situation. It was in November 1982 that the Ontario Law Reform Commission was urged to report to the Attorney General on the legal implications of the new reproductive technologies, including donor insemination and "surrogate" motherhood. The impetus for the OLRC study came from the much publicized case of a Florida "surrogate" mother who was to sell her baby to a Scarborough couple. In the 1982 Ontario case, the $20,000 transaction was arranged by Noel Keane of Michigan. The woman came to Canada for the birth but left suddenly and the child was seized by the Metro Toronto Catholic Children's Aid Society (CCAS). In July, Ontario Supreme Court Justice George Walsh ruled that the Scarborough man was the legal and biological father of the child. Family Court Judge Ball later ruled the genetic father was entitled to permanent custody of the boy, rather than the Florida woman's husband. Public discussions soon followed.

A 1983 forum featured Bernard Dickens, the University of Toronto specialist in medical law who was briefly Research Director of the OLRC investigative project. Perhaps the most interesting point of view articulated in that discussion was that of Suzanne Scorsone, Director of the Archdiocesan Office of the Catholic Family Life and spokesperson during the Metro

Toronto CCSA action claiming custody of the child born to the Florida "surrogate" mother:

> Essentially what we are looking at here is the recreation of concubinage. The idea of a childless man, a man whose wife cannot bear children, taking a second-class wife on a contract basis of one form or another and using her reproductive services is something as old as Abraham and Hagar, and older, and it's not just within the Judeo-Christian tradition, it's right across the world. Now one of the evolutions within the Judeo-Christian tradition and, I think, one of the really good things about our society generally, at this point, is that women have not, any longer, been placed in that secondary class position with their reproductive services being used, and the woman herself being treated as an object. If we start having surrogate mothers who can be contracted for this, what we are doing is recreating a sanitized form, without the sexual intercourse, of this second-class concubine status.[8]

Dickens responded: "I think you're missing the nature of contract, which is a free arrangement among equals; that is, if women achieve autonomy over their reproductive capacity, then they are free to offer that as they wish."[9] Scorsone countered:

> Ah! but I doubt they will be equal. First of all, the fact that the woman needs the money, and the man who's giving it doesn't, means that already there is a class situation involved. In many cultures women were perfectly happy to become concubines because they were in a position of needing money, needing the position, needing the respectability of at least being a concubine if they couldn't be a first class wife.[10]

Dickens spoke of women who perform this "service" out of compassion, and of the need not to impose criminal sanctions in a pluralistic society. Another male discussant felt that the usual situation of a "surrogate" mother would likely be a "low-income person or perhaps a housewife who has another child and she wants to stay at home to raise it, but the family could use some money,"[11] and in that case this woman shouldn't be deprived of this opportunity to earn income. Dickens used the analogy between wet nursing and "surrogacy" as a way to validate the concept.

Although she seeks refuge from patriarchal abuses in a protectionist Old Deal, Scorsone is right to question the laissez-faire model of market regulation for relations of reproduction. It is indeed unlikely that wage-laboured birth will mean any more power for women than sexual service. Feet in the stirrups is not the best bargaining position. A feminist approach to the question of "surrogate" motherhood must be based on concerns relating to the economic as well as reproductive and sexual subordination of women. Our politics must not be reduced to a reactive support of an opposite position; it must be one of resistance and creation. The Pope says he is for peace and the redistribution of wealth: are we to oppose this, and similarly endorse surrogacy because he is now against that? We must also examine the social construction of the desire for a child, and how it is that a woman can be humiliated if she is infertile. At the same time, it is necessary to notice that some people's desires are held to be better than others': it is argued that married women's desires for IVF children must be met, or it is said that severe psychological trauma will result. But a "surrogate" mother's desire to keep her child indicates the serious moral flaw of contractual unreliability. A couple's desire for a child, if met, could save a marriage. These examples illustrate that in this and other things, male and heterosexual desire is better recognized and better funded.

The Ontario Law Reform Commission on Human Artificial

Reproduction and Related Matters reported in 1985. These proposals have not become law, but they are important because they indicate the direction official discourse is taking. The report opts for a consumer choice and social stability model for reproduction and family structure. It contrasts two ideological techniques: "private ordering" of reproduction, appropriate for donor insemination and in vitro fertilization, and "state regulation" for surrogate motherhood. Thus, masculine dominance is assured by professional codes and legislative sanctions. In the case of donor insemination, the discretion of the medical profession becomes sanctified and privatized. Donor insemination, which afforded some control to women by disrupting traditional controls over paternity, is medicalized because of the supposed seriousness of the procedure. The Commissioners are of the opinion that "the injection of semen into the uterus could cause a severe reaction, and possibly death."[12] Although donor insemination is being institutionalized, and self-insemination criminalized, the actions of the medical profession are being privatized in order to absolve doctors of liability under the Charter of Rights in case they are charged with practising discrimination based on marital status. Nor would the Ontario Human Rights Charter provide a basis to charge doctors with discrimination according to marital status, since "suitability to parent"[13] could be argued.

While the behaviour of medical practitioners as moral decision-makers is being privatized, that of women as "surrogate mother" is to be subject to regulation. This is achieved first by the Report's equation of motherhood and sperm donation in terms of intentionality: "she wishes to have nothing further to do with the child."[14] In the political ideology based on a total but "neutral" male model of male body and ethics, women shall be allowed to donate their children, as men do their sperm. It is certainly not the intention of the Report to strengthen women's abilities to keep and care for their children through recommendations for improved social services, housing or economic conditions for women.

The all-male Law Reform Commission stresses the genetic importance of the "surrogate" mother to the child, and conjures away the centrality of birthing, which traditionally established a woman's relationship to a child. The Report emphasizes that the transfer of custody is the key feature of "surrogate" motherhood. Simple transfer of custody, however, would logically suggest a model similar to adoption, except that under current adoption law, women retain the decision-making capacity before birth. Clearly, it is the sperm that is at issue here, and paternal rights. Therefore, the "surrogate" is seen as potentially disruptive, capable of a sudden impetuous decision not to surrender her child. Thus, the surrogacy arrangement devised by the Commissioners is based on "contract law, and, in particular, the law respecting specific performance."[15] A command performance, that is, to return the tiny Sperm made Flesh to its "social parents." Interestingly, throughout the Report, the contractors are referred to as the "social parents" of the fetus. This establishes the "social parents" as Culture, and the "surrogate" mother as Nature (ever capricious). The Commission recommends that "where a surrogate mother refuses to transfer custody, she could be compelled to do so by court order."[16] And if, during the pregnancy, she begins to waiver or indicate some attitudinal change, then "where the court is satisfied that the surrogate mother intends to refuse to surrender the child upon birth, the court, prior to the birth of the child, should be empowered to make an order for transfer of custody upon birth."[17] Indeed, the "unreliability" of Mary Beth Whitehead was put forward as an important consideration for denying her custody.[18] She was described by Judge Sorkow as "narcissistic, controlling, unstable, exploitative and lacking in empathy."[19] William Stern, who represents Culture and the good of the community, was applauded for a supposed "ability to make rational decisions in the most trying of circumstances."[20]

This division of the pregnant woman into a freely contracting and entrepreneurial – but altruistic – individual also establishes the fetus as the property of another party, which has implications for abortion. What are the consequences for women if current legal controls over female procreativity, such as the abortion laws, extend to "surrogacy" and embryo transfer? Bernard Dickens approves of Judge Sorkow's decision, and has admonished women: "Women have come of age. If you enter into a contract, don't be surprised that you will be kept to it."[21] Will female lawyers continue this attitude? Already, lawyers such as Linda Silver Dranoff have offered to draw up contracts controlling a woman's smoking, drinking, nutritional, sexual and aerobic behaviour. She recognized, in a January 1984 advice column in *Chatelaine,* that under current laws any mother can change her mind and refuse to give up her baby for adoption. Nevertheless, she offered to draw up contracts for readers that would require the surrogate to:

> Undergo psychological, medical and genetic tests before artificial insemination; forgo sexual intercourse with her husband or lover for at least two weeks before and two weeks after artificial insemination; follow specified nutritional guidelines, get proper rest, not smoke, drink alcohol, take drugs or expose herself to other possible hazards and keep you informed of her medical condition during pregnancy; attempt another artificial insemination or terminate the contract if the first artificial insemination doesn't work or if she miscarries involuntarily; seek your permission if she wants to abort, either because of medical problems or second thoughts.[22]

The Centre for Bioethics in Montreal has approved of "surrogate" motherhood and finds it morally acceptable because "it doesn't necessarily depersonalize motherhood or human sexuality or violate the integrity of the marital relationship .... The practice doesn't trivialize pregnancy or childbirth because it helps a couple fulfill one of the purposes of marriage."[23] The major concern of Dr. David Roy of the Centre is whether or not "surrogate" motherhood jeopardizes the marital relationship. It is the "surrogates" who could act immorally, and who must be regulated and penalized. Dr. Roy finds that "the profit-making aspect of surrogate motherhood can render it immoral, and he calls for regulatory legislation with sanction against women who accept anything more than expenses associated with the pregnancy."[24]

As feminists have pointed out,

> The most victimized character in the courtroom dramas is unquestionably the surrogate mother. Most of the public censure is directed toward her for accepting a fee, while everyone expects doctors and lawyers to charge for their services. "We want to avoid the money-hungry types," said the attorney who is holding up the book he wrote in every photo I saw. Women who list money as the only motive on their application forms are not selected. They must be able to provide reasons more compatible with public opinion: they truly enjoy pregnancy, they want to "give life"; they want to share their happiness with total strangers.[25]

Abortion rights do not figure in the OLRC recommendations, even though, as the Report itself acknowledges, "At present, it is usual in medical treatment and research for patients and subjects to be free to withdraw their consent at any time." The Commission refused to resolve the question of whose "rights" are paramount: the contracting or delivering party. With respect to ineffective lavage (the technique to wash the embryo from the womb) after in vitro fertilization, the Report considers: "We suggest that it would be salutary if, upon diagnosis of the pregnancy, the woman were to be allowed to agree with the couple that, upon birth, the child will be surrendered to them, and that she will continue her pregnancy as a surrogate mother."[26] One may only choose to become a "surrogate" mother (if you pass the screening tests) but, under Canadian law, it is not obvious that one may choose otherwise, once pregnant. Are we to be relieved that the Commissioners do "not find it undesirable"[27] that a woman retain the right to back out of a signed agreement, before insemination or embryo transfer take place? Even this measure of autonomy would be annulled if Judge Sorkow's reasoning comes north. As *The Globe and Mail* reported, "He used the same principle that upset U.S. anti-abortion laws – the right to control what a person does with his or her body – to find that men have the constitutional right to use their sperm to reproduce via a surrogacy contract."[28] In New Jersey, the sperm as entrepreneur has now acquired constitutional rights. The rights of women to abort this sperm are denied by the laws of the marketplace. In this way, men have a greater right to reproduce than women have to their corporal autonomy. In Canada, then, we would have to be as outraged that men have to leave the country to find mothers for their sperm as we are that women often have to leave for safe abortions.

Forced to choose pregnancy, forced to surrender our children, these are the choices offered by a liberal democratic patriarchy which, while urging women to exercise individual will and consumer choice, resists women's real autonomy and collective control. Susan Ince's experience in the American surrogate industry as a "surrogate" mother revealed to her that "The careful screening process was a myth. I encountered no evidence of real medical or psychological safeguards, just enough hurdles to test whether I would be obedient."[29] These are the realities of women's lack of control under which we must contextualize medical promises of consumer choice in childbirth. It is the freedom of women to bear and keep children that is at stake. And we cannot allow the theft of child-birth to become the theft of "surrogate" women's children.

Interestingly, it is not women, but male lawyers and commissioners who are posing the issue in terms of compassion versus commercialism ("surrogate" mothers as humanitarians or prostitutes), and who are championing women's "rights" to reproductive prostitution. Osgoode Hall Law Professor Allan Hutchinson accuses his colleague, Allan Leal, Vice Chairman of the Ontario Law Reform Commission, of sexism. Hutchinson is right that Leal's dissent, and his rejection of artificial insemination and surrogate motherhood, is based on a conception that childbearing and rearing must take place in a marital union, and therefore Leal's objections do, as Hutchinson argued in *The Globe and Mail* in 1985, "draw their force from the dominant male view of sexual roles and family relations."[30] But Hutchinson's own model of equality for women is a package deal: if we want abortion rights, we must accept surrogacy. The idea that abortion rights must be bought with surrogacy, the proposition that if we want choice we must be ready to be chosen from the surrogate mother photo files, is increasingly being put forward, as the following newspaper account illustrates:

> And imposing outright legal sanctions against surrogacy in Canada will drive more couples across the border, predicts David Roy, director of the Centre for Bioethics in Montreal and co-founder of a reproductive technology workshop also slated to report next month. Dickens, another co-founder and the consultant expert for the Ontario commision, agrees, "Oh no, we are not going to make the same mistake we made with our abortion laws," he vows, referring to the large number of Canadian women forced to go outside the country every year for abortions.[31]

And, as Allan Hutchinson proclaims,

The freedom of men to control their own sexual lives
must be extended to women. This is nowhere more
urgent than in procreative decisions. The traditional
views of motherhood and sexual exploitation are male
… Any improvement must begin with opportunities for
women to reclaim and redefine their sexual roles and
responsibilities. Motherhood is one place to begin. And
surrogacy is a first step.

One is tempted to ask – a baby step? But this extension to
women of a male conception of freedom, freedom in the marketplace, freedom as male-defined "sexual liberation," is neither non-sexist nor neutral. It obliterates women's "reproductive consciousness," which is a source for the elaboration of a
way of knowing and being which is not one of separation,
violence and control.[32] The liberal, masculinist approach
silences through ridicule, renders inaudible, out of order
women's experiences, desires and relationships to maternity.
Maternity must now, like sexuality, only be spoken of with
patriarchal words. The step we are urged to take, in this masculine ordering of control over our procreative processes, is to
confess and repudiate our anachronistic maternal consciousness.

The defense of a woman's "right" to sell her child depends
on an equation of the sperm and "the final product," the child.
As one disingenuous headline in *The Guardian* reads, "No
one makes a fuss about artificial insemination by donor. So
why all the bother about surrogate births?"[33] Actually, the
favourite example for the justification of surrogacy is "Suppos-
ing two sisters …." But surely we can remember that the family is no guarantee of agreement and harmony. There is so
little evidence of sisters anxious to make this arrangement that
The London Times was forced to resort to printing a story of
two sisters who were very much in the preliminary stage of
considering embryo transfer, depending upon their boy-

friend's, husband's and sons' approvals. Glenda remarked of her sister Jacki: "We are just using Jacki as a suitcase, really, an incubator to carry it. At the end of the day it's our child."[34]

Surrogacy is big business. For example, Harriet Blankfeld wants to see her Bethesda, Maryland *National Centre for Surrogate Parenting Inc.* become the "Coca-Cola of the surrogate parenting industry"[35] with branch plants worldwide. Genetics is likely to replace economics as the key political issue of the future. With embryo transfer, Women of Colour could be used to carry white babies, and Gena Corea has already discovered some evidence that this is happening in Central America. She has also pointed out that the new reproductive technologies could be used to extend the brothel model of social control over women: "Women can sell eggs, ovaries and wombs as they can now sell vaginas, breasts and buttocks."[36] Andrea Dworkin captures the patriarchal liberalism behind this new commodification of women and children:

> The arguments as to the social and moral appropriateness of this new kind of sale simply reiterate the view of female found in discussions of prostitution: does the state have the right to interfere with this exercise of individual female will (in selling use of the womb)? If a woman wants to sell the use of her womb in an explicit commercial transaction, what right has the state to deny her this proper exercise of femininity in the marketplace? Again, the state has constructed the social, economic, and political situation in which the sale of some sexual or reproductive capacity is necessary to the survival of women, and yet the selling is seen to be an act of individual will – the only kind of assertion of individual will in women that is vigorously defended as a matter of course by most of those who pontificate on female freedom. The state denies women a host of other possibilities, from education to jobs to equal rights before the law to

sexual self-determination in marriage; but it is state intrusion into her selling of sex or a sex-class specific capacity that provokes a defense of her will, her right, her individual self – defined strictly in terms of the will to sell what it is appropriate for females to sell.[37]

It is crucial that we understand why this legislation is being developed now, and not some other time after the late 1800s when donor insemination was first practised. Donor insemination is a relatively simple technique: the difficulty when it is applied to surrogate wives is that there is currently no legislation assuring paternity rights. The institution of access to DI through the medical system would criminalize women's self-insemination networks. Nor can we ignore the assertion of "other rights" in this context that challenge women's struggle for abortion rights. And clearly the implications of these proposals are different in terms of a woman's race and class. Mary O'Brien has argued that "Reproductive technology makes the marriage of capitalism and patriarchy fecund."[38]

Feminists have responded wryly to conservative attempts to "protect" women against the exploitation of surrogacy. Renate Duelli Klein points out that the Warnock report in England on reproductive technologies focuses on the rights of the embryo and the moral dilemmas of manipulating and exchanging eggs and embryos. Her position on surrogacy is

the practice of offering one's uterus to another (for money or free) could – at least theoretically – be under the control of women. That is, surrogacy could be arranged between the two women themselves and without the interference of exploitative baby agencies. It appears that the Warnock Committee advocates the strictest control in those two areas where women can act without any technological interferences (AI-D and surrogacy) … It is very interesting to see the moral outrage towards the "hiring of a uterus for money," and it shows

154 The Future of Human Reproduction

once again – independent of how we personally see the problem of surrogate mothering – that women's control over our bodies is severely opposed.[39]

And English feminist Jalna Hanmer agrees: "The outcry against surrogacy in Britain is interesting. No doubt women can be abused by the spread of this practice, but surrogacy, like AI-D, can put power in women's hands. Could this explain the vehemence of the opposition to *all* surrogacy, not just the money making agencies?"[40] Other feminists perceive both artificial insemination and surrogacy as similar movements in a process of commodification, and therefore reject women's self-insemination networks, including the needs and perspectives of lesbians. Louise Vandelac argues that changes in reproductive technologies are less significant than the elaboration of an economy of human reproduction which has the same androcentric values and rhythms as production. The objectification of male sperm is part of the same process as the exploitation of women as surrogates.[41] Klein and Hanmer also resist the Taylorization of childbirth, but argue that women can disrupt and confuse certain aspects of patriarchal control. Whether this fracturing of masculine dominance necessarily empowers women, and puts us on the path to a feminist future, is less certain.

Françoise Laborie's article, "Ceci est un éthique,"[42] romanticizes "surrogate mothers" as modern witches, disruptive outlaws who taunt science's inability to develop an artificial plancenta, wild women who intervene and interrupt a context of scientific rationality by speaking of love and the gift of life. Yet Laborie's attention remains fixed on the Lacanian look: she is caught in reaction to the masculinist discourse and in conversation with the hysteria surrounding "surrogate" motherhood. Accepting patriarchal dualism, she equates opposite with opposition, trick with resistance. For "surrogate mothers" are liminars; their ambiguity is assured of resolution because it is fundamentally linked to social norms. The absorption of "sur-

rogate" motherhood does not require permanent or fundamental changes in the patriarchal social order. Rather, it is a
legal technology which assists the patriarchal appropriation of
children, now updated to include children from donor
insemination. Laborie attempts to make surrogacy the child of
the women's movement because she accepts a masculine
reproductive and sexual consciousness of exteriority:

> Because here, it seems to me, at the moment of having a
> child in the traditional manner, where sexuality is
> involved, there is ejaculation from the man to the
> woman, the sperm exits, as a separate part of the male
> body and nine months later: birth, parturition, a separate
> part of the mother's body, which it is necessary to detach
> in cutting the umbilical cord. There can be, therefore, at
> the moment of conception, a structural imaginary equiv-
> alence between sperm and child.[43]

Laborie's solution is that legally, surrogacy should be
treated like DI. In a context of masculine dominance, where
divisions of race and class still penetrate the best-intentioned
feminist politics, surrogacy as power for women is ultimately
myopic, a naive delusion, the true science fiction. Surrogacy is
not individual imaginary physiology, but big business.

This is a period of ideological as well as technological war-
fare over women's procreativity, and our feminist response
must not be defined in reaction to whichever variation of
patriarchal ideology we are addressing. A feminist critique of
the philosophy of science and of liberal individualism is necessary to avoid a reactive politics which would be ultimately
connected to the fixed norms of patriarchal culture: liberal or
neo-conservative. These decisions and discourses indicate
that it is as much maternity as paternity that is being redefined.
An integrative understanding of birth does not see parturition
as a technological event, children as commodities or women
as suitcases. Maternity is the challenge of the century to femin-

ists, a challenge taken up by Mary O'Brien, whose work makes visible an epistemology which is not one of separation, a consciousness which is not fundamental hostility to otherness, and a dialectics which does not proceed through negation. For without this philosophy of birth, we will be constrained to imagine and perform maternal desires, processes, experiences and relationships to children with patriarchal language and tools. Women are being offered a surrogate reproductive consciousness, a masculine one, where freedom is alienation, and where the cultural primacy of exteriority – male genitals and science – implies our inferiority. Our challenge is to resist childbirth as alienated waged labour, and the patriarchal assertion of rights to children and control over female procreativity and corporal autonomy.

NOTES

1   An earlier version of this paper appeared in *Broadside,* vol.8, no. 7 (May 1987), pp. 8-9. See also "Off the Pedestal and Onto the Bloc? Motherhood, Reproductive Technologies, and the Canadian State," *Canadian Journal of Women and the Law,* vol. 1, no. 2 (1986), pp. 407-423.

2   "Custody of Baby M given to father, judge upholds surrogate contract," *The Toronto Star,* 1 April 1987, sec. A, p. 4.

3   "British mom wins fight for her surrogate twins," *The Toronto Star,* 14 March 1987.

4   Margaret Atwood, *The Handmaid's Tale* (Toronto, McClelland and Stewart, 1985).

5   Rosemary Agonito, *History of Ideas on Women: A Sourcebook* (New York, G.P. Putnam, 1977), p. 47.

6   This is based on Mary O'Brien's outstanding and original philosophy of birth. Her Marxist, feminist and radical theory of a universal, genderically differentiated, historical consciousnesses of reproduction and species continuity is elaborated in Mary O'Brien, *The Politics of Reproduction* (London, Routledge and Kegan Paul, 1981); Mary O'Brien, *Reproducing the World* (Boulder, Colorado, Westview Press, 1989).

7   O'Brien, op. cit., 1981, p. 54.

8 "The borrowed-womb debate," *The Globe and Mail,* 2 August 1983, p. 8.

9 Ibid.

10 Ibid.

11 Ibid.

12 Ontario Law Reform Commission, *Report on Human Artificial Reproduction and Related Matters,* 2 volumes (Toronto, Ministry of the Attorney General, June 1985), p. 33.

13 Ibid., p. 49.

14 Ibid., p. 72.

15 Ibid., p. 250.

16 Ibid., p. 252.

17 Ibid., p. 252.

18 "Custody of Baby M" sec. A, p. 1 and p. 4.

19 Ibid., sec. A, p. 1.

20 Ibid., sec. A, p. 4.

21 Dorothy Lipovenko, "Baby M ruling a milestone for surrogate motherhood," *The Globe and Mail,* 2 April 1987, sec A, p. 7.

22 Linda Silver Dranoff, in "Free for the Asking," *Chatelaine,* January 1984, p. 26.

23 Marine Strauss, "Surrogate birth acceptable, medical ethics expert says," *The Globe and Mail,* 2 May 1983.

24 Ibid.

25 Mary Kay Blakely, "Surrogate Mothers: For whom are they working?" *Ms,* March 1983, p. 18.

26 Ibid., p. 61.

27 Ibid., p. 265.

28 Lipovenko, op. cit.

29 Susan Ince, "Inside the Surrogate Industry" in Rita Arditti, Renate Duelli Klein and Shelley Minden, eds., *Test-Tube Women: What Future for Motherhood?* (London, Pandora Press, 1984), p. 110.

30 Allan C. Hutchinson, "Surrogate motherhood: why it should be permitted," *The Globe and Mail*, 12 July 1985, p. 7.

31 Sarah Jane Growe, "Surrogate mothers: legislators haven't decided whether they're humanitarians or prostitutes," *The Toronto Star*, 23 March 1985, sec. L, p. 1.

32 O'Brien, op. cit., 1981.

33 Clare Dyer, "Baby Cotton and the birth of a moral panic. No one makes a fuss about artificial insemination by donor. So why all the bother about surrogate births?" *Guardian Women*, 15 January 1985, p. 20.

34 "Why I am having a baby for my sister," *The Times*, 23 November 1984, p. 11.

35 Sarah Helm *et al.*, "Nothing Left to chance in 'rent-a-womb' agreements" *The Toronto Star*, 13 January 1985, sec. H, p. 1.

36 Gena Corea, "How the New Reproductive Technologies could be used to apply the brothel model of social control over women," *Women's Studies International Forum*, vol. 8, no. 4 (1985), pp. 299-305, p. 299.

37 Andrea Dworkin, *Right-Wing Women* (New York, Perigee Books, 1983), p, 182.

38 Mary O'Brien, "State Power and Reproductive Freedom," *Canadian Woman Studies / les cahiers de la femme*, vol. 6, no. 3 (Summer / Fall 1985), pp. 62-66, p. 63.

39 Renate Duelli Klein, "Taking the Egg from the One and the Uterus from the Other," *Development: Seeds of Change*, vol.4 (1984), pp.92-97, p. 92.

40 Jalna Hanmer, "Transforming Consciousness: women and the new reproductive technologies," in Gena Corea *et al.*, eds., *Man-Made Women* (London, Hutchinson, 1985), pp. 88-109, p. 96.

41 Louise Vandelac, "Sexes et nouvelles technologies de la reproduction humaine ... Songes et mensonges," *Resources for Feminist Research / Documentation sur la recherche féministe*, vol. 15, no. 4 (November 1986), pp. 28-31.

42 Françoise Laborie, "Ceci est un éthique. Bon dos? bon ventre? Les mères porteuses ..." *Les Temps modernes*, no. 462 (janvier 1985), pp. 1215-1255; "Ceci est un éthique (II), Des mères porteuses encore ..." *Les Temps modernes*, no. 463 (fevrier 1985), pp. 1518-1543.

43 Ibid., no. 463, p. 1541, translation by Somer Brodribb.

Small "p" Politics: The Midwifery Example

Patricia O'Reilly

IF YOU WERE A TWENTIETH century woman expecting to bear a child and you lived in the Netherlands, or Nigeria, or France, or Brazil, or England or almost any country of the world, you could choose both your type and location of parturient care. But unlike most women, if you lived in twentieth century North America, you would have little or no control over either of these choices. Regardless of the level of risk your pregnancy presented, you would be attended by medical personnel and you would give birth in a medical institution – where available.[1] And your overall chances of a healthy outcome would be among the lowest in the developed world.[2]

However, some North American women do defy the authorities. Where normal birth is indicated, a small but growing number have placed their care with a midwife (usually in association with a medical doctor in case of emergency or medicine needs), and have given birth wherever they felt most comfortable doing so (either at home or in a hospital). In recent historical times the midwives who attend these women in Canada have been shut out by the medical profession and endangered by the law. Unlike the medical doctor who faces disappointment over the normal death of an occasional newborn, the midwife, party to the same unfortunate event, faces imprisonment. The charge of criminal negligence hangs heavily over her head.

Following the 1985 Ontario death of a newborn two days

159

after a midwifery-assisted birth, a coroner's inquest was held. However, after reviewing the case (and the story and facts about midwifery practices), the jury recommended not criminal conviction of the midwife but rather that midwifery be granted both legal recognition and incorporation into the existing health care system. The Ontario Minister of Health subsequently announced the Ministry's intention to establish midwifery as a regulated health profession. A task force was set up to study the issue. Its recommendations include self-regulation for an autonomous midwifery profession and access to the present hospital system.[3] Based on extensive research, which included study of many other countries' systems for childbirth, the task force came out in favour of a proposed midwifery profession, as well as acceptance of home-birth.[4]

Given their strong approval of the technical abilities and compassionate and considerate care of midwives, one wonders how it was that midwives ever came to be so maligned and misunderstood by competing professionals as well as by a great deal of the public. The politics of this injustice is very telling. Like all of the past and present struggles for reproductive assistance and choices surrounding birth control devices, abortion and new issues created by developing technologies, various factors come into complex interplay. Nevertheless, there are common political themes, and it is these on which I wish to concentrate.

By "political" I mean much. Within the ordinary stories of ordinary people's lives is a lived politics articulated daily in their most simple acts and everyday language. Reality is both concrete and theoretical: analysis of this reality ought to be both concrete and theoretical. By this I mean simply that when we look to our own and others' lives, we must inevitably balance out what is often misconstrued as two separate things: the events of life, and the ideas and beliefs within which they are embedded. Fancy theories about human nature and socialization, reason and moral responsibility, individual freedom and collective identity, liberalism and democracy, are all being experienced daily by each of us. There is a tendency to think of these things as "out there" – fodder for intellectuals. But if we are to understand the positions within which society has constrained us, then we must grapple with what lies behind, and has provided sanction for, those constraints; that is, the political and philosophical claims that provide the "theoretical" foundation for the social and political controls within which we must draw our every breath.

Our contemporary Western political system has won its ethical legitimacy mainly on the basis of concepts of liberalism and democracy, both of which necessitate the interaction of human beings capable of reason and morality. However, women have historically been assumed to be deficient in both of these realms. We have paid a heavy price both theoretically and practically for such false assumptions. In order to understand the historically-based set of ideas and beliefs upon which our present, and therefore future, situation rests, we must at least attempt to unravel a very complex set of dynamics. We sometimes fall back into the old way of thinking of politics in terms of institutionally recognized organizations and actors only, that is, public things like parliament, political parties and the courts, and public figures like the prime minister and parliamentarians, arguing over the heads of ordinary people about public political issues. But politics as lived experience is, and has always been, much more than this. While the earlier institutionally oriented type of analysis does cover one important element of political struggle, it can only take us so far towards gaining a better understanding of all of the political forces concomitant to any public decision. As we will see, too many things get left out.

It is also inadequate in helping us to formulate an alternative vision on which to build our political ethics. It does nothing to help us define "the Good," or the ends of our political community. Politics is about how the goods and bads of our shared existence get defined and distributed. A careful political analysis might provide us with some direction towards the formulation and means to feminist ends. The Canadian midwifery case can provide such an example.

In the twentieth century, control over the traditionally female-dominated practice of midwifery was won over completely by the medical profession. Unlike most other countries (with the exception of the United States which parallels the Canadian experience), childbirth was moved almost entirely from the home to the hospital: a location from which midwives were to be excluded. At first glance it appears as a good example of traditional political institutional battling. (Who do the traditional institutions of the legislature and the courts grant legitimacy and / or funding to?) However, it is important to recognize this institutional battlefield as only the overt manifestation of all that lies fermenting beneath it. Several crucial elements come into play. This story of political struggle for control is, first and foremost, a story of political struggle for social / political definitions of the constitution and usefulness of expertise and knowledge, the role of ethical and altruistic guardianship, the maintenance of traditional gender, class and race hierarchical positions and their "moral" and "intellectual" baggage, various territorial claims in relation to economic and political monopoly and, finally, individual and collective identity and survival in the midst of all this struggling.

All of these dimensions interact and overlap. They can be unravelled only very carefully, as one might try to guess the personal history of a life by sifting through the contents of an old trunk found in the attic. To look only to the institutional legislation and laws of midwifery would be like trying to know a personality only from the furniture in that person's house. So let us look also to the closets and trunks.

The historical institutional battle in North America has been well documented.[5] Professionalized medicine had won a social and political monopoly over childbirth by the early 1900s – *before* its emergency measures were scientifically safer than non-technological, midwifery-assisted birth.[6] Today, in Canada, midwifery and homebirth are again being fought against by the medical profession on the false grounds of better safety associated with medical hospital birth.[7] How the medical profession has been able to convince the public that they are the better guardians of normal birth as well as emergency birth situations which would necessitate technological intervention, despite all evidence to the contrary, is the real political story.[8] And it is a story that is being retold throughout all of today's reproductive issues.

One of the main factors in the medical profession's gaining of access to all of childbirth was its monopolization of the realm of scientific expertise. They became the expert definers not only of what constituted scientific and technologically necessary intervention in physiologically problematic childbirth, but also, in the North American case especially, of acceptable intervention and practices in normal childbirth. The latter was most significant in that it was the application of new scientific medical tools, for example, forceps, anesthesia, aseptic drugs and Caesarean surgery (somehow assumed to be the exclusive territory of men), on which justification of male intervention rested. Midwives were not opposed to interventionist medicine where necessary. Then, as now, they welcomed emergency help. But how was it that only medical professionals were seen as capable of handling the new scientific tools? Any use of interventionist birth technology could only have been justified in terms of its effectiveness in reducing mortality and morbidity risks in birth outcome. Given the circumstances in which the first of these tools, the forceps, was introduced (in Europe circa 1700), this justification was certainly debatable. Male attendants, because they attended only difficult births, knew considerably less of the normal birth process and thus were apt to cause much damage by unnecessary intervention. Throughout the Western world, injury to mother and infant was even more pronounced when birth started moving into the hospital in the mid 1800s. Due to a lack of understanding of septic infection which was being passed on to women during birth by unscrubbed doctors, puerperal fever raged, leading to a dramatic increase in maternal mortality rates. "In Europe hospital birth was roughly six times more dangerous than home birth in the 1860s."[9]

Despite all this, a very strong climate of uncritical acceptance of scientific progress as "good" seemed to obfuscate the "details." The new god spoke and almost everyone listened. As elsewhere, he spoke in a male voice with a decidedly White Anglo Saxon Protestant (WASP) accent. The new technologies became the "science" or "knowledge" of the day, not because they were based on proven fact, but because they were presented and accepted as such. Today the Canadian medical profession is so strongly entrenched in the position of health "expertise" as to feel little need to even bother with scientific data to support their claim, for example, that non-medical birth is dangerous for all women. As I have documented elsewhere, the recent fight in Ontario has been most striking in that it has been the midwives who have made use of relevant scientific studies (found in the doctors' own academic journals) to argue their case, whereas the medical professionals in general have provided little more than rhetoric.[10] The political battle is not about facts: it is about who gets to define the construction and use of "facts."

These "experts" have also gained legitimacy through their assumed role of altruistic and ethical guardianship. This elevated position is, of course, intricately linked to the glorification of professional expertise. There is a tendency for the public to grant a kind of moral authority to the professional which goes well beyond the realm of his or her technical expertise. Throughout a recent Ontario Medical Association discussion paper on childbirth, emphasis was placed on the association's "responsibility to its members to help maintain a position of leadership" (in the community).[11] Why it is they feel the public needs, or would wish, to be led at all in these matters (especially by scientists), is never addressed. Furthermore, the doctor's role as altruistic guardian is seriously called into question by the profit orientation of the medical business. It is an altruism with a hefty price tag.

This caretaker role is very much linked to the paternalism of the medical profession. Unlike the midwifery model of care which advocates a mother-centred decision-making orientation, the medical model of care has historically been based on a hierarchical, if not authoritarian, orientation, whereby the patient is reduced to the moral level of a child. And, of course, all of this is exacerbated by traditional Western gender, race and class biases around which public support is rallied. Ideas about such socially and politically constructed notions as the rightful place and potential danger of women and persons of particular race and class were given the totally unjustified professional sanction of "value-neutral" science. Such intellectual smugness could only have come from something as untouchable as the new scientific mode of thought, a mode whereby the scientific discoveries of the day were fast becoming the only criteria for health management. For example, one of the major turning points in North American medical history came with the recommendation of the Flexner Report in 1910[12] which was commissioned by the philanthropic Carnegie Foundation, and which was to carry a great deal of weight with later government funding. Flexner found that only those schools teaching the new scientific medicine to well-to-do males were "fit" establishments. All of the women's training colleges and most of those for blacks were left to die. The American Medical Association could hardly have been turned to for support, since they had themselves included in their 1870 Code of Ethics a clause which held physicians in violation of the code "if they consulted with sectarian (that is, traditional, alternatively-trained) physicians or female or black doctors."[13]

These kinds of prejudices set the tone which we have seen carried into the present day in terms of the translation of such non-medical issues as sexuality, intellect and moral responsibility into supposedly medical areas of judgement. It is sometimes argued that medical professionals, being a product of a particular social climate, cannot be held any more responsible than anyone else. I would argue that just as their claim to scientific expertise leaves them open to intellectual and moral criticism for the cover-up or abuse of inconvenient scientific facts, so too can they be held more responsible for sex, class, and race biases *because* of their claim to scientific objectivity and humanitarianism. To their discredit, they are party to these biases in an active way by using bad science to lend credence to bad assumptions. They were granted political institutional backing on the assumption they were to uphold the public trust; they have abused that trust.

These biases of the medical professionals often lend credence to what they see as their natural territorial rights. Recognized experts seem to have a tendency, once having won support for a particular realm for their own activities, of first turning this support towards sanction for their exclusive claim to this self-defined territory, and then, after a bit of time and lazy public memory, assuming their unquestionable right to judge others unfit for entry even into the fringes of "their" realm. Unfortunately, a great deal of the public buys this rather arrogant stance, but there is no reason to assume that historically-based territorial justifications are valid today. The medical profession itself has a rather selective memory. In a recent fight with the Ontario Ministry of Health over "extra billing" it was loudly protesting against government interference in publicly-funded "medical territory." Just a few decades ago, when the association was fighting for a monopoly over this very territory, it was lobbying heavily for exactly such "interference" – which it then referred to as "support."

The medical orientation to birth has not gone unchallenged. Resistance has always been present in some form or other,[14] but it has taken on a new strength in Canada today. Individual midwives (who always practised to some extent) and small collective midwifery practices have become politically organized in opposition to their vulnerable non-legal status. Alternative medical practitioners in general continue to gain access to previously inaccessible areas.[15] And the public is increasingly seeking greater access both to less technologically and bureaucratically oriented care and to the political means of institutionally guaranteeing this access.

While there is a tendency for politicians to ignore issues related to women's reproduction, or to leave them to the courts, the recent activities in Ontario surrounding the midwifery debate may symbolize an opening up of the political process in two major directions, both of which would be important for feminist strategy. First, it may point to a new type of politics whereby the process is expanding to meet the increased political demands of a disenchanted public. In keeping with the relatively recent populist orientation of the Ontario Ministry of Health,[16] the task force described its mandate and process thus:

> [We] gathered information about how midwifery is practised inside and outside Canada, how Ontario midwives and other health care providers envision the integration of midwifery care into the health care system, and how the public perceives its needs. We consulted extensively with organizations representing physicians, nurses, hospitals, health sciences educators, and midwives, and we held public hearings [in various cities].... Submissions

were received from more than 500 women's groups, consumer organizations, and individuals. We assembled an
extensive collection of literature.... [W]e chose to visit
places [internationally] where midwives function auton-
omously and have clearly defined roles in the health care
system, as well as places where midwives have difficulty
functioning to their full potential and find their roles
threatened or not yet fully realized ...[17]

Those familiar with the public policy process will recognize
this as a relatively broad and sensitive effort at solicitation and
consideration of public concerns. This effort provided access
points for individuals and small groups into a system from
which they are usually covertly excluded by their lack of the
economic and political clout necessary for the game of
"power politics." The forum set up by the task force encouraged discussion at a level well beyond that possible in the
ordinary courts or legislatures. It was an arena where small "p"
politics could be practised by ordinary people; where they
could challenge standard notions of expertise; and where
they were listened to.

Secondly, in relation to a new political direction, more than
just providing a model of greater democratic participation,
this process can be seen to symbolize a new way of thinking.
Considerable sensitivity was brought to bear on the whole
process. First, the selection of the task force members was
geared towards a weighting favouring women's lives. The
chairperson, Mary Eberts, is well known for her work in this
area. Second, the actions undertaken by the task force itself
showed considerable sensitivity for the women who would
be affected by the conclusions of the report.

Unlike election voting processes or populist-type opinion
polls which fail to differentiate between irrational and
reasoned democratic opinion and which give equal weight to
the opinions of those who will not be called upon to bear the

consequences of the decision, a task force process is designed to elicit a more reasoned and balanced assessment. The Task Force on the Implementation of Midwifery in Ontario went to great lengths to do just that. Its members travelled to other countries and to remote regions of the province for comparative analyses, and they presented ample opportunity to the midwives and interested parents to argue their positions. And, since women's lives and the lives of their newborns were to be affected most by the report, the task force members weighted their concerns towards these lives. Midwifery was not seen as a general public issue. Rather, it was seen, more correctly, as the concrete and specific issue it is; an issue concrete enough to have real-life consequences for specific people – ordinary people usually given little access to the normal channels of institutional public policy making.[18]

The whole process exemplified a new perception of legitimate political experience. An experience mirrored by the midwifery model itself; a model which holds central its concerns for nurturance and assistance, for care and respect for women as responsible, ethical adults, and for humane rather than bureaucratic treatment. These are the kinds of concerns articulated daily in the language of the midwives and their clients and political supporters. And this was the kind of politics aimed at by this task force: a politics based on respect for ordinary people's lives and experiences. A politics where there is room to speak not only a feminist critique, but also a feminist vision: room for more than "expert" facts and institutional rights, room for a feminist vision, a happy vision based on love and friendship, co-operation and wholeness, compassion and nurturance, understanding and empathy. This is a politics we should be fighting for.

NOTES

I wish to thank Gordon McRae, Jack Grove, Christine Overall and Katherine Scott for their support for this project.

1 In Canada midwifery-trained nurses have long been used in the North where M.D.s and hospital centres have been reluctant to locate.

2 Of the industrialized nations the Netherlands, where midwives attend over half of all births, has the lowest mortality and morbidity rates. Canada and the U.S. both come very near the highest. Caesarean section, which involves the increased risk of surgery, is considerably higher in North America than in Holland (14-18% in the former and 3.8% in the latter). William Johnson, "What are the Dutch doing right?" *The Globe and Mail,* 18 July 1983, p. 8; Diony Young, ed., *Obstetrical Intervention and Technology in the 1980s* (New York, The Haworth Press, 1983), p. 186.

3 Ontario Task Force, *Report of the Task Force on the Implementation of Midwifery in Ontario* (Toronto, Ontario Ministry of Health and Ontario Ministry of Colleges and Universities, 1987), pp. 19-22.

4 Ibid., p. 14.

5 See, for example, Richard W. Wertz and Dorothy C. Wertz, *Lying-in: A History of Childbirth in America* (New York, Schocken Books, 1979). For a good historical account of the institutional battles in Britain, and to some extent the Continent, see Jean Donnison, *Midwives and Medical Men: A History of Inter-Professional Rivalries and Women's Rights* (New York, Schocken Books, 1977).

6 Patricia O'Reilly, *Midwifery and the Medical Monopoly* (M.A. Thesis, Queen's University at Kingston, 1986), pp. 32-37.

7 Ibid., pp. 105-114.

8 The medical profession itself recognizes most births as medically safe. For example, the Ontario Medical Association categorizes pregnancies as:
Level I – 85% of pregnancies with no identifiable risk;
Level II-12% presenting identifiable risks at a moderate level;
Level III-2-3% of the pregnancies at high risk and requiring very special, rare or expensive facilities for management. Ontario Medical Association, "Discussion Paper on Directions in Health Care Issues Relating to Childbirth" (Toronto, 1985), p. 15.

9 Edward Shorter, *A History of Women's Bodies* (New York, Basic Books, 1982), p. 130.

10 O'Reilly, op. cit., pp. 116-122.

11 Ontario Medical Association "Discussion Paper," p. 5.

12 Canada's McGill University was included in this study.

13 E. Richard Brown, *Rockefeller Medicine Men* (Berkeley, University of California Press, 1979), p. 88.

14 O'Reilly, op. cit., pp. 37-43.

15 Canadian Holistic Medical Association, Canadian Chiropractic Association, Ontario Naturopathic Association, and Ontario Herbalist Association, *Submissions to the Health Professions Legislation Review Board* (Ontario, 1983-1989).

16 Ontario Ministry of Health, *Health Care in the 80s and Beyond: Seeking Consensus* (Toronto, Queen's Printer, 1983), p. 6.

17 Ontario Task Force, "Report," p. 11.

18 The dynamics of this participation are complex. While it can be interpreted (as here) in a positive light, it can also be seen as somewhat problematic – in that this solicitation is state controlled. The Ministry both sets up the composition and mandate of the Task Force, and has acceptance and veto power over its recommendations. This raises serious concerns about institutional co-optation. I do not mean to make light of these concerns: only to reserve such discussion for another time. For, while the midwifery case may be problematic in terms of requiring more in-depth political analysis, it nevertheless serves as an example of reproductive public policy we would do well to investigate.

III
SOCIAL POLICY
QUESTIONS

PREGNANCY AS JUSTIFICATION FOR LOSS OF JURIDICAL AUTONOMY

Sanda Rodgers

MARGARET ATWOOD'S APOCALYPTIC novel *The Handmaid's Tale* describes a society in which women are valued and used in direct relation to the reproductive services they can provide. To fail to conceive leaves a woman vulnerable to expulsion and possible death. The last section of the novel, entitled "Historical Notes," purports to be a learned review of the historical context of *The Handmaid's Tale* which is delivered at an academic conference in 2195. Here, a fictional professor comments that prior to the period described in *The Handmaid's Tale:*

> The need for ... birth services was already recognized ... it was being inadequately met by "artificial insemination," "fertility clinics," and the use of "surrogate mothers," who were hired for the purpose.[1]

Atwood's novel is disturbing exactly because she recognizes and extends towards its inherent conclusion our contemporary manifestation of cultural and political attitudes towards women's reproductive capacity. Nowhere is this attitude more chilling than in recent developments in legal doctrine that allow interference with a pregnant woman's autonomy wherever her behaviour is seen to be detrimental to the fetus she carries.

Increasingly, academics and judges have taken the view that pregnancy results in diminished juridical capacity. Courts in eleven American states have ordered Caesarean sections for unconsenting women in the alleged conflicting interest of the fetus she carries. Several Canadian provinces have recognized the fetus as entitled to protection under child welfare legislation. Two of those provinces have interfered with the liberty of women in late pregnancy or early stages of labour. Only a handful of these decisions have been reported and are therefore available for public scrutiny. Those for which there is a record are dismal examples of the worst form of legal reasoning.

A pregnant woman has full legal rights only so long as her behaviour corresponds with norms acceptable to others in positions of power. Pregnancy takes on the markings of a status, not unlike infancy, that allows others to determine what is best, and to impose those views upon her. Failure to conform to behavioural norms considered appropriate for sacred reproductive vessels entails the possibility of arrest, confinement and imposed surgery.

I argued against this development in the 1986 volume of the *Canadian Journal of Women and the Law,* which issue was devoted to "Women and Reproduction."[2] Since that time, the assertion that the rights of the pregnant woman may be compromised in the interests of the fetus that she carries has continued, both in the courts and among academic writers. Few are the voices raised on behalf of the woman's continuing autonomy despite her pregnant state. While increasing numbers of courts have imposed some form of state interference upon pregnant women, no court has yet ensured a hearing of the issue in a way that would allow an opportunity for careful juridical review of the many legal principles that protect the autonomy of all human beings, including those who are pregnant. Few who argue for diminished maternal autonomy have turned their attention to those whose activities jeopardize the health of pregnant women and the fetuses that they carry. Among them are workplace and other polluters; those who fail to provide adequate access to nutrition, housing and income; and those who market products known to negatively impact on fetal and maternal health, among them alcohol and tobacco.

State interference with maternal autonomy has taken several forms. In all cases precedence is given to the alleged interests of the fetus, as determined by officious intermeddlers, rather than to decisions made by the pregnant woman on her own behalf and on behalf of the fetus she is carrying.

Several courts have imposed Caesarean sections on unwilling women. An allegation by medical professionals that the fetus is in a state of distress which can be alleviated only by imposed surgery is generally perceived as sufficient grounds to justify surgery. Little heed is paid to the pregnant woman's decision to decline surgery on grounds that are convincing to her. Attenuated hearings are held, often in the labour room, often in the absence of the woman herself. There is ordinarily no opportunity to fully argue points of constitutional law, rights of inviolability and integrity or religious conviction. Careful proof of medical facts, on which the prediction of fetal injury is based, is rare.

Where a judicial decision is made to impose a Caesarean section on a woman who is not in judicial custody, the order is often unenforceable. In some cases, the pregnant woman simply ignores the order to attend and submit to surgery and, in an act of classic civil disobedience, gives birth vaginally. Often the medical prediction of dire consequences for both mother and child proves inaccurate. Where the woman is in custody because in labour, surgery is imposed.

The legal principle upon which unconsented surgery is imposed upon a pregnant woman is often unclear. However, some judges have argued that the legal justification for denying pregnant women autonomy available to all other persons lies in the State's obligation to protect the interest of the unborn child. This is an interest not previously recognized by the law in the absence of viable birth of the fetus. Other courts have stretched child welfare legislation designed for the protection of children in the custody of parents unable to care for them by arguing its applicability to the fetus.

This was the approach taken recently by the Provincial Court of British Columbia. In this case, the definition of "child in need of protection" was extended, without legal justification, to include a child in the process of being born. Earlier Canadian cases had held that an unborn child is a child in need of protection, that an unborn child can be abused during the gestation period and that a guardian could be appointed on behalf of an unborn child of eighteen weeks' gestation.

In the recent decision in British Columbia, the unborn child was in a breech position with a threat of oxygen deprivation, resulting in concern for the safety of the fetus. The mother declined to consent to a Caesarean. Contact with the Ministry of Social Services was made. On the advice of the treating physician, a social worker gave permission to the doctor to do "... what was medically required for the child but that he was not consenting to any medical procedure to be performed on the mother." This is a distinction which, in the context of the medical facts presented to the Ministry of Social Services, strikes one as tortuous in the extreme. The judge pointed out that some two hours later the mother appeared to change her view, and gave her consent to the surgical intervention. For this reason he concluded:

> This is not a case of women's rights, Mrs Roininen consented without coercion or threat to the operation. This case in my humble opinion ought not be a concern for the right to life of the unborn person as suggested in argument.... This is simply a case to determine what is best for the safety and well being of this child.[3]

It is impossible to view Ms. Roininen's apparent consent as

informed or uncoerced under the circumstances. It is also important to note that the request to override the maternal decision refusing surgical intervention was made on the basis of the uncontested and unexamined recommendation of a sole physician. Nor does the legal reasoning stand up to rigorous analysis. Nothing in the language of the child welfare legislation supports the court's conclusion that the purview of that act can be extended to the fetus prior to viable birth, regardless of the imminence of the birth.

Equally disturbing is the recent use of the provisions of the Ontario Mental Health Act to override maternal behaviour considered harmful to the fetus. In Re: Children's Aid Society of City of Belleville, Hastings County and T.[4] the provisions of the Act were used to apprehend a woman whose behaviour was alleged to jeopardize the health of the fetus she carried. Under the provisions of the Child and Family Services Act the unborn fetus was held to be a "child" in need of protection. The fetus was also held to be a "person" within the provisions of the Mental Health Act. Whereas the rules of statutory interpretation are quite precise, and despite the existence of a legal tradition determining that the unborn fetus is not entitled to protection in law, the judge dealt with this complicated legal issue by concluding, "I am prepared to find that the child is a person, as I have already concluded in the proceedings under the Child and Family Services Act, 1984." No reference is made to previous decisions refusing to recognize the status of the fetus, nor to the very complex constitutional arguments as yet untried under the Canadian Charter of Rights and Freedoms.

A last disturbing trend can be identified in the move toward recognition of feticide as a criminal offence and the laying of criminal charges against the pregnant woman herself for the criminal injury she has allegedly done to her fetus. In 1986, Pamela Stewart was charged by the State of California under child support legislation designed to provide for the support of children and pregnant women. The basis of the allegation was that Ms. Stewart had failed to follow medical advice to avoid street drugs, stay off her feet, refrain from sexual intercourse with her partner and contact her physician in the event of any bleeding. Of these four imperatives, only the activity first described is not legally available to all other persons as an exercise of their legal and constitutional rights.

The choice to prosecute under this particular piece of legislation avoided two problems that would likely have arisen under the homicide provisions of the California Criminal Code. First, the child support legislation had been specifically amended to refer to "a child conceived but not yet born." This addition had been included to allow prosecution of a male partner who failed to make financial contribution to the upkeep of the pregnant woman. Furthermore, prosecution for homicide under the Criminal Code would have required proof beyond a reasonable doubt that the actions of Ms. Stewart had caused the death of the child; proof which is notoriously difficult to get. Wilful disregard of medical instructions and the failure to follow medical advice constituted Ms. Stewart's crime. Ms. Stewart's partner was not charged. The court dismissed the charges against Ms. Stewart but left open the question whether specific legislation to deal with maternal behaviour alleged to jeopardize fetal status was appropriate.

In three American states, South Carolina, Massachusetts and Kansas, courts have interpreted state penal code provisions to include the fetus. In each of these, the extent of the scope of the increased offence is unclear. In other states, the legislature has chosen to include the fetus within the purview of state penal legislation. In addition to the California provision relied upon in the Stewart case, the homicide offence specifically refers to "the unlawful killing of a human being, or a fetus, with malice aforethought." Courts have limited this language to the viable fetus. New York State defines homicide to include "death of an unborn child with which the female has been pregnant for more than twenty-four weeks." Each of these raises the possibility of prosecution of the pregnant woman for lifestyle offences, for insistence on religious objection to treatment or for disregard of professional medical advice.

Finally, four states to date have enacted specific feticide offences. These include Illinois, Indiana, Iowa and Minnesota. Only the Illinois and Minnesota provisions specifically exclude behaviour by the pregnant woman herself.

The trend of courts, legislatures and legal commentators to interfere with the autonomy of the pregnant woman, wherever there is a medical impression that the woman's behaviour risks the fetus she carries, is of serious concern. These decisions pit woman against fetus, and make of women mere reproductive units breeding on behalf of the state and subject to state regulation and control. Behaviour that is constitutionally protected for all other persons is denied to pregnant women. State protection of fetal interests against the wisdom of maternal decision reinforces anti-abortion positions and threatens the progress made by pro-choice proponents. The women subject to state-imposed treatment, surgery, incarceration or criminal charges are invariably from poorer economic backgrounds, or from marginal religious persuasions. In no reported case, to date, has there been a careful reasoned consideration of legal and constitutional precedents. Most of the cases are unreported, and therefore subject to severely limited scrutiny. Appeal, for the purposes of a complete review of legal precedent and legal principles, does not occur, either because the surgery has been performed, or because the birth has occurred. In only one case of the several with which commentators are familiar has the autonomy of the pregnant woman been respected by the courts.[5]

If we are concerned with ensuring the birth of healthy babies to women who can freely choose to continue pregnancies, we must provide state services in housing, income, education and support. Medical interference in pregnancy, litigation against pregnant women, state incarceration of pregnant women in the interests of fetal health and criminal charges against women who give birth to damaged infants – all these acts effectively defeat women's claims to autonomy and full participation in the affairs of the state and the economy. They do little to ensure the birth of healthy, wanted babies. For this reason, the motivation for such interference with the autonomy of women must be questioned.

In the fall of 1987 the District of Columbia Court of Appeal, Washington, D.C., ordered a Caesarean section for a woman we know only as A.C. A.C. had successfully fought bone cancer as a child, losing a leg to that disease. She had married and, in June 1987, was pregnant. That pregnancy was interrupted by a diagnosis of recurring cancer; the prognosis was measured in days only. The fetus she carried was twenty-six weeks old.

Over the objections of A.C., her partner and her family, the George Washington University Hospital applied for and received permission to impose a Caesarean section on A.C. The fetus, when delivered, died immediately. A.C. died two days later, the surgery a contributing factor. The court upheld the state's obligation to rescue a potential life from a dying mother. "Condolences," said the court, "are extended to those who lost the mother and the child."

NOTES

1 Margaret Atwood, *The Handmaid's Tale* (Toronto, McClelland and Stewart, 1985, Seal Edition, 1986), p. 287.

2 Sanda Rodgers, "Fetal Rights and Maternal Rights: Is There a Conflict?" *Canadian Journal of Women and the Law,* vol. 1 (1986), p. 456.

3 *In the matter of the Family and Child Service Act and in the matter of Baby Boy Roininen,* no. 876215, 8 Sept. 1987, Prov. Ct. B.C. (unreported).

4 (1987) 59 Ontario Reports (2d) 204.

5 *Taft v. Taft* 446 North Eastern, 2nd Series 395 (1983).

Prenatal Diagnosis: Reproductive Choice? Reproductive Control?

Abby Lippman

Reproductive technology probably dates back to the seventeenth century and the first use of forceps during labour.[1] Since then, various other technical tools and procedures have been applied to the whole process of reproduction from conception (or its prevention) through delivery, with recent developments such as in vitro fertilization, embryo transfer and surrogate motherhood attracting growing attention in professional and lay literature. Unfortunately, the focus on these dramatic and overtly controversial procedures appears to have distracted attention from other technical interventions in pregnancy that, because of their widespread use, may have even more impact on our attitudes and social policies with respect to pregnancy and to pregnant women. These are the techniques used for prenatal diagnosis.

In speaking of prenatal diagnosis, I am referring generically to all the methods and techniques that can be used to obtain information about a fetus during pregnancy. Included are already widely-used procedures such as amniocentesis and ultrasonography, methods currently under assessment such as chorionic villi sampling, and methods under development such as fetal cell sorting.

Recent biomedical discoveries and technological developments have rapidly expanded both our genetic knowledge and our ability to obtain information about the fetus in utero, vastly increasing the possibilities for prenatal diagnosis. This expansion in the availability and application of prenatal diagnosis and the widespread adoption of these specific reproductive technologies by professionals have not been accompanied – much less preceded – by thoughtful deliberation about their social policy implications. However, because some form of prenatal diagnosis is here to stay, and because all women planning a pregnancy are already potential candidates for prenatal diagnosis, it is still important to identify some of the implications that appear especially problematic.

Prenatal diagnosis had its beginning in the development of tests for couples at known, quantifiable risk for having children with certain specific genetic disorders that would interfere with their health or intelligence. Most of these disorders were considered "serious." Although "serious" was never rigorously defined, it was rapidly accepted as a physician-imposed criterion for testing.[2]

This orientation primarily to genetic conditions whose severity and consequences were generally agreed upon, and for which there was no effective treatment, now seems less and less the case given the enormous broadening, over the years, of the scope of conditions considered appropriate for prenatal diagnosis. With many of the tests that can now be carried out, we can identify fetuses with conditions that have little effect on, or uncertain implications for, postnatal health and functioning. Often we can tell if the fetus has the relevant genes that increase its susceptibility to some illness, but not whether it will be exposed to the environmental circumstances that will interact with these genes to actually create a problem. As well, we can sometimes give a fetus a general diagnostic label – neural tube defect, for example – but we cannot tell how serious its disability will actually be. We can diagnose conditions for which effective treatment is available and can also detect a number of conditions that are not even genetic.

To date, this expansion has resulted largely from the

choices physicians and scientists have made about the tests they would develop and make available. These choices have resulted in some selected conditions being labeled not only as "serious," but as "undesirable": undesirable enough to warrant testing and the possible abortion of affected fetuses. Before further expansion occurs, it is timely to consider carefully both the conditions we want to have diagnosed and the process by which we want decisions about access to testing to be made.

To begin these difficult and complicated tasks of establishing objectives for prenatal diagnosis programs[3] and defining a decision-making process, we might first try to learn why we seek knowledge about the fetus. Unlike mountains, climbed just because "they are there," information about the fetus ought not necessarily be sought or provided just because we can do so. Thus, what is it we want to predict – and why? Are there any basic objectives of testing we can agree on that will prevent its banalization?[4] This question is becoming increasingly pertinent as information about fetal status can be obtained earlier and earlier, and at less and less risk to the pregnancy, perhaps even at no risk at all, if fetal cells in the mother's blood can be found and analyzed. Are there principles regarding prenatal testing that we should honour, irrespective of the nature of the test or when it is carried out? For example, what if we can do prenatal diagnosis even before there is a pregnancy by examining an egg fertilized in vitro? What ground rules would we want to see in place?

Answering these questions will require us to determine the kind of information we want to obtain and the responses to this information we will tolerate as individuals and as a society. Can we harness the technologies and apply only those that conform to our common values, limiting the diagnoses we will make? Or will we continue as we have been doing, letting our ability to make diagnoses early in pregnancy lead automatically to extensions in what is called "undesirable," changing our values as we redefine what we consider to be a "disability" whenever our technical skills expand the list of diagnosable conditions? Past experience does not lead to optimism. But we must at least begin to consider the objectives of testing and insure that choices about its extension or restriction reflect the social and moral values not only of the health professionals who will provide the testing, but also of the women who will seek it.

Adding urgency to this need for open, broad-based consideration of the objectives of prenatal diagnosis are not only the recent developments allowing earlier testing for a longer list of conditions but, perhaps more importantly, the changing emphases in health care and especially the growing popularity of what is called "predictive medicine." Predictive medicine involves the search for genetic or other markers that identify individuals who will develop some disorder in the future. It may also involve the search for markers that identify those who are only predisposed to develop some disability; those who will develop the condition only if the circumstances (for example, some environmental or occupational exposure) are "right." Both kinds of markers – for diseases *and* for predisposition – can now be diagnosed in the fetus. This means we must be concerned not only about objectives of prenatal diagnosis that reflect obviously malign eugenic policies, but also about those that may originate in more insidious, but no less dangerous, programs to identify, while still in utero, children who are "susceptible," so that they may postnatally experience "preventive" measures aimed at minimizing the harmful effects of their genetic characteristics.

For example, depending on the condition, testing is now or will probably soon be available to identify those who, after birth, may be at greater than average risk for the development of a disorder of adult onset, a disorder such as diabetes, heart disease, cancer or mental illness; a disorder likely triggered by some gene-environment combination. Once again, the early

186 The Future of Human Reproduction

identification of those thought to be genetically susceptible is not just to gather this knowledge for its own sake. Rather, it can be a basis for suggesting to these individuals behaviours and lifestyles that are believed to decrease their probability of future disability. As such, it sounds fairly benign and, properly used, employing interventions of known effectiveness, it may be. But the predictive information could also be used as a basis for *prescribing* a path for each individual to follow (what jobs to avoid or favour and what habits to avoid) to prevent future disability, with, for example, penalties for non-observance of the guidelines, discrimination in hiring or refusals of insurance for those with known susceptibilities.

Knowledge of an individual's susceptibilities prenatally could result either in establishing the "best" program to decrease future risks after birth, or in deciding to abort the "susceptibles" because of the added burden this special programming could entail. Unfortunately, we and our children are *all* susceptible to something. Consequently, all fetuses are potential candidates for screening for predictive purposes, and we must not be seduced by this seemingly rational approach to dealing with health problems before closely questioning its assumptions. As currently practised, predictive medicine emphasizes primarily how the individual must act to reduce her probability of later disability. Do we accept this approach, or shall we favour the alternative and look at how the environment can be changed to accomodate the most susceptible among us? The latter appears politically disfavoured today, but it *is* a choice.

Another worrisome aspect of uncritically expanding prenatal diagnosis in the guise of predictive medicine is that the mass screening programs being established to test pregnant women will call into question many more pregnancies than will actually later be diagnosed as affected.[5] These are the initial "false positives" – fetuses who are at first thought to be affected but are later shown by confirmatory diagnostic tests to be unaffected. We have no solid data on the effects of early knowledge of fetal status on the individual subsequently born or on her family, but it is not unreasonable to be concerned about them.[6] What does it mean to a woman to have her fetus' health called into question, however temporarily, early in pregnancy? Can the anxiety this may create have an effect either physiologically, on the pregnancy itself, or socially, on parent-infant relations? What does it mean to the child born subsequently to have had her health questioned? To know she might not have been born had she not met certain standards?[7] Are we at risk of creating an entire generation of "vulnerable children" among those who were "false positives" on an initial battery of screening test?[8] Or among those who are selected to be born? Even if a false positive diagnosis per se only rarely causes a problem, the number of false positives in most screening programs is likely to be sufficiently large to make this an important concern. Certainly, any policies implemented in the context of predictive medicine using the new genetic technologies must take this factor into consideration. A separate question is how often women will take action, usually by choosing abortion, following the provisional results of screening tests without waiting for diagnostic confirmation.

To date, reproductive technologies used for prenatal diagnosis have been developed as a "professional resource." Professionals alone have set the context for their use by assuming the power to decide when and by whom they will be used.[9] As well, professionals have defined those situations in which they will permit "consumer" input and, in particular, have specified those procedures which members of the public can request or reject.

The breadth of these definitions has then determined how much opportunity there is for individual autonomy.[10] For example, amniocentesis for fetal diagnosis, supposedly a means for enhancing women's reproductive choices, is not available to all women, though this would appear to be a logical albeit debatable consequence of an autonomy argument.[11] It is allowed to women over thirty-five years of age, who can choose whether to be tested in most jurisdictions, but it is not allowed to women under thirty-five who may also want testing. Similarly, amniocentesis is allowed to be chosen by women wishing to diagnose trisomy 21 (Down's syndrome), but it is not made available in Canada (or the United States) to those wanting to learn fetal sex in the absence of a specific medical need for this information. By contrast, ultrasound screening, most often overlooked as an approach to prenatal diagnosis, is frequently carried out with *no* input from women, some of whom might reject this testing if they had a choice.

So far, professionals alone have established the criteria for access to all these techniques and it is appropriate to question not merely the criteria but the entire process of decision-making. Who should establish objectives and criteria for prenatal diagnosis, through what processes, and how do we want policies made in this domain? Again, none of this has ever truly been the subject of public discussion that it should be.[12] Even if the techniques used for prenatal diagnosis are "professional resources"[13] insofar as licence to use them is concerned and even though, to date, professionals alone have decided on their use, these decisions about their actual application are rarely, if ever, strictly medical. For example, the almost universal choice of thirty-five years as *the* minimum age requirement for entry to prenatal diagnosis has no clear biological or other medical justification; it is, in fact, a strictly arbitrary threshold probably chosen for economic reasons.[14]

Recent non-medical developments which physicians have labeled as threats to their professional control[15] highlight other social-policy factors that influence the application of prenatal diagnostic techniques. Unfortunately, these developments – cost containment requirements, profit motive, government regulation, fear of medical malpractice suits[16] – are unsuitable bases on which to establish criteria for testing. Paradoxically, they may further exclude women from the process of decision-making on both individual and policy levels, and tighten rather than relax medical constraints on them. The opportunities for decision-making by pregnant women may be threatened even more than those of their physicians – as has already occurred with respect to decision-making in other areas of genetic medicine.

Thus, in the field of genetic screening, the progression from viewing a test as voluntary to viewing it as mandatory has tended to be fairly rapid. This transition is most evident with respect to newborn screening: professionals viewed its benefits as so far outweighing its costs as to require that all infants be tested for selected disorders, even when the efficacy of some interventions was unproven. In this situation, overt professional paternalism replaced individual autonomy with few exceptions.[17]

More subtle transitions have occurred as a procedure gains wide use. In these situations – and amniocentesis for women thirty-five years and over is again an example – the use of the procedure itself establishes a standard of care to which other professionals believe they must adhere to avoid litigation. In turn, this very availability is interpreted by the lay public as meaning that the test is routine and sanctioned and "must" be done.

This leads to further restraint on the contribution of pregnant women to decision-making about prenatal diagnostic techniques, a restraint reinforced by the trend towards "defensive medicine" – the tendency of physicians to make clinical decisions based as much on the possibility of a future lawsuit should something go wrong as on the chance that the test results will lead to some effective intervention.[18] Here, two factors are especially relevant in the context of prenatal diagnosis. First, since most parents in our society wish – and may even be led to expect – that their babies will always be healthy, the birth of an infant with a disability leads to a search for an explanation and, perhaps, for someone – self or other – to blame for what has apparently "gone wrong." Physicians are aware of this and, in their desire to insure that they are blameless, may routinely suggest prenatal testing to all patients. A.R. Feinstein suggests that this strategy of choosing the option "whose wrong result will cause the least chagrin" is commonly applied in clinical decision-making, and it would certainly appear to apply here.[19] Second, the very availability of a prenatal test may pressure physicians to offer it to insure that their practice conforms with local standards of care for legal purposes.

Given this context, the use of prenatal diagnosis may come less and less to reflect either physicians' efforts to reduce the birth prevalence of some disorders or women's control over the quality of the children they bear, both previous (though arguable) justifications of prenatal diagnosis.[20] Instead, the techniques may be integrated into obstetric practice by physicians who merely want to comply with perceived medical-legal standards of care. One effect of this will be to trivialize the implications of these new techniques and this is, I suggest, the situation now with the extensive – and still growing – use of ultrasound. The latter is *not* recommended for routine use since its efficacy has not been demonstrated,[21] but it is nonetheless so used, probably as a component of a defensive, if not "aggressive," medical approach. This attitude may also explain how ultrasound has become the first method of prenatal diagnosis for which informed consent is not obtained. Physicians alone determine when and by whom it will be used.

So it would not be surprising if public discussion and open processes of policy evaluation for other prenatal technologies continued to be precluded by the quick and universal application of newly-developing diagnostic approaches by physicians wishing either to "keep up" with colleagues or to avoid any possibility of a law suit, should a patient who was not tested subsequently give birth to a child with some disability that a test might have identified. In fact, professional association advisories and state regulations requiring physicians to inform all pregnant women of maternal serum alpha-fetoprotein screening tests seem to have been enacted in the United States just to protect physicians, rather than out of concern for the pregnant woman.[22] A similar trend in Canada is not unlikely. And, given the growing frequency in both countries of court-ordered obstetric interventions often requested to protect health professionals, one must ask if mandatory prenatal diagnosis and other attempts to regulate women's behaviour during pregnancy are really unlikely.

Furthermore, while professionals may still insist that prenatal diagnosis is voluntary, and though *they* may be able to distinguish between "routinely" making prenatal diagnosis available for patients to accept or reject and "routinely" testing everyone,[23] this distinction may be too subtle for most of us to recognize.[24] How often do patients really feel they can themselves decide about having a test the physician recommends? How many women can reject tests "recommended" by their physicians, especially if the advice is couched in terms suggesting the tests are "for the baby's good."[25] There may be alternatives, but is there truly a choice for the woman whose physician "recommends" – or even mentions – prenatal diagnosis? For many women, the answer is clear. Already, when asked why they decided to have amniocentesis, they respond: "I didn't have a choice." Unfortunately, they often don't.

Given that prenatal diagnostic techniques will continue to be developed – and not just for serious disabling conditions – and that at least some women will continue to request them, we need to change the process of decision-making about the individual and collective use of this technology if fetal testing is to "work" to serve the needs of women and to provide them with real choices, not hypothetical alternatives. To start, prenatal diagnosis needs to be seen *not* apart from, but as a component of, a social policy that guarantees comprehensive care for all pregnant women and all children. This should include a guarantee of adequate care for those born with a disability and for their families. This means limiting, if not severing, the connection between prenatal diagnosis and genetic medicine, and viewing these interventions as part of an array of potential health services for women.

In this context, the basis for, and effects of, prenatal diagnosis could be compared with those of other "preventive" programs to assess their relative impacts on the health and well-being of children and parents. Such an exercise would help de-mystify prenatal diagnosis. And, by making us directly confront its role versus, for example, the role of nutritional supplementation, parent education or anti-smoking interventions in the improvement of reproductive health, it would require us to explicitly consider its objectives. Perhaps if prenatal diagnosis were seen in this broader, more appropriate context as a possible addition to, rather than as a substitute for, caring, relevant and effective preventive and health promotion services, its objectives and its social and policy implications could be clarified and ways found for it to truly begin to simultaneously expand women's choices and women's control.

NOTES

1   A. Oakley, *Becoming a Mother* (New York, Schocken Books, 1979), p. 16.

2   Among the several possible explanations of this, two seem most relevant. 1) Prenatal diagnosis carries some risk to the fetus. Thus, physicians may have been unwilling to jeopardize a clinically normal pregnancy in the absence of what was, to them, a compelling reason to do so, such as a serious fetal abnormality. 2) Abortion has historically (if myopically) been

isolated as *the* ethical or sociopolitical question of paramount importance with regard to prenatal diagnosis, perhaps because the prenatal diagnosis technology available has meant that any resultant pregnancy terminations would have to be carried out in the second trimester. Health professionals, the gatekeepers for prenatal diagnosis, may have considered only "serious" disabilities to be compelling justifications for the procedure this late in pregnancy. In addition, the fact that only "serious" fetal abnormalties are legally accepted grounds for abortion in many countries, though not in Canada, may also explain why seriousness or severity became grounds for access to testing.

3 There has never really been a broad-based attempt to define the objectives of prenatal diagnosis. This has not impeded the establishment and proliferation of guidelines or criteria for access to testing, however.

4 B.K. Rothman, *The Tentative Pregnancy: Prenatal Diagnosis and the Future of Motherhood* (New York, Viking Press, 1986).

5 This is because these screening tests, for technical reasons, can almost never be a hundred percent accurate in detecting either the affected or the unaffected pregnancies; there is usually some overlap in the test results for these two groups.

6 A preliminary study of parents of infants screened in the newborn period failed to reveal increased anxiety or depression in those awaiting confirmatory tests after an initial abnormal test (J.R. Sorenson, H.L. Levy, T.W. Mangione and S.J. Sepe, "Parental Response to Repeat Testing of Infant with 'False Positive' Results in a Newborn Screening Program," *Pediatrics,* vol. 73 (1984), pp. 183-187), but the generalizability of these results to the prenatal period is unknown.

7 J. Fletcher, "The Brink: The Parent-Child Bond in the Genetic Revolution," *Theological Studies,* vol. 33 (1972), pp. 457-485.

8 J.C. Levy, "Vulnerable Children. Parents' Perspectives and the Use of Medical Care," *Pediatrics,* vol. 65 (1980), pp. 956-963.

9 A. Oakley, "The History of Ultrasonography in Obstetrics," *Birth,* vol. 13 (1986), pp. 8-13.

10 D. Dickson, "Public Interest Criteria for Technology," *GeneWatch,* vol. 4, no. 3 (May / June 1987),pp. 1-2; 14-15.

11 A. Lippman, "Access to Prenatal Screening Services: Who Decides?" *Canadian Journal of Women and the Law,* vol. 1 (1986), pp. 434-445.

12 President's Commission for the Study of Ethical Problems in Medicine, *Screening and Counselling for Genetic Conditions* (Washington, U.S. Government Printing Office, 1983).

13 Oakley, op. cit.

14 Lippman, op. cit.

15 S. Elias and G.J. Annas, "Routine Prenatal Genetic Screening," *New England Journal of Medicine,* vol. 317 (1987), pp. 1407-1409.

16 Ibid.

17 It is possible, though arguable, that screening programs carried out in high schools in Quebec or through health maintenance organizations in the United States reflect a similar paternalism via professional control.

18 This is "defensive" medicine on the individual level. It is probably not stretching the term too far to suggest that defensive medicine on the societal level is reflected in the growing reliance on cost-benefit arguments to support medical interventions. Here, early screening "defends" the public purse against future medical costs of care of the disabled.

19 A.R. Feinstein, "The Chagrin Factor and Qualitative Decision Analysis," *Archives of Internal Medicine,* vol. 145 (1985), pp. 1257-1259.

20 Lippman, op. cit.

21 Consensus Conference, "The Use of Diagnostic Ultrasound Imaging During Pregnancy," *Journal of the American Medical Association,* vol 252 (1984), pp. 669-672.

22 S. Elias and G.J. Annas, "Maternal serum AFP: Educating physicians and the public," *American Journal of Public Health,* vol. 75 (1985), pp. 1374-1375.

23 Elias and Annas, op. cit.

24 M.H. Shearer, "Does This Work? We Don't Know, but it Pays," *Birth,* vol. 14 (June 1987), pp.73-74.

25 Ibid.

THE FUTURE OF ABORTION IN CANADA: A LEGAL VIEWPOINT

Sanda Rodgers

ON 28 JANUARY 1988 the Supreme Court of Canada decided the *Morgentaler* case. The Court held that the provisions of the Criminal Code of Canada that allowed restricted access to abortion were unconstitutional. Those provisions made obtaining an abortion a criminal offence except under certain precise conditions. The result of the Supreme Court decision is that abortion is no longer a crime under Canadian law, so long as it is performed by a qualified medical practitioner.

Until the decision of the Supreme Court in the *Morgentaler* case,[1] a woman who determined that an abortion was necessary needed the permission of a therapeutic abortion committee before she could have an abortion. Therapeutic abortion committees were to approve the abortion where the criteria of the provisions of section 251 of the Criminal Code were met. These criteria required that the woman's life or health be endangered before she could legally be excused from continuing the pregnancy. If, in the opinion of the therapeutic abortion committee, those criteria were met, she could have an abortion at any time within the pregnancy. If, in the opinion of the committee, she did not meet those criteria, no abortion could be obtained legally. Any abortion without the permission of a committee raised the spectre of a criminal prosecution and of incarceration.

The provisions that were struck down by the Supreme Court were a liberalization of the Criminal Code provisions that preceded them. Their passage in 1969 had been part of a major revision of the Criminal Code. Nonetheless, Canada's laws on abortion were significantly less liberal then those found in most countries and particulary those of Western Europe, most of which allowed liberal access to abortion in the first twelve weeks of pregnancy, at a minimum. In the United States the criminal law provisions of the various states with regard to abortion had been ruled unconstitutional by a series of decisions of the United States Supreme Court. The most famous are *Roe v. Wade* and *Doe v. Bolton*.[2]

Almost immediately following the 1969 amendments to the Criminal Code, concerns were raised as to the provisions of section 251. In 1975 the Minister of Justice appointed a blue-ribbon committee comprising Robin Badgley, Denyse Fortin Caron and Marion G. Powell to report as to whether the new provisions were operating equitably across Canada. The findings of the Badgley Committee were devastating. The committee concluded that the procedure purportedly provided for by section 251 was practically "illusory" for most Canadian women. Although the number of deaths from illegal abortions dropped following the amendment to the Criminal Code, the type and number of complications could have been further reduced if the abortions performed had been performed earlier, in specialized units. The criteria of danger of life or health were applied differently from location to location and committee to committee, and other criteria not referred to in the Criminal Code were being imposed. These included such criteria as consent of spouse, gestational limits, residency and quota requirements. Many hospitals did not have committees; some had committees on paper which failed to meet and consider applications for the procedure.

Some communities had no hospitals of the size and kind in which committees could be established. The four hundred-page report was comprehensive and detailed. It clearly indicated that the operation of the provisions of the Criminal Code that appeared to make abortion available to the woman whose life or health would be jeopardized by the continuation of her pregnancy proved illusory protection for most Canadian women.

In the years following the Report of the Committee on the Operation of the Abortion Law[3] dissatisfaction with the *Criminal Code* provisions remained high. The medical and legal professions were unhappy with the requirements of section 251, as were supporters on both the pro-choice and anti-choice sides of the issue. At the same time Dr. Henry Morgentaler instituted a series of challenges to the legality of the section. In a private Montreal-based clinic, Dr. Morgentaler offered therapeutic abortions to women who made no formal attempt to establish compliance with the requirements of threat to life or health specified in the Criminal Code, and without first requiring an application to, and permission of, a hospital-based therapeutic abortion committee. While Dr. Morgentaler argued that the provisions of the Criminal Code under which he had been charged were unconstitutional within the terms of the Canada Act, 1867 and violated the Canadian Bill of Rights, he was unsuccessful in so convincing any court in Canada, including the Supreme Court of Canada. Nonetheless, Canadian juries steadfastly refused to convict Dr. Morgentaler of unlawfully performing an abortion in violation of the criminal law. The penalty for a doctor who performed an illegal abortion was life imprisonment, while the penalty for the woman who underwent the procedure was two years' imprisonment.

In 1981 Canada repatriated the Canadian Constitution and added the Canadian Charter of Rights and Freedoms to its constitutional documents. The Charter contained a list of the fundamental human rights of all Canadians, now recognized in a constitutional document that applied to both federal and provincial governments and from which they could not derogate easily. Charged with illegally performing an abortion by the Province of Ontario where he had opened a new clinic, Dr. Morgentaler responded by raising these new constitutional protections. He argued that the provisions of the Criminal Code governing abortion violated his constitutional rights and the constitutional protections afforded to Canadian women by the provisions of the new Charter. On 28 January 1988 the Supreme Court of Canada agreed.

Ideally, particularly in contentious constitutional matters, the Supreme Court of Canada speaks with one voice. The reasons for judgement are written by an unidentified member of the Court and signed by all members participating in the case. This uniformity of thought assists Canadians who must adjust their behaviour to take into account the views of the Supreme Court as to the legality or constitutionality of any given issue. In the *Morgentaler* decision, the Supreme Court of Canada spoke with four separate voices; an indication of the complex responses that the issue of abortion can raise. As a result we know that section 251 of the Criminal Code is unconstitutional, but that various members of the Court so decided for very different reasons. Therefore, if the task that the federal or provincial government sets itself is to redraft a rule on access to abortion that meets the requirement of the Charter, four different views as to what would be required must be considered.

Counsel for Dr. Morgentaler argued that the Criminal Code provisions governing abortion violated several provisions of the Charter, including section 7 which protects the right to "life, liberty and security of the person," section 2(a) "freedom of conscience and religion," section 12 prohibiting cruel and unusual treatment, and section 15(1) which prohibits discrimination on the basis of sex. Various members of the Court found that the Criminal Code provision violated section 7.

Madame Justice Wilson alone found a violation of section 2(a), protection of freedom of conscience. No member of the Court commented on the impact of the section 15(1) prohibition of discrimination on the basis of sex on the regulation of abortion; nor was there comment on some of the other constitutional arguments raised by counsel including the argument that the Criminal Code provisions on abortion constituted cruel and unusual treatment or punishment under section 12 of the Charter.

Chief Justice Dickson, writing for himself and Mr. Justice Lamer, held that section 251 was unconstitutional. In his view, section 7 protects the woman's right to control of her body. Such a violation can occur where the interference by the state is by way of increased psychological stress. He said:

> [A]t the most basic, physical and emotional level, every pregnant woman is told by the section that she cannot submit to a generally safe medical procedure that might be of clear benefit to her unless she meets criteria entirely unrelated to her own priorities and aspirations. Not only does the removal of decision-making power threaten women in the physical sense; the indecision of not knowing whether an abortion will be granted inflicts emotional stress. Section 251 clearly interferes with a woman's bodily integrity in both a physical and emotional sense. Forcing a woman, by threat of criminal sanction, to carry a foetus to term unless she meets certain criteria unrelated to her own priorities and aspirations, is a profound interference with a woman's body and thus a violation of security of the person.

Madame Justice Wilson took an even broader approach to the issue of women's autonomy. In holding that section 251 violated both sections 2(a) and section 7 of the Charter she said:

[T]he right to liberty ... guarantees to every individual a degree of personal autonomy over important decisions intimately affecting their private lives. The decision of a woman to terminate her pregnancy undoubtedly falls within the class of protected decisions. It will have profound psychological, economic and social consequences ... the circumstances giving rise to it can be complex and varied and there may be and usually are powerful considerations militating in opposite directions. It is a decision that deeply reflects the way the woman thinks about herself and her relationship to others and to society at large.... It is not just a medical decision; it is a profound social and ethical one as well.... Woman's reproductive capacity must be subject to her own control.... She is truly being treated as a means – a means to an end which she does not desire but over which she has no control. She is a passive recipient of a decision made by others as to whether her body will be used to nurture a new life. Can there be anything that comports less with human dignity and self-respect? How can a woman in this position have any sense of security with respect to her person?

I have quoted extensively from the reasons for judgement of Chief Justice Dickson and Madame Justice Wilson because the language used by these two justices of Canada's highest court is extraordinary, and extraordinarily important, in its emphasis on issues of autonomy and self-determination for Canadian women.

Mr. Justice Beetz, with whom Mr. Justice Estey concurred, took the view that section 251 violated section 7 of the Charter. In his view, the therapeutic abortion committee structure that section 251 required was, in fact, often unavailable to many women. The delays that the committee structure entailed significantly increased the physical and psychological risk to the woman requesting the procedure because continuation of the pregnancy would jeopardize her life or health.

Mr. Justice McIntyre, with whom Mr. Justice La Forest concurred, found section 251 constitutional in all respects. In his view, delays were caused by the numbers of women who requested abortions from therapeutic abortion committees knowing that they did not meet the criteria. In so doing, in his view, they caused queues that negatively impacted on access by those women who were legitimately entitled. His view is a classic example of blaming the victim.

What next for abortion law in Canada? Following the decision of the Supreme Court in the *Morgentaler* case, what governs the abortion procedure? It is wholly inaccurate to identify Canada as being without laws on abortion. In the absence of a Criminal Code provision, abortion is a medical procedure and is regulated in the myriad complex ways in which all other medical procedures are regulated. Provincial regulation of doctors, hospitals and access to health care services all apply to that medical procedure as to any other. The only thing that has changed is that providing an abortion can no longer be the basis of a criminal charge and conviction.

Second, since the decision of the Supreme Court the importance of the provincial governments in the provision of abortion services has been highlighted. Provision of health care services is a matter within provincial jurisdiction. Federal input into the health care area is tenuous at best. The federal government is free to criminalize behaviour that is appropriately the subject of criminal law. Its jurisdiction in the provision of health care services is otherwise non-existent. However, the federal government does make significant funding available to the provinces to assist them in financing provincial health plans.

This is done through the Canada Health Act, which is the legislative mechanism that forms the basis for medicare in Canada. This funding is offered to the provinces on certain conditions only. Failure to meet these conditions can result in the withholding of federal funds to the province which is in breach. In order to qualify for federal funding, provincial health care services must be universally accessible and must be comprehensive in scope. Failure to provide access to abortion to all provincial residents could result in an action to force the withholding of funds at the federal level. Other legal challenges against provincial governments for failure to provide access to abortion could well be brought, alleging the same kinds of Charter violations that struck down section 251.

A great deal of attention has rightly turned to the provincial response to the provision of abortion services. These responses have differed dramatically to date. Ontario provides abortion as a medical procedure and funds it under the provincial health insurance plan. Abortion may be performed in hospital or in free-standing clinics, including the Morgentaler clinic in Toronto. Other provinces severely limit access to therapeutic abortion in ways which may be unconstitutional. Newfoundland limits abortion to the first twelve weeks and requires counseling by a psychiatrist, gynecologist, social worker and registered nurse. New Brunswick and Alberta require referrals from two doctors. Prince Edward Island performs no abortions and will pay for out-of-province abortions only where five doctors approve.

Will the federal Parliament act to recriminalize abortion? The Supreme Court of Canada suggested that a provision in the Criminal Code that proscribed abortion some time after the beginning of the second trimester might withstand Charter attack. Any such provision would have to be carefully scrutinized for Charter conformity. In July 1988 the government motion was defeated that would have allowed for termination of pregnancy in the "earlier" stages where the woman's physical or mental wellbeing was threatened and in the "subsequent" stages of pregnancy only where her life or health would be seriously endangered. At the same time, a pro-choice amendment that would have allowed abortion where the woman, in consultation with her physician, considered it appropriate, as well as an anti-choice amendment that would have prohibited abortion except where the woman's life was endangered by continuation of the pregnancy, were both defeated. New legislation at either the federal or provincial level could require continued legal challenge at significant cost and time for the women of Canada.

Recriminalization is, in my view, an inappropriate solution. It is difficult to imagine a provision that would meet the constitutional parameters described by the Supreme Court of Canada. To impose upon women the burden of continuous litigation simply to establish their constitutional rights is an unfair burden. Abortion is a matter of conscience for women who are best placed to determine whether a pregnancy can be continued. Regulation of access to abortion at the provincial level as a health care service is appropriate, although litigation will likely be necessary to ensure provincial compliance with the constitutional protections women are entitled to.

The decision of the Supreme Court of Canada in the *Morgentaler* case was a major victory for Canadian women. It remains to be seen whether the federal and provincial governments will feel compelled to impose new restrictions on women's reproductive autonomy. Any such attempt must be assessed against the constitutional protection of sections 2, 7 and 15 of the Charter.

Finally, abortion policy and rhetoric must be measured against actuality. Even given the delays that resulted from the cumbersome mechanisms imposed by the Criminal Code provisions struck down by the court, 88.9 percent of all abortions in Canada occurred prior to the twelfth week of the pregnancy. Only .03 percent occurred after the twenty-fourth week. A policy that is designed to restrict access to early abortions would likely violate the constitutional rights of Canadian women as defined by the Supreme Court of Canada in *Mor-*

gentaler. Recriminalization of abortion that purports to be concerned with the prohibition of late-term abortions must be carefully scrutinized. Given the minimal numbers of such procedures, and the fact that such procedures are performed only in the case of gross fetal abnormality such as the absence of a brain incompatible with existence after birth, a policy that is directed to preventing procedures of that nature appears to say more about how we feel about women's reproductive autonomy than about respect for the late-term fetus.

NOTES

1 *Morgentaler, Smoling and Scott* v. *Attorney General Canada,* Supreme Court of Canada, 28 January 1988.

2 410 United States Reports 113 (1973).

3 Minister of Supply and Services Canada, 1977, Ottawa, Canada.

The Home Birth Alternative to the Medicalization of Childbirth: Safety and Ethical Responsibility

Paul Thompson

> To birthing, as to dying, we bring our histories, our relationships, our rituals, and the deepest values and hopes that give meaning to our lives. We bring needs and values that relate to intimacy, sexuality, the quality and style of family life and community, and our deepest beliefs about birth, life and death.
>
> Judith Dickson Luce

DURING two decades there has been an increasing demand by parents – particularly women – for greater autonomy over where they give birth and the procedures employed. With few exceptions, physicians have opposed the attempts of parents to secure this increased autonomy over the procedures employed and have refused to accept home birth as an alternative to hospital birth. Admittedly, a few obstetrical practices in some hospitals have been modified to reflect some of the concerns that have led to parental dissatisfaction. These modifications, however, have been minimal, very slow in coming, and not altered the institutional and psychological constraints on parental participation in decision-making.

One of the main reasons given by physicians for their opposition to home birth is that it is unsafe and, therefore, unreasonable and morally irresponsible. The claim that it is unsafe is based on the existence of avoidable risks – avoidable, that is, in hospital – to the child and to the woman. However, the concern expressed by these physicians for the welfare of the woman is extremely problematic because it, in effect, involves restricting the choices of a competent woman *for her own good*. The restriction of one's choices for one's own good is seldom morally or legally acceptable. Hence, the most important factor in this rationale is concern for the welfare of the child. Even this basis for opposition, however, is problematic and, ultimately, inadequate.

There are two fundamental problems which undermine the adequacy of this basis for opposing home birth. First, determining whether something is safe is more complex than simply demonstrating that an action involves avoidable risks. It also involves using moral and social values in comparing the risks associated with an action with those associated with available alternatives. Hence, an action is usually more safe or less safe than alternative actions rather than being simply safe or unsafe. In addition, assessing the safety of an action is not simply a technical matter – the values of the family involved are an important factor. When one seriously considers the comparative nature of determining safety as well as the value elements involved, home birth does not seem less safe than hospital birth. It is also obvious that determining the safety of home birth is not only – probably not most importantly – a technical medical issue.

Second, whether an action involves taking an *unreasonable* risk is a complex issue within law, ethics and social theory. An accepted definition of "reasonableness of risk taking," says that taking the risks associated with a home birth does not involve the taking of unreasonable risks on behalf of the fetus. Let us examine these problems in more detail.

SAFETY AS COMPARATIVE AND VALUE LADEN

Assessments of safety are usually not straightforward and uncontroversial. For an assessment to be straightforward and uncontroversial, an action that is assessed as safer than available alternatives must avoid at least one risk which is present in all available alternatives, and involve no greater likelihood of other risks than are involved in any of the other available alternatives. Most actions do not satisfy the second of these conditions.

When an action does not satisfy the second condition, the assessment of its safety depends upon the relative *undesirability* of the occurrence of the risks associated with it in comparison with the risks associated with the available alternatives. The assessment of the *undesirability* of a risk is, however, a function of moral and lifestyle *values* and goals; "desirability" and values are fundamentally connected. Consequently, in all cases where the second condition is not satisfied, the safer action can only be determined by reference to moral and lifestyle values and goals. The assessment of the safety of hospital birth compared to home birth is not straightforward and uncontroversial because the second condition is not satisfied. Hospital birth, while reducing the likelihood or severity of some risks which are present in home birth, introduces new risks and increases the probability of the occurrence of some other risks.

Roberto Caldeyro-Barcia, former president of the International Federation of Gynecologists and Obstetricians, has stated this point most succinctly:

It is a fact that in the last forty years more artificial practices have been introduced which have changed labour from a physiological event into a very complicated medical procedure, in which all kinds of drugs and maneuvers are done, sometimes unnecessarily. Many of them are potentially damaging for the baby and even for the mother.[1]

What seems undeniable is that intervention in the birthing process is high in hospital birth[2] and low in home birth. For example, the use of analgesics and anesthesia is considerably more frequent in hospitals. The use of such drugs involves risks to the child; a number of studies[3] have shown that the use of analgesics and anesthesia during labour produces, in newborns, detectable effects – some lasting several months – whose clinical significance is unknown. In addition, rupturing of the amniotic membranes (breaking the waters) to artificially initiate labour is quite frequent in hospitals and results in increased risk of infection.[4] Also, while recent research[5] has cast doubt on earlier claims about the importance of "bonding," the controversy underlines an important risk factor, namely, that there are conflicting views about the consequences of many obstetrical interventions. Hence, many obstetrical interventions are inherently risk laden – we know far too little about the consequences of such interventions.

One extremely significant feature of interventions is that one intervention often initiates a chain of others. Each new intervention in the chain is required to counteract the effects of previous ones.[6] Hence, the total negative impact of an intervention is often considerably greater than the negative impact of that intervention considered in isolation. For example, the risks associated with epidural anesthesia (injecting a pain killer into a space – an epidural space – in the spinal column in order to locally "freeze" the abdomen) also include: increased likelihood of forceps delivery due to decreased voluntary effort and, as a consequence, fetal intercranial injury (injury to the brain), increased likelihood of induction (artificial initiation of labour) due to slowing of labor which increases the risk of fetal bradycardia (decrease in the fetal heart rate) resulting in fetal distress (endangered physical state) and increased morbidity (long term ill health).[7]

These examples – and the list could be substantially expanded[8] – lead one to the conclusion that the greater the intervention, the more likely it is that some consequence of the intervention will adversely effect the woman or fetus. Therefore, for women screened as low-risk (screening tests such as the Goodwin Scoring System[9] are highly accurate predicators), obstetrical interventions in hospitals introduce risks to the fetus and mother which are not usually a feature of planned home birth. Hence, the assessment of the safety of hospital birth compared to home birth is not straightforward and uncontroversial, and whether hospital birth is safer than home birth can only be determined by reference to moral and lifestyle values. The determination involves value judgements about the relative desirability of the very different risks associated with the alternative places of birth. Physicians have no special expertise in these matters and their assessments may reflect their moral and lifestyle values and goals. These, however, may not be the same as the moral and lifestyle values and goals of parents and there is no reason to believe that the values and goals of physicians should take precedence over the values and goals of other members of society.

The important remaining question is: Who should make the assessment on behalf of a fetus? In effect, one is asking: Whose moral and lifestyle values and goals should be employed in assessing the relative undesirability of risks? My answer is: the parents. And their assessment should be over-ridden only when it can be shown to be *unreasonable*.

"REASONABLENESS" IN TAKING RISKS

It is a fundamental feature of the moral and social fabric of North American society that decisions made on behalf of children are made by the parents of those children. Of course, sometimes a parental decision can be overridden by legislation or a legal decision. This, however, happens very rarely and only when compelling reasons for doing so can be given. One such compelling reason is that the parental decision involves taking *unreasonable* risks on behalf of the child. What this fundamental feature means in connection with a parental decision to have a home birth is that the decision should be accepted unless it can be shown that it involves taking unreasonable risks on behalf of the fetus. Certain criteria have to be applied to determine whether the risks involved in a particular decision are reasonable or not.

The most promising analysis of the reasonableness of risk taking has been developed by Joel Feinberg.[10] In his analysis, some risks are small enough to warrant running them for a greater gain (pleasure, achievement, etc.), and no one would be considered unreasonable were he or she to make the decision to take the chance. Other risks, however, are too likely to occur, or the harm is too serious should it occur to make taking the chance reasonable. In those cases, it might be acceptable for a third party to intervene to protect the person from his or her own recklessness and unreasonableness. This intervention would be especially appropriate if one person is being protected from the harm posed by the unreasonable risk taking of another person, as is the case with a fetus and its potential parents.

Feinberg's analysis takes into account five variables:

1. the probability that the harm risked will occur;
2. the seriousness of the harm should it occur;
3. the probability of achieving the goal for which one takes the risk;
4. the value of achieving the goal;
5. the existence of alternatives.

These five variables capture the important features of any

assessment of "unreasonableness of risk." Consider, for example, the case of driving one's child to the house of her maternal grandparents. The grandparents live 200 kilometres from the child's home. If the car has been properly maintained, the driver is not in any way impaired or inexperienced, the child is properly restrained and road conditions are acceptable, the probability that the harm risked will occur is small. However, should the person be involved in a moderate-to-high speed accident, the seriousness of the harm is great (i.e., death or serious physical or mental injury). The goals for which one takes these risks are largely a function of intangible lifestyle and moral values. The achievement of most of these goals by driving one's child in a car is highly probable and the value of achieving them, while subjective and highly variable, is, for most people, also high. In addition, in this case, viable alternatives do not seem to be available. Hence, what we have is a case in which the probability that the harm risked will occur is low, and in which taking the risk will most likely result in the achievement of a highly desired goal which cannot be achieved by any available alternatives. It is unlikely that anyone would consider the decision to take this risk on behalf of one's child to be unreasonable. Hence, there is no reason to override the parental decision.

Now consider the case of home birth. The probability of harm for a low-risk woman is very low if she is attended at home by a competent midwife or physician who has available certain drugs such as methylergobasine (a drug used to decrease severe uterine bleeding) and who is living within a fifteen-minute ambulance ride from a hospital. However, as in the case of driving a car on the highway, sometimes the harm risked will occur and sometimes it will be severe – perhaps the death or significant retardation of the child.

The goals for which people take these risks are varied. For some the goals are a function of intangible lifestyle and moral values – much like the goals to be achieved by taking the risk of driving one's child to visit with grandparents. For example, the goals of home birth might be a family centred experience, a less clinical approach, a desire for more intimate contact with the child and a sense of personal contribution to the process. These goals are admirably expressed by Luce:

> To birthing, as to dying, we bring our histories, our relationships, our rituals, and the deepest values and hopes that give meaning to our lives. We bring needs and values that relate to intimacy, sexuality, the quality and style of family life and community, and our deepest beliefs about birth, life and death.[11]

It is for reasons similar to these that people take numerous risks every moment of every day on behalf of their children and themselves. Failure to recognize their importance can only be regarded as resulting from a self-centred arrogance based on the belief that one's own values are the only right and reasonable ones to hold. This position would be difficult to defend and it is unlikely to be accepted or tolerated even by physicians.

The goal of home birth for others, perhaps the largest number, will be avoidance of interventions which are prevalent in hospitals and for which the associated risks for low-risk women are arguably greater than the risks of home birth. Even for those with this goal, however, the above mentioned intangible benefits of home birth are often embraced as goals worth striving for.

The probability of achieving such goals by means of home birth appears, from the experience of those who have chosen it, to be high. Of course, those few who have problems will not achieve their goals. But this is no different from a person who sets out with a child for the home of the child's maternal grandparents and has a serious mechanical breakdown of the car midway, or, worse, is involved in a collision in which the child is seriously injured or is killed. This in no way undermines the reasonableness of taking the risks, nor does it justify overriding the parental choice to take the risks in either case.

The final consideration in Feinberg's scheme is the existence of alternatives. In the case of home birth, the only alternative that might achieve some of the goals for which home birth is sought is a birthing centre. These centres are either separate from a hospital but close enough to one to permit speedy transfer of emergency cases or an addition to a hospital. In either case, the centre is equipped with emergency equipment. At present, very few such centres are in existence and any substantial increase seems unlikely as most physicians are rather negative about them – an attitude that speaks volumes about their commitments and biases.

However, if there were more birthing centres, they would provide, for some parents, a viable alternative to home birth. The percentage for whom they would constitute a viable alternative would depend on the degree to which the current medical practices of physicians could be changed. As should be clear from what has been said on this point, the choice of home birth for many is less a choice about the *place* of birth than it is about the *medical* nature of birth. The features of hospital birth that many families wish to avoid by choosing home birth are the propensity to intervene, the depersonalization of the process, the decision-making structure, and the interference with the after-birth relationship between parents and child. Unfortunately, these features are fundamental to the current medical practices and attitudes of most physicians. Hence, they are likely to infect the birthing centre environment unless the current practices and attitudes of physicians change, or midwives, rather than physicians, have primary and *independent* responsibility for low-risk births in birthing centres.

At present birthing centres are not numerous enough to be a viable option. In addition, it is unlikely that building more birthing centres will provide a viable option unless accompanied by some rather fundamental changes in the care of low-risk labour and delivery.

Hence, on the basis of the five criteria set out by Feinberg, taking the risks associated with home birth is no more unreasonable than taking the risks associated with driving a child 200 kilometers to her maternal grandparents' home for a visit. Numerous other cases of *unreasonable* risk-taking on behalf of a child could also be compared with taking the risks of home birth. To do so would further strengthen the claim that taking the risks of home birth is not unreasonable.

CONCLUSIONS

I hope it is now clear that when one gives serious thought to the comparative nature of determining safety and to the value elements involved, home birth does not seem less safe than hospital birth. It is also obvious that determining the safety of home birth is not only – probably not most importantly – a technical medical issue. Also, whether an action involves taking an *unreasonable* risk or not is a complex issue within law, ethics and social theory. And using a widely accepted definition of "unreasonableness of risk taking," taking the risks associated with home birth does not involve the taking of unreasonable risks on behalf of a fetus.

NOTES

1 R. Caldeyro-Barcia, "Some Consequences of Obstetrical Interference," *Birth and the Family Journal,* vol. 2 (1977), p. 34.

2 H. Brody and J.R. Thompson, "The Maximin Strategy in Modern Obstetrics," *Journal of Family Practice,* vol. 12 (1981), pp. 977-986.

3 Y. Brackbill, J. Kane, R.L. Manniello *et al.,* "Obstetric Meperidine Usage and Assessment of Neonatal Status," *Anesthesiology,* vol. 40 (1974), pp. 116-120; T.B. Brazelton, "Psychophysiologic Reactions in the Neonate: vol II, "Effect of Maternal Medication on the Neonate and his Behavior," *Journal of Pediatrics,* vol. 58 (1961), p.513; G. Stechler, "Newborn Attention as Affected by Medication During Labor," *Science,* vol. 144 (1964), pp. 315-317;

J.W. Scanlon, "Neurobehavioural Responses of Newborn Infants After Maternal Epidural Anesthesia," *Anesthesiology,* vol. 40 (1974), pp. 121-128.

4 Brody and Thompson, op. cit., pp. 977-986; S.N. Beydoun, "Serious Postpartum Infections" in A.C. Fadel, ed., *Diagnosis and Management of Obstetric Emergencies* (Melano Park, CA, Addison-Wesley, 1982).

5 S.B.G. Campbell and P.M. Taylor, "Bonding and Attachment: Theoretical Issues," *Seminars in Perinatology,* vol. 3 (1979), pp. 3-13.

6 Brody and Thompson, op. cit., pp. 977-986.

7 Ibid.

8 For another obvious example see J.Lumley, "Editorial: The Irresistible Rise of Electronic Fetal Monitoring," *Birth,* vol. 9 (1982), pp. 150-152.

9 J.W. Goodwin *et al.,* "Antepartum Identification of Fetus at Risk," *Canadian Medical Association Journal,* vol. 101 (1979), pp. 458-464.

10 J. Feinberg, "Legal Paternalism," *Canadian Journal of Philosophy,* vol. 1 (1971), pp. 105-124; and *Social Philosophy* (Englewood Cliffs, Prentice-Hall).

11 Judith Dickson Luce, "Ethical Issues Relating to Childbirth as Experienced by the Birthing Woman and Midwife," in H.B. Holmes *et al.,* eds., *Birth Control and Controlling Birth* (Clifton, New Jersey, The Humana Press, 1980), p. 240.

REPRODUCTIVE TECHNOLOGY AND SOCIAL POLICY IN CANADA

Deborah C. Poff

THE DISCUSSION ABOUT reproductive rights and reproductive technology has been generated primarily by religious fundamentalists, ethicists, medical practitioners and feminists. Although these categories are not mutually exclusive, they do indicate different interests and different orientations. As a feminist, my concern is with the well-being of women, and the thrust of my discussion will be on how best to provide reproductive technology in a safe, non-exploitative and economically feasible manner.[1]

On 28 January 1988 the Supreme Court of Canada struck down the federal abortion law as unconstitutional. From 1969, when therapeutic abortion in Canada was legalized, until the 1988 Supreme Court decision, access to a therapeutic abortion in Canada was largely and arbitrarily determined by regional location and economic status. The Supreme Court decision involves the formal recognition of the injustice of the previous legislation where poor rural women in many parts of Canada *de facto* could not obtain abortions while wealthy urban women could. Although it is unclear what legislation will be introduced to replace the previous law, the intent of the Supreme Court ruling is clear. The Supreme Court upheld the position that a woman's right to decide what to do about a pregnancy should not be determined by economic status and regional location.

The decision to strike down the therapeutic abortion legislation is central to many other feminist concerns regarding other types of reproductive technology.

This paper begins with the general assumption that various reproductive technologies will continue to be developed and utilized in Canada. This may make some feminists unhappy because it appears to bypass some theoretical debates among feminists about whether certain if not all reproductive technologies are inherently harmful (or beneficial) to women. Elsewhere[2] I have written on the social and political contexts in which reproductive technology develops, and have argued that it is highly unlikely that much of the reproductive technology currently available would have been developed in a non-patriarchal environment. However, I believe that it is important to begin with the assumption that reproductive technology is a part of Canadian medical technology and then try to set national social policy guidelines which will guarantee that issues such as accessibility, informed consent and safe, quality medical treatment be formulated in a manner consistent with Canada's Charter of Rights and Freedoms. Beginning with such an assumption does not preclude raising questions about various kinds of technology.

Nor does it preclude ruling *some* types of technology inadmissible on the grounds that there is sufficient evidence that such technology is harmful to the status of women. However, if feminists refuse to consider policy guidelines within the current Canadian context, they will be formulated by persons far less concerned with women's rights.

I will consider the policy implications of reproductive technology by addressing two key types of medical interventions: donor insemination (DI) and in vitro fertilization (IVF).

Before doing so, however, it is important to discuss the desire to reproduce, especially within the context of the

Canadian commitment to universal health care. There is no doubt that many women and men have a strong desire to raise children who are their own biological offspring. Over the past decade, studies in Canada, the United States, Britain and Australia have documented the expressed psychological and emotional costs experienced by many infertile couples. In one such study, Singer and Wells[3] documented the extended, painful and costly medical intervention which women are willing to undergo in an attempt to overcome infertility problems. On the face of it, wanting to give birth to a child seems like a legitimate kind of want or desire to have. One would think that it is at least on a par with such desires as the desire to be happy or the desire to live a long and healthy life. However, wants or desires are not self-certifying and may not always be based upon values which we, as a society, wish to endorse. For example, one assumption about women's desire to reproduce is that women want to give birth because it is a part of women's nature to do so. Generally, those who argue in this manner move from arguing that it is part of women's nature to give birth to arguing that it is morally good to have such a want.

There are a number of objections to such arguments. One objection is that even if it were true that women have such naturally based desires, it does not follow that such desires are morally good. If "natural" means such activity is compelled or not rationally chosen but biologically required, then morality is irrelevant. But if this natural activity is chosen, then the moral worth of the activity has to be independently argued for. Furthermore, many feminists have questioned the assumption that the desire to reproduce is an essential, biologically driven and natural desire in women. They have questioned this claim for two reasons. First, it is theoretically impossible to confirm or disconfirm such claims given that women are shaped by both biology and environment. Second, most feminists are well aware of the inherent ideological conservatism of such sociobiological accounts. We know that many women want to have children. However, given women's socialization within patriarchy, we cannot always take a woman's avowed desire to have a child at face value. A precondition for choice is a meaningful alternative. This requires that women and men cease to be conditioned to believe that child-bearing is essential to the definition and nature of being a woman. It also requires that women have meaningful alternative choices to motherhood, such as equal access to education, equal career or job choices, equal pay for the same jobs and equal pay for work of equal value. Until such conditions are met, it will be extremely difficult to judge whether childbirth is a choice made because of the desire to have children or merely a socialized response to being female.

"CREATED WANTS" VERSUS NATURAL DESIRES OR WANTS

Having said this, something should be said about what philosophers call "created wants." The problems associated with created wants have been discussed for centuries. Currently, created wants is a hotly debated topic in advertising ethics. The economy of the developed world is based, to a great extent, on the marketing of created wants. There is considerable literature in business ethics about whether it is morally defensible or not for corporations to create "wants." One moral issue raised in this context involves who gets to have these wants satisfied and who does not. Creating wants usually means creating or exacerbating social inequities. Everyone is led to believe that the created wants are good wants; that is, that they will improve the quality of life or increase the level of happiness in life. However, many such wants can be fulfilled only by the economically privileged members of society. This is not problematic to everyone; some regard the fact that the rich have more material goods than do the poor as "just the way the market economy operates." Those who object to this point out that the poor contribute disproportionately, through low wages, harsh working conditions, and so on, to the ability of the rich to satisfy created wants, but often cannot satisfy such wants for themselves.

With respect to the created want to have children, in countries like the United States those who can afford to pay for costly reproductive technology have had access to it, and those who cannot afford to pay for it have not. This situation has important implications both for how Canadians view access to health care and for how the Canadian government will frame social policy with respect to women's reproductivity. My own view regarding reproductive technology and social policy in Canada is that publicly funded, universally accessible treatment will mitigate many of the social inequities which created wants in general serve to perpetuate. That is, it is not the created want that is inherently problematic but the social and economic inequity that such a want may foster. However, my deeper conviction is that our society would be healthier-minded if fertility were not seen to be of such importance, and if infertility were not treated as a disease in need of a cure.

DONOR INSEMINATION (DI)

For feminists, DI may theoretically be the least problematic of all reproductive technologies. It is low level technology which can be performed without medical expertise. However, as feminists have noted,[4] DI has generally been regarded by the medical community as a "treatment" or "cure" for a "disease." As such, access to DI has been controlled by the medical establishment. In the United States, DI is usually done either in a hospital or a private clinic. Treatments are costly and usually not covered by private medical plans. In addition, access to DI has sometimes been denied to single women. "Self-insemination" groups composed primarily of lesbians have consequently been formed in the United States. Such groups rely on volunteer donor sperm.

Part of the problem with DI, in terms of both who gets access to it and who pays for it, is that DI as a procedure is understood in complex and not necessarily consistent ways. First, it is considered to be a medical treatment. Therefore, it must be controlled and supervised by the medical profession. Second, it is not considered to be a necessary medical treatment but rather a choice, and is therefore not covered by medical plans in the United States. Third, it is considered to be not just a choice, but a choice with serious social implications. Consequently, clinics and doctors set up criteria concerning who is appropriate for, or deserving of, such treatment. This general interpretation of DI has led to an interventionist, discriminatory procedure which limits access on the grounds of marital status, sexual orientation and ability to pay.

There is no reason for Canada to adopt the U.S. approach to DI. However, recent decisions of hospital boards suggest that a discriminatory policy already exists. In Nova Scotia, for example, the policy of the Grace Maternity Hospital on both DI and in vitro fertilization is that such treatment is reserved for legally married couples. Such policies rest upon unquestioned and unsupported assumptions about who should and should not become mothers. Although sexual orientation and marital status are not included in the protections of the equality clause of the Canadian Charter, it is imperative that feminists continue to argue that such protections are consistent with the intent of that clause.

Further, there is no reason for DI to be costly. As already stated, it is low level technology which does not require a doctor's supervision. A medical history should be taken for the possible future benefit of the child (for example, in the case of genetically transmitted diseases). A more controversial but nonetheless crucial requirement is that the donor be tested for acquired immunodeficiency syndrome (AIDS). Such tests are available and would not put undue stress on universal health care.

Since DI will continue to be utilized in Canada, it should be available to all Canadian women and covered by universal health care. It should be made available at neighbourhood clinics and not necessarily performed in hospitals. Those who would suggest that such loose criteria do not discriminate between "fit" and "unfit" potential parents should note that no one applies *any* criteria to the majority of heterosexual married women who become pregnant through intercourse. To set up separate criteria for those women who need DI treatment is to discriminate against them.

IN VITRO FERTILIZATION (IVF)

IVF is a more complicated and costly medical procedure than DI. It involves removing eggs from the woman's body, fertilizing them outside of the womb and then implanting them in the womb. IVF is usually unsuccessful, and when it does result in pregnancy there is a high rate of spontaneous abortion. IVF often involves hormone therapy to produce more eggs. Implanting numerous fertilized eggs in the womb increases the likelihood of premature birth and multiple neonatal deaths. Many women who have undergone repeated unsuccessful IVF treatments say that the procedure is both psychologically and physically difficult. However, despite the psychological, physical and economic difficulties, access to IVF is often sufficient to prompt women to spend years trying to become pregnant through treatment.

Because of these difficulties, some feminists question the value of IVF. The availability of such technology in a patriarchal society still reinforces women's reproductivity while simultaneously undervaluing it, and fosters a desperation in some women to be mothers. This desperation is the result of a strongly socialized self-definition that views motherhood as necessary to both womanhood and personhood. However, many women who undergo IVF deny such depictions. One woman who called in while I was appearing on a talk show argued that although IVF was psychologically painful and it took some time before she became pregnant, she was not acting out of desperation. She is a professional, a happily married woman who now has two children as a result of IVF. As feminists, we must come to terms with such women if we are to argue convincingly that IVF is detrimental to women. Women in IVF programs argue that they are freely choosing to participate in such programs. The fact that their choice may be conditioned by a created want does not *prima facie* make it an unacceptable choice. Nor does the pain endured for the low probability of success mean that we can rule the choice out of order because a woman is choosing against her own self-interest or well-being. We allow many more obviously harmful choices in our society where there is no beneficial outcome comparable to the birth of a child (for example, cigarette smoking and alcohol consumption).

IVF seems to raise more concerns than DI mainly because the costs are higher: both the cost to the woman who undergoes the treatment and the cost to the state if such treatment is state-subsidized. The history of medicine has in large part been a history of limiting women's choices and intervening in their well-being "for their own good." If feminists are not to fall prey to a similar maternalism we may have to allow women the freedom to make choices that we wish they would not make. Further, since it cannot be shown definitively that IVF is harmful and since many women consciously choose IVF, such treatment will undoubtedly continue to be available in Canada. Consequently, it is essential that, as with DI, the government be pressured to implement standards for treatment which do not violate basic equality principles. This necessarily includes equal access to treatment. IVF is costly, but to privatize the treatment is to set up an infertility treatment guideline with classist and probably racist implications. Consequently,

IVF, like any other reproductive technology, must fall within the mandate of the universal health care system.

THE POLITICAL CONTEXT OF CANADIAN SOCIAL POLICY

I have argued that the Canadian government should subsidize the technology of both DI and IVF through the universal health care plan. Since the Supreme Court decision on abortion was handed down, the provinces of Saskatchewan and British Columbia have stated that they will violate that decision and set up punitive and restrictive criteria for access to abortion. This kind of response is precisely what feminists feared when the Meech Lake Accord (an agreement between the Canadian federal government and the provinces which would grant significantly more autonomy to the provinces in public policy legislation) was introduced. What freedom would provinces have to set up social and medical programs which violated the intent of the federal government's commitment to standardized universal health care? There is a precedent for the Government of Canada to stop transfer payments to provinces when those provinces violated national standards. However, that precedent predates Meech Lake. If Canadian women are to benefit from the Supreme Court amendment, it is necessary that provinces not be allowed to violate the integrity and purpose of that ruling.

This undoubtedly means two things. Not only must Canada introduce the social policy that I have outlined in this paper, but also, if such a policy is introduced, it will be as a consequence of women's active political lobbying for such legislation.

The future of women's reproductive autonomy is at stake. It is imperative that Canadian women focus on reproductive justice for women now.

NOTES

1 Also, the audience that I am most interested in addressing is feminist. Consequently, I am addressing the issue of reproductive technology as a feminist talking to feminists.

2 D. Poff, "Content, Intent and Consequences: Life Production and Reproductive Technology," *Atlantis,* vol. 13, no. 1 (1987), pp. 111-115.

3 P. Singer and D. Wells, *The Reproduction Revolution: New Ways of Making Babies* (Oxford, Oxford University Press, 1984).

4 G. Corea, *The Mother Machine* (New York, Harper & Row, 1985).

Some Minimal Principles Concerning the New Reproductive Technologies*

Margrit Eichler

In the spring of 1987, a group of concerned individuals met to discuss the implications of the new reproductive technologies (NRTs),[1] including new social arrangements, for women and society at large. They agreed that NRTs are extremely important to women but extremely difficult to get a grip on due to (a) a lack of available information (for example, what hospitals use what techniques?), (b) a collective lack of knowledge about the consequences and implications of some of the techniques and arrangements, and (c) the complexity of the issues involved.

This being the case, those present felt that the best way of addressing NRTs was to try to move the federal government to establish a Royal Commission which would examine the entire syndrome for its social (not just legal and medical) significance. The Canadian Coalition for a Royal Commission on New Reproductive Technologies was born that day. It presently includes a wide range of individuals and organizations across the nation.

In talking with supporters of the coalition and other interested groups and persons, it became obvious that there was some need to situate the coalition politically and publicly as a feminist-oriented one. The feminist community has not yet developed any clear set of stances about NRTs. We, therefore, tried to identify a set of minimal guidelines which would provide a start as to how to approach NRTs. These principles are meant to be preliminary (pending further discussion, more knowledge-generation and dissemination of this knowledge) and non-exhaustive (they do not address some of the important issues that need to be addressed), and they must be seen in conjunction with each other, rather than in isolation. Taking any of the principles as self-contained would lead to problematic interpretations.[2]

THE PRINCIPLES

1. *Each reproductive technology needs to be evaluated separately with respect to its overall social desirability.*

There are various stances on NRTs. At one extreme is a complete rejection of all NRTs, which is manifested by some feminist groups. At the other extreme is an attitude that suggests: "what can be done should be done," which is exhibited by some of the medical research teams and legal experts working in the area.

Both these approaches are global in their acceptance or rejection of NRTs. This is problematic given the wide range of techniques and arrangements included in the overall descriptor "new reproductive technologies" and the different uses a particular technique can be put to. To provide just one example of the latter: In Canada, the first clinic for sex pre-selection of babies opened in Toronto in 1987. The clinic operates on a franchise basis. While it is highly problematic to introduce a franchise principle into medical services, and while there are serious problems in allowing sex pre-selection of babies on a large scale, there are other situations in which the availability of such techniques must be seen as highly desirable. Such a situation would occur if the gametes of a couple carried a genetic illness that appears in one sex but not in the other.

What is problematic with respect to sex pre-selection techniques, then, is the use to which they are put as well as the manner in which they are offered, rather than the development or employment of all such techniques in principle. That is, it is necessary to consider the social desirability of each technique in its various manifestations separately, rather than as a complex.

2. *In choosing a particular technology, in all instances the safest, least invasive, simplest technique available should be employed before others are tried.*

In vitro fertilization (IVF) is sometimes used for male fertility problems. As IVF is extremely intrusive, and as yet of unknown safety, there seems to be no justification for such use. Gamete interfallopian transfer (GIFT) is an alternative technique in which eggs and sperm are injected into a woman's fallopian tubes so that fertilization can take place there, rather than outside the woman. This technique is somewhat less intrusive than IVF and would be appropriate for some women who are approved for IVF. This principle would specify that IVF can be used only when the other techniques are not helpful. The same would hold for any other technique when a simpler, safer and less intrusive alternative exists.

3. *Any woman or man has the sole right to accept or refuse all treatments affecting her or his reproductive processes.*

This principle is perhaps the most important one for feminists. It must, however, be read in conjunction with the other principles. This is not a blanket endorsement of all currently existing technologies; all of them need to be evaluated for their overall social desirability (see principle 1). It simply means that no woman or man should be forced to undergo a treatment which she or he has not explicitly agreed to. This confirms, among other things, the right of women to agree to, or refuse, an abortion.

It also states clearly that it is the woman or man in treatment who has the final say in whether an operation or procedure is undertaken. This is particularly important in light of a 1987 Canadian court decision which declared a fetus to be a child in need of protection. As a result, the fetus was "apprehended." How does one apprehend a fetus? One clearly does not – it is the woman who is apprehended. This decision is extremely worrying, since, by declaring the fetus a patient, it threatens to remove the woman as a patient.

The recent decision of the Supreme Court of Canada which struck down the until then existing abortion law does not settle this particular issue. Madam Justice Bertha Wilson states in her comments:

> ... the fetus should be viewed in differential and developmental terms. This view of the fetus supports a permissive approach to abortion in the early stages where the woman's autonomy would be absolute and a restrictive approach in the later stages where the state's interest in protecting the fetus would justify its prescribing conditions.
>
> The precise point in the development of the fetus at which the state's interest in its protection becomes "compelling" should be left to the informed judgement of the legislature ...

Finally, in the light of recent developments in fetal surgery, it is most important that the woman have the sole right to agree to such treatments. The same would also apply to aspects of treatments that have been agreed to. In the case of IVF, this would mean that the woman – rather than the doctor, as is currently the case – would determine how many embryos get implanted in her. In all instances the doctor should advise, but the woman or man undergoing treatment should have the sole right to agree to, or refuse, treatment.

4. *Stringent criteria as to what constitutes informed consent /
decision-making must be developed and enforced.*

This principle is related to the preceding one. If the sole right
to accept or refuse treatment rests with the woman or man
undergoing treatment, then it is necessary to develop checks
and procedures which ensure that the patient is informed, in
an adequate manner, of the decisions that she or he is called
upon to make. In addition, it is necessary to develop safeguards which will prohibit implicit and indirect coercion. For
example, such possible indirect coercion would occur if a
doctor who performed IVF were to offer continued treatment
on the condition that the woman "donate" her "spare" eggs to
an egg "donation" system.

5. *Legislation should prohibit individuals and organizations
from arranging, for their own profit, transactions involving
genetic materials and reproductive processes, and provide
penalties for those who do.*

This principle would curtail the commercialization of reproduction. In particular, it would make commercial contracts for
the production of children illegal, without penalizing individual women who have received money because they bore a
child for someone else. The individuals or organizations who
have arranged the transaction for their own profit would be
the ones liable for punishment. The logic behind this is parallel to the logic of prosecuting pimps.

If companies that arranged so-called surrogate contracts
were banned, if placing advertisements for surrogates were
illegal, and if lawyers were not permitted to bring together clients who wanted to buy and sell babies, presumably any such
transactions would be severely circumscribed.[3] On the other
hand, so-called altruistic surrogate arrangements involving no
money would not be affected by this prohibition.

Contracts for the production of a child are not the only

transactions that would be involved if this principle became translated into law. Profit-oriented, commercial selling of eggs, semen and embryos – as currently practised in the U.S.A. – would be illegal, although free donation would be permitted. The relevant analogy is our current practice concerning organ donation.

6. *Semen, eggs and embryos can be used only with explicit informed consent of the donors.*

This principle must be read in conjunction with the preceding one, which would prohibit the sale of gametes, embryos and babies. (This would imply a change from our present approach to semen "vending," often labeled semen "donation," as practised in donor insemination (DI). This principle does not specify for what purposes or in what manner gametes can be used. Here principle 1 is relevant, as it would determine the social desirability of every specific technique or social arrangement. Principle 6 does specify that any use of the gametes (DI, embryo transfer, experimentation, etc.), can take place only with the donor's explicit informed consent.

7. *National standards must be set for compulsory short-term and long-term follow-up of all reproductive technologies.*

Again, this principle must be read in conjunction with the others. It does not imply a blanket endorsement of all technologies or arrangements nor does it condemn them. But whichever technologies are employed, they require follow-up on all involved parties. For instance, to my knowledge there is not a single study which has examined the consequences of contracts for the production of children on the biological mother, her husband (where applicable), her other children (where applicable), the child in question, the social parents, and other affected parties (e.g. other halfsiblings, grandparents).

In the cases of IVF and other high-tech approaches, it is

imperative that careful follow-up procedures be developed and used to study any long-term consequences for the woman and the child (where applicable), for instance due to the very powerful drugs used on the woman. Such screening should also involve, as a central aspect, a follow-up on unsuccessful IVF candidates: What are the physical and psychological consequences for the approximately eighty to ninety-three percent of IVF patients who do not walk away with a baby in their arms after years of trying?[4]

In DI, it is imperative to monitor how many children are generated from one donor and whether they are free of genetic illnesses.

It is extremely irresponsible to permit wide-scale application of techniques without prior evaluation of their consequences.

8. *Everybody has the right to an environment free of agents which create and contribute to infertility.*

This is a blanket statement, but an extremely important one. Principles are not meant to suggest specific remedies, but to identify in which direction remedies should be sought.

How much of current infertility has been induced by work environments, by the overall environment and by previous medical treatment? It is crucial that these questions be answered, that infertility be prevented and that heroic efforts to produce children be restricted to such cases where idiosyncratic factors have resulted in infertility.

CONCLUSIONS

These eight principles concerning NRTs provide some demarcation that seems sensible. For instance, they clearly endorse the right of a woman to choose an abortion – unfortunately one of the dividing lines in this debate that can be expected to become increasingly important. They neither endorse nor reject all NRTs, but rather argue that each technology or arrangement must be examined in terms of its own social merits.

The principles do leave some open areas. For instance, the questions of fetal tissue transplants or genetic experimentation are not covered except by principle 1. These are difficult issues which must be discussed at the national level, in an open forum, with input from as many Canadians as possible, for they will certainly affect the quality and type of life of the entire nation.

We are left, then, with questions instead of answers. It is crucial that these questions be addressed before we go further. These questions include the following:

– Should everyone have a "right to procreate"?

– Should existing treatments be covered by public health insurance programs?

– Is it ethical to deliberately generate children in such a manner that they will not be able to identify their genetic parents? Should there be a right of children to know their biological parents?

– Should fetal tissue be used in treating patients? If so, in what manner and by what means can it be obtained? (There was a recent case of a woman who deliberately became pregnant so that her fetus could be aborted and the tissue used for a transplant for her father who was suffering from Parkinson's disease. Should this be permitted?)

– How should the status of the fetus be legally conceptualized?

– How can semen, eggs and embryos be obtained if commercial transactions involving them are prohibited? (France has an interesting system whereby a semen user must also supply a semen donor.)

– Should egg transfers be permitted? (Sweden has outlawed them.) If so, under what circumstances?

– Should manipulation of human genes be permitted? If so, what type? For what purpose? Who will decide what constitutes the "perfect" human gene? How will we safeguard against abuses, including the creation of new categories of human beings?

- Should embryo experimentation be permitted? For what purposes, and for what length of time?
- What is the current range of techniques that are practised in Canada? Who does, and who should, decide what techniques are used? Who decides on the selection criteria for patients? Who supervises the doctors?
- What are the short-range and long-range effects of the various techniques and arrangements for all participants (including those indirectly affected, such as siblings in contractual arrangements for the production of children, offspring in donor-gamete procreation, effects on spouses, parents, and others)?
- What constitutes informed consent and decision-making? (In the Baby R case, the mother "agreed" to a Caesarean section while in labour and pressured by a doctor who had already applied for legal permission to perform the operation without her consent.)
- Should the sale and purchase of gametes be permitted? Should the sale and purchase of embryos be permitted? Should the sale and purchase of babies be permitted?[5]
- What are the reasons for infertility? What proportion is due to prior medical treatments? What proportion can be traced to environmental factors? What proportion is due to idiosyncratic factors?
- Is it ethical to spend large amounts of public resources on generating a few children for a few people while condemning others to a substandard life with a high likelihood of medical and social problems, possibly including an increased chance of infertility? (About one fifth of all Canadian children currently live below the poverty level).
- Should we, as a nation, make a concerted and conscious effort to develop and foster types of parenting other than

just parenting one's own biological or adopted children? These are just a few of the questions that need to be addressed – soon. Failing widespread public debate and eventual political and legislative action, our choices in answering these questions will become more and more circumscribed.

NOTES

* Since this was written, the federal government has announced in its throne speech of April 1989 that it will set up a Royal Commission on New Reproductive Technologies.

1 Not all techniques included in this term are new (for instance, donor insemination (DI)), nor are they all technologies (for instance, contracts for the production of children, so-called "surrogate arrangements"). Nevertheless, the entire group of techniques and arrangements tends to be called new reproductive technologies, and that language is adopted here in spite of its slight inaccuracy.

2 Although the principles have been discussed among coalition supporters, these elaborations are strictly my own. In formulating the principles, we tried to reach a consensus. My own views are in accord with the principles as stated, but would occasionally go further if I were to develop my own personal set as well as include others.

3 Personally, I would simply outlaw selling or buying of humans, or eggs, semen and embryos, and of so-called "reproductive services," on the principle that humans or parts of them should not be for sale. A similar sentiment governs the current Canadian attitude to blood and organ donations – blood and organs, also, are not for sale.

4 The percentages vary depending on whether one assumes the success rate is twenty percent or seven percent – the current range of estimates.

5 Most advocates argue that surrogate contracts do not involve the sale of children, but merely of a service: letting oneself be impregnated and carrying the child to term. Since it is the child that is at stake, this seems a spurious argument. For a more extended discussion of this argument, see Margrit Eichler, "Preconception Contracts for the Production of Children – What are the Proper Legal Responses?" in *Sortir la maternité du laboratoire* (Gouvernment du Québec, Conseil du statut de la femme, 1988), pp. 187-204.

IV
LOOKING TO THE FUTURE

PRINCIPLES INTO PRACTICE: AN ACTIVIST VISION OF FEMINIST REPRODUCTIVE HEALTH CARE [1]

Vicki Van Wagner and Bob Lee

THIS IS A STORY AND an essay – fictional and analytical – about what feminist reproductive health care of the not-too-distant future could be. We try to sketch out a vision of care that would empower women. Such care could best be centred in community clinics providing education, counseling and services for the whole cycle of women's reproductive lives – from safe and effective contraception to abortion, from birth and midwifery to well-woman and well-baby care, and from sexuality counseling to reproductive technology developed according to women's needs and priorities. We tell some stories to illustrate the guiding principles within which such a women's reproductive health centre could work.

A vision of feminist reproductive care is widely held within the women's health movement. Common fragments and images of a future model of feminist care are shared by many. But these hopes and dreams have seldom been pulled together into a coherent political vision and the importance of clear long-term goals and ideals to our ongoing political struggles has only rarely been discussed. That is what we hope to do here.

As we tried to articulate these fundamental goals, we reflected on the political history of the movements for community midwifery and abortion rights that we have worked in. We recalled the stories we have heard of women's experience of health care and their dreams of the future, and tried to imagine what feminist reproductive care could be and what a woman-controlled reproductive health care centre would look like. We kept coming back to a number of central principles: it would be care that covers the whole spectrum of women's reproductive lives, is universally accessible, integrates services and counseling, respects and validates all sexual and reproductive choices, and is accountable to the women of its community. Most fundamentally, this means health care that empowers women – that provides what women need, comes from women's lived experience and enhances their control over their lives.

THE WAITING ROOM

As usual, the Windsor Women's Reproductive Health Centre is busy. The waiting room, walls covered in posters, is filled with women.

Two talk quietly to each other. Both are pregnant. Michelle explains she is about to meet her clinic worker, who will describe the abortion services available. Kanwaljit has come for prenatal counseling to help decide whether she will give birth at home or at the birth centre attached to the clinic.

Audri, passing through to drop off eight-year-old Lalu at the centre's day care, greets the women. She joins in the discussion. Lalu asks why Michelle is having an abortion. Michelle explains that she doesn't plan to have children. Kanwaljit tells the girl about how she chose to have an abortion two years ago and, pointing to her pregnant belly, how she is now choosing to have a baby. They begin to discuss how they have come to rely on the centre's staff and services for information and care: Michelle recalls how difficult it was for women in the early 1980s to find and afford care before women's reproductive health centres were opened in every community. Kanwaljit mentions that she is on the centre's board and that new members are needed. The conversation drifts to include Hannah, a new mother bouncing a baby on her hip, who has just been in for a well-baby check up. They discuss the agenda of the next meeting, when the main topic will be the centre's alternative insemination program. Hannah mentions how important this program has been to her as a lesbian wanting children. As the adults try to keep straight faces Lalu solemnly and proudly declares that her mother, Audri, is a lesbian and that she herself was conceived by donor insemination.

A local high school student comes through the door to look over the large bulletin board. She signs up for the Thursday night workshop on birth control options for teenagers and stuffs a flyer into her pocket for her mother. The flyer is about a guest lecture on nutritional treatment for menopause.

Audri and Lalu hurry downstairs to the daycare. Michelle and Kanwaljit are met by clinic workers and go into their appointments. Hannah bundles up her baby, getting ready to leave.

COMPREHENSIVE CARE

An integrated and comprehensive women's health service is based on the philosophy that women need quality care during all phases of the reproductive life cycle, and aims to educate women about all aspects of fertility and the choices available to them. Education and counseling for puberty, contraception and conception, sexually transmitted disease, abortion, miscarriage and menopause all occur at the centre. The centre emphasizes the importance of open acceptance of all kinds of choices in women's lives.

The bulletin board of the Vancouver Women's Clinic has this week's classes and activities posted, as well as a listing of basic services available. A glance reveals that prenatal classes are available in Chinese and English. Pregnant women can choose between classes for first-time or experienced parents, for single mothers, teenage parents or lesbian mothers. Multi-coloured flyers on the board announce educational self-help support groups focused on specific topics/concerns: for women with sexually transmitted diseases, for young women approaching menstruation, for older women in the midst of menopause. In one of the centre's big rooms, a class on understanding the menstrual cycle is in progress. Classmates find each other there for a wide variety of reasons. Two women have histories of infertility and hope what they are learning will help them to get pregnant. Many in the class are learning to understand fertility in order to avoid pregnancy more effectively. Others hope to use alternative insemination effectively.

By integrating services for lesbian and heterosexual women, single women, women of all ages, women choosing to have children and not to have children, the simple existence of the clinic validates a wide range of reproductive choices.

Universal Access

What would be needed to ensure that the centre was accessible to all women? First of all, the centre would be fully funded, with all services free of charge. We imagine a clinic conveniently located in every community or neighbourhood and designed for women of all physical abilities and ages. Because access involves much more than cost, the centre would provide services in the languages of the local community and attempt to provide culturally appropriate care, sensitive to the values and needs of particular groups of women.

Free on-site childcare facilities would help to make health care accessible to women who look after children.

> The last community council meeting of the Moncton Women's Clinic had been stormy. A number of women did not want men to be allowed in the clinic. Others felt that women who wanted to be supported by men should be able to. At the same time, they recognized that this may feel intrusive to others.
>
> Francoise had opened the discussion: "I am a lesbian mother and the last thing I want to see when I come in here for my prenatal classes is some bloody man playing at being supportive."
>
> June had been concerned about the way this type of argument got presented for some time: "Hold on now – I am also a single mother and a lesbian, but that doesn't make me infallible. For myself, I share childcare with my daughter's father and he often brings her here to day-care. But I know how the presence of men can make many of us uncomfortable and I wouldn't want this imposed on women. Can we sort out some kind of compromise? Some days and classes for women only, and some in which women can bring men to support them if they want."

The centre would attempt to balance the open acceptance of all choices and the general provision of services for all stages of the reproductive cycle with the recognition that care must also be provided for women with specific needs and wishes. The women who use the clinic would determine what the appropriate balance should be.

Informed Choice

The centre's philosophy would place women at the centre of reproductive decision-making. What is needed for women to really have informed choice? Not only must all services be accessible, but they must be provided in such a way that each individual woman has the power to decide what she needs for herself. This rests on respect for her ability to make choices in health care appropriate to her values and her life circumstances. It also implies a certain kind of counseling – counseling that would ensure that women know the risks, benefits and alternatives of all care and services. Such counseling is an integral part of physical care, rather than fragmented from it. Choices such as having an abortion or giving birth are never purely "medical" or physiological events, but are processes with social and emotional meaning. In helping women arrive at the appropriate decision, health care workers focus their attention on the woman's whole life situation, instead of just on medical procedures and routines. Every effort would be made to allow women to make their decisions without the pressure of arbitrary time limits or restrictions. Because neighbourhood clinics would be staffed by workers with ethnic and class backgrounds integral to the community, counseling, education and services would take into account cultural background and attitudes towards birth customs, abortion and contraception, and baby care.

> Theresa is pregnant with her first baby. Because she was born with disabilities which are hereditary, Theresa is planning to undergo prenatal screening through her well-women's clinic. She has spent several visits discussing the risks and benefits of a variety of screening techniques and done a great deal of research for herself in the clinic's resource centre. She is hoping that knowing whether her child has inherited her disabilities will help her to prepare the best possible support systems for her child and herself.

> Marussia has come for an abortion. She schedules it for the next day, to give herself some time to think over the kind of procedure she wants, to consider pain relief and

to talk to her partner. At home they decide that they will return to the clinic the next day, rather than have a menstrual extraction with a clinic worker in her own home. Marussia wants the choice of using pain relief which the clinic setting offers.

A clinic worker closes the door of Room 3 behind her, leaving two women talking quietly. Shabat Kaur has been working towards decisions about her infertility, after trying to conceive for three years. Mary is an adoptive mother who has come to share her experiences with Shabat Kaur. Shabat Kaur and her clinic worker have discussed both treatments for infertility and the social meaning of motherhood and how it affects choices. She has decided that it is not being a biological mother that is important to her and wants to understand more about women's experience of adoption.

Continuity of Care

As much as possible the staff would also attempt to provide continuity between services. Ideally a woman would have the same worker for contraceptive or conception counseling, and perhaps later for abortion and / or birth care. This kind of continuity not only prevents health care from becoming mechanistic and impersonal but also increases safety and effectiveness as the woman becomes an active participant in, rather than a passive recipient of, her health care.

Training health workers to provide all aspects of reproductive care benefits not only women needing care but the workers themselves, helping prevent the burnout resulting from repetitive, fragmented care.

Maria is having a primary herpes attack. Upset and angry, she is grateful that the clinic worker who has always been her birth control counselor is there to examine her, give her advice and just talk. Maria is especially distraught because she had planned to have a child in the next five years and wanted to give birth at home. Thinking that she is now automatically high risk in pregnancy and will have to have a C-section, the tears roll down her cheeks. Jalna puts her arm around her and reassures her that it is fine to give birth at home, as long as Maria does not have an outbreak at the time of labour and tests for herpes are negative. Jalna says that she hopes she will be attending births when Maria is pregnant so that she can be there with her. They go on to discuss how diet and stress can affect herpes outbreaks. Jalna describes the many women she has worked with who have herpes and how most have had normal, healthy births.

Nancy is 52 and going through her second year of difficult menopausal symptoms. She decided she would not use medication but needs the support of the clinic's self-help group and individual counseling when she gets discouraged. After working hard over the past few months to become more fit, she's made a connection between her worst symptoms and her activity and exercise patterns, and wants to share her insight with other women in the group. She leaves smiling.

THE CLINIC AND THE COMMUNITY

The monthly council meeting of the Sherbrooke Women's Health Centre is in the process of getting underway. Judy, a council member, begins by explaining the basic structure of the clinic for new community members attending the meeting.

"All women who use and work at the centre are members and can sit on the council or the committees. Council meetings are open to all members. They are the forum where the overall direction of the clinic is decided.

"The council and committees all work collectively. It's

taken a long time for us to evolve this structure. We have found that we need a stable organization to involve the greatest number of women possible, but we don't want to get too bureaucratic. Every year brings changes – who knows what we'll look like in five years. Let's start with committee reports."

Lucy has come with a report from the Outreach Committee. The centre acts as a neighbourhood resource centre and her committee organizes services for women in their homes. "The clinic workers providing care for pregnant women in their homes have been doing more sexuality and birth control counseling in the past six months, in addition to prenatal and postnatal care and home births. We have found that women in this neighbourhood, many of whom have recently moved from rural areas, prefer to have counseling in their own or friends' homes rather than at the clinic. Soon we will have to consider getting another van for our mobile counseling service." She reports that the Home Help program is running smoothly – providing meals on wheels and help with cleaning, shopping and cooking to about thirty-five elderly women, ten new mothers and between five and ten ill women per month. Workers have been very pleased with the cooking project – bringing groups of elderly women together in each other's homes to prepare meals together and socialize.

The Research and Evaluation Committee report next. Helene outlines a research proposal to test for lead levels and evaluate the impact on the health of the community. She explains to the new members at the meeting that all research proposals have to be accepted by the council.

"The centre's philosophy stresses that all research must be relevant to, and defined by, the women who use the clinic. We use research to help integrate feedback from users into our policy decisions. This keeps us accountable to community needs and also provides data on the effectiveness of our reproductive health services. I think we generate some of the best women-centred research around. This not only helps staff and users, but is a way to use our experience to influence the wider health care system. It's my opinion that in this case the research project alone is not enough. We need to decide if we are committed to use the findings to press for greater environmental protection. Can we take on another political project?"

After the report of the Staff Committee, Simone, who has been training at the clinic for two months, expresses concern that her background as an MD has not prepared her for the integration of counseling with the technical aspects of care. Celine, previously trained as a midwife, offers reassurance, saying that she too had been nervous when she first started: "It has been an adjustment to attend a birth one day and to do an abortion the next. It was also such a challenge to become skilled at decision-making counseling, really knowing what information and support women need to be active in their health care. But the rewards are so great. And although it's a change for some of us to work with women on every-thing from puberty to menopause, it's worth it. I've just come back from attending the birth of a woman who I first met five years ago when she came to our birth con-trol workshop for teenagers. Being able to provide that kind of continuity and personal connection means a lot to our clients."

"What frustrates me," adds Zakia, who has worked at the centre for six years, "is that sometimes I feel I can offer all of the information, outline the choices, educate women about risks and benefits, but the options avail-able are often still so far from ideal. I feel I'm sometimes just helping women to accept what shouldn't have to be acceptable – to choose the least bad of a range of limited alternatives."

Celine continues, "That's why our commitment to organizing for wider change is so essential. I liked what Helene was saying earlier, about the important link between our research and our political projects. The same with counseling – we can provide some women with reproductice choices here, but outside this clinic women still face inequality and exploitation. Counseling for women's individual situations is not enough. How do we work for changes that will make the choices better for all women?

"The women we work with want choices. Isn't our centre all about empowering women to work for changes that will make the choices better for the next woman? Knowing our political work is part of how we define health care work helps keep *me* from burning out.

"The biggest success of the clinic is that the users become so actively involved. You know one of my clients has just taken on organizing a meeting on reproductive hazards at her workplace. Remember yourself from years ago, Zakia? You started as a sceptic, coming in here looking around suspiciously, wondering if we could help you get pregnant. Look at you now – Coordinator of the Outreach Committee and teaching the best fertility classes we've ever had."

Community-based care means being solidly based in a particular community, responsive to its needs and accountable to its users. We imagine that each centre would have a community board or council representing the diversity of the local neighbourhood. It would be the primary forum for setting policy directions and priorities and for ensuring high standards of quality and accessibility. Through outreach and working committees of the centre, users and community members would be involved in areas such as self-care, health education and promotion, developing and maintaining health support networks and organizing for change in the social, political and environmental conditions which affect women's health.

CONCLUSIONS

The ideal women's reproductive health centre we have sketched out here is firmly utopian – we try to capture the reproductive rights movement's guiding principles, ultimate goals and hopes, and images of the future. We have tried to envision a system of health care which gives women all the information and services needed to control their bodies.

But such visions are not really for the future at all; we have found that a clear and attractive sense of what we are struggling for is an indispensable part of our current politics.[2] A vision of health care that empowers women can seize people's imagination by showing that there are realistic alternatives to the existing system. It can inspire activists to keep fighting and draw new people into the movement. Clearly defined long-term goals can also help us to negotiate the inevitable tactical compromises, strategic adjustments, and ebbs and flows of long campaigns. In these ways – as inspiration and touchstone – a vision of the possibilities of future reproductive health care can contribute directly to our current struggles.

Radical Visions and Movement Building

Visions of future goals and possibilities are neither precise blueprints of what is to come nor utopian dreaming. Rather, they are an indispensable means of challenging and transforming contemporary culture and consciousness. Images or ideals of what could be are expressions of people's needs and desires that cannot be met within society as it is. Visions of alternative arrangements and relationships are means of imagining how these needs could be met.[3] As such they are a critique of the present; but to be effective we have to be able to make these radical visions come alive as practical and realistic alternatives to the existing order.

We think this model of a future reproductive health centre can do this largely because its elements have arisen out of, and speak to, the concrete experience of our movements and struggles. The value of this particular model is that all of its components are easily understood in terms of present-day knowledge and practice. Instituting such centres does not depend on new technology still to be invented or medical advances still to be achieved. They will only come about as part of a transformation of the social relations of reproduction and the relations of power surrounding health, gender and women's positions in comtemporary society.

Because this vision of the future contrasts so starkly with the situation women face now, it serves to dramatize existing inequality and oppression. This can inspire people to join the movements seeking to bring the necessary changes to pass. Clearly laying out what could be also helps us to highlight what stands in the way of health care that empowers women: the dominance of organized professional medicine over the provision and very definition of health care; the multifaceted state regulation of women's reproduction, from abortion law to family allowance benefits; an ideology of women that defines women as selfless nurturers and mothers; and the opposition of those diverse right-wing forces that work to buttress the patriarchal family and women's "rightful" place within it.

A clear delineation of long-term goals helps us to understand our ongoing struggles in their proper political and historical context; to see current situations, even when problematic and contradictory,as stages in a long struggle. This can temper the unavoidable frustrations and disappointments of political activism. For example, without legal recognition, midwives in Ontario remained outside the public health care system, and this meant women had to pay for their care. We knew that this limited access. But we also felt that practising midwives were the crucial base upon which to build a consumer and feminist movement to pressure the provincial government to legalize and fund the profession. So we accepted a situation that inevitably could not meet the principle of equal access in the short-term, in order to build a broader movement to win community-based midwifery.[4]

We also need to be able to evaluate which strategies and directions move us towards our long-term goals and which immediate changes could seal us off from further progress. Such a long-term perspective is vital to avoid co-optation; to identifying those government proffered reforms that could diffuse and divert our movements. For example, advocates of greater choice in childbirth saw that designating certain hospital rooms for "family" maternity care and humanizing their decor did not fundamentally change the power of doctors of the interventionist ethos of contemporary obstetrics.[5]

Such a long view is also important as we evaluate the direction of our current politics. Over the years campaigns we are involved in for legal midwifery and free-standing abortion clinics had been criticized in ways that seemed to miss the complexities of our political situations.[6] For example, midwives' demand for legalization was criticized as playing into the hands of state and professional bureaucratization and regulation.[7] Similarly, Ontario Coalition for Abortion Clinics was criticized because the first free-standing clinics were privately owned rather than controlled by the women's community. It seemed that our struggles were being evaluated – perhaps unconsciously – against some image of a "perfect world" in which reproductive health care was provided in a woman-centred environment. But this is a very imperfect world, and you cannot judge immediate practice against ultimate goals without taking into account the complexities and pressures the reproductive rights movement faces in a very hostile political and ideological environment. Put most simply, we had to decide whether to wait until conditions would allow us to create the "perfect" women's health service or begin our struggle from the situation at hand. We decided not to wait, believing that ideal conditions would never arise by themselves; that only political struggle would enable us to win our demands.[8]

The campaigns we have been involved in tried to develop strategy that works at two levels simultaneously: that can both radically address immediate conditions and build a consciousness and movement to transform the existing oppressive relations of reproduction. In the Ontario Coalition for Abortion Clinics, for example, we tried to pose the argument for free-standing abortion clinics in this double way. The Morgentaler and Scott clinics provided indispensable services to women. They dramatized daily how unfair and unworkable the existing law was, and showed the solution in the most concrete and immediate fashion possible. The clinics provided a vital spark to building the choice movement and a focus around which to mobilize. At the same time, we stressed our longer-term goal of publicly funded centres in every community providing care for the full spectrum of women's reproductive lives, from contraception to midwifery, from abortion to sexuality counseling.

Similarly, by always bearing in mind the fundamental principles of feminist reproductive care, we can try to be prefigurative of our ultimate goals in our current practice and strategy. These principles cannot be seen as axioms that can always be attained, but rather as guidelines or standards by which we orient our work. So, as mentioned above, access to midwives will remain unequal as long as they must practice outside the public health care system. Nonetheless, without waiting for legal recognition, most midwives use a sliding scale to make their care accessible regardless of income. The Midwives Collective of Toronto, for example, has developed a project to provide free midwifery care for high-risk teenage mothers.

You Can't Get There From Here

However attractive and inspiring such a vision of future possibilities can be, the women's reproductive health centre we have sketched out here cannot be achieved in a simple or direct fashion. The struggle for reproductive freedom is a complex process involving many stages, many difficult strategic and tactical choices in the face of powerful opponents, and many differing coalitions, alliances, campaigns and issues.

This final story is true.

In February 1989 Vicki and Bob were sitting in Vicki's kitchen, talking and writing. We were discussing a set of problems that is quite unique – and no doubt envied – in the women's movement. Both the campaigns we have been involved in had won immediate demands: on 28 January 1988 the Supreme Court had thrown out the oppressive abortion law and in effect made legal the clinics in Ontario that we had been fighting to defend, and the Ontario government was moving, albeit ponderously, to legalize midwifery.

But we both had known that even these most positive outcomes would not be the end of our struggles. Immediately after the Supreme Court ruling a number of provinces tried to refuse funding for abortions or attempted to impose other restrictions; and a year later access remained horribly inequitable. While the Court decision was a major advance and a historic victory for abortion rights, we knew that it really was only the beginning of the next stage of a long struggle.

Here again, the strategic interchange between these two movements proved invaluable. Midwives had been grappling for several years with issues that were now pressing on the choice movement: How to avoid being strangled by the state's regulatory and medical framework? How to win comprehensive woman-centred care within a hostile medical system? How to avoid getting drowned in the red tape of funding and administrative procedures when the existing clinics were brought into the public health system? And how to make sure this did not prevent our goal of community clinics? How to pressure the state so that sufficient public resources are committed to ensure that every woman has free and equal access to abortion and all the other reproductive care she needs in her own community?

We also found that these movements faced a number of common problems, the most crucial being the question of fetal rights. The powerful and emotive symbol of the innocent and defenceless fetus had long been the lynchpin of anti-choice political strategy.[9] After the Supreme Court, the more lurid anti-choice fanatics raised the spectre of countless feckless women having abortions right up to the time of birth and the federal government had been using concern over late abortion to promote legislation restricting abortion past certain gestational limits. Simultaneously, doctors had been using their self-appointed role as guardians of fetal interests to justify increasing obstetrical – and most ominously, court-ordered – intervention, even against the woman's will. All of this was highlighted when the Law Reform Commission, a federal legal policymaking body, released a report in February 1989 provocatively entitled "Crimes Against the Fetus." Their recommendations would not restrict access to abortion, but legitimize increasing state and medical surveillance and control of pregnancy and birth in the name of fetal protection.

We thought that the best response was to stress preventive approaches to reproductive health care, as opposed to criminal or medical regulation. So the answer to late abortions was to eliminate needless delays, ensure timely and equal access, and provided comprehensive sex and contraceptive education. "Star Wars" high-tech obstetrics has not been able to prevent premature babies and infertility. What is needed is comprehensive prenatal care and the elimination of those social, environmental, work-related and iatrogenic factors that cause these problems in the first place.

Underlying both the anti-choice reification of the fetus and the medical championing of its interests is the insidious message that women could not be trusted to make responsible decisions themselves without "expert" regulation or legal restrictions. We thought it vital to challenge this dominant viewpoint. It is crucial to fashion and popularize a competing feminist discourse of reproductive freedom, based upon the premise that women's ability to control their sexuality and reproduction is an essential precondition of self-determination and autonomy. We need to shift the focus of public debate back from the fetus to women's well-being and circumstances, women's capacity to make the most appropriate decisions about their reproductive lives and health for themselves, and the conditions needed for them to be able to do so.

We had no final answers that night. There will be no final answers to the political problems our movements face for some time yet.

We have tried to outline a model or framework within which reproductive health care could be empowering for women. But, of course, this vision will not be achieved simply because it is more rational and effective than the existing system; it will have to be won through political struggle. A precondition of winning this type of women-centred care, of bringing the development of reproductive health care under women's control, and ultimately, of challenging and transforming the social relations of reproduction, is a strong reproductive rights movement. This movement must bring together our diverse campaigns for abortion rights, midwifery, daycare, employment equity and sexual self-determination; galvanize and embolden the largest number of women through direct political activism; and put the maximum pressure on the state to meet our demands.[10]

We have also been arguing that a clear sense of future goals and possibilities is an essential part of building such a movement. A clear vision of ultimate goals is vital to building the energy and insight our movements need in the long struggle for sexual and reproductive freedom. It to this end that we have sketched out a model of what feminist reproductive health care could – and should – be.[11]

NOTES

1 We have both been working in the reproductive rights movement for many years. One of us is a practising midwife, involved in the campaign for legalization of independent midwifery; the other is active in the Ontario Coalition for Abortion Clinics. We would like to thank Mariruth Morton and Mary Gellatly for their work with us.

2 Agnes Heller argues, "Utopias are in the present, not in the future. The more a utopia captures the imagination of people in the present, the more it is transformed into a new utopian mentality which can transcend the dominant social imagination." Patrick Wright, "A Socialist in Exile" interview with Agnes Heller, *New Socialist* (July 1985), p 39.

3 Sheila Rowbotham, "Hopes, Dreams and Dirty Nappies," *Marxism Today,* 11 (December 1984). Directly relevant to this chapter, she argues: "In considering utopias as stories it is not so much their fixed virtues as ideals but a means of putting time aside to jog the imagination and let fancy roam. It is the *process* of intertwining hopes for the future and analysis of the present which can shift seemingly immutable realities." See also her "What Do Women Want? Women-centred Values and the World As It Is," *Feminist Review,* 20 (June 1985).

There is also a rich tradition of feminist science fiction; one theme of which is to hold existing relations of reproduction, sexuality and power up to scrutiny by imagining totally different forms and relationships. See Patrocino Schweikart, "What If ... Science and Technology in Feminist Utopias" in Joan Rothschild, ed., *Machina Ex Dea: Feminist Perspectives on Technology* (New York, Pergamon Press, 1983); and Ruby Rohrlech and Elaine Hoffman Baruch, eds., *Women In Search of Utopia: Mavericks and Mythmakers* (New York, Schocken Books, 1985).

4 Vicki Van Wagner, "Women Organizing for Midwifery in Ontario," in Sue Findley and Melanie Randall, eds., *Feminist Perspectives on the Canadian State: Resources for Feminist Research,* 17:3 (September 1988), pp.115-118.

5 We addressed these issues in an interview: Midwives Collective of Toronto and Ontario Coalition for Abortion Clinics, "Visions for Reproductive Care," *Healthsharing* (Spring 1988), pp.30-32. We discussed how certain reforms proposed by the provincial government, such as hospital birthing rooms and hospital-based women's health centres, were not based on the type of principles we have sketched out in this article and were in fact explicitly directed to diffusing support for autonomous midwifery and free-standing abortion clinics.

6 Connie Clement, "The Case for Lay Abortion," *Healthsharing* (Winter 1983); and Kathleen McDonnell, *Not an Easy Choice: A Feminist Re-examines Abortion* (Toronto, Women's Press, 1984). For an insightful critique of the latter see Lorraine Gauthier's review in *Canadian Women's Studies,* vol. 6, no 2.

7 Jutta Mason, "Midwifery in Canada," in Sheila Kitzinger, ed., *The Midwifery Challenge* (London, Pandora, 1988), pp. 98-129.

8 See a number of articles on the history of our struggles for free-standing abortion clinics and autonomous midwifery: Patricia Antonyshyn, B. Lee and Alex Merril, "Marching for Women's Lives: The Campaign for Free-Standing Abortion Clinics in Ontario" in Frank Cunningham, Sue Findlay, Marlene Kadar, Alan Lennon and Ed Silva, eds., *Social Movement / Social Change: The Politics and Practice of Organizing* (Toronto, Between the Lines, 1988); Ontario Coalition for Abortion Clinics, "State Power and the Struggle for Reproductive Freedom: The Campaign for Free-standing Abortion Clinics in Ontario," in Findley and Randall, eds., op. cit., pp. 109-114; and Van Wagner, op. cit.

9 Rosalind Pollack Petchesky, "Foetal Images: the Power of Visual Culture in the Politics of Reproduction" in Michelle Stanworth, ed., *Reproductive*

Technologies: Gender, Motherhood and Medicine (London, Polity Press, 1987), pp. 57-80.

10 We have discussed how we attempted to do this in the campaigns for abortion rights and autonomous midwifery in articles cited earlier. For broader material on the politics and strategy of the reproductive rights movement see Rosalind Pollack Petchesky, *Abortion and Women's Choice: The State, Sexuality, and Reproductive Freedom* (New York, Longman, 1984); Adele Clark and Alice Wolfson, "Socialist-Feminism and Reproductive Rights," *Socialist Review* 78 (1984), pp.110-120; and Committee for Abortion Rights and Against Sterilization Abuse, Susan Davis, ed., *Women Under Attack: Victories, Backlash and the Fight for Reproductive Freedom,* (Boston, South End Press, 1988).

11 Behind this particular schema of what feminist reproductive health care could be, of course, is a broader vision in which the material inequalities and subordination women face and the straightjackets of contemporary gender relations are transformed. The outlines of this vision are another story, but see Lynn Segal, *Is the Future Female? Troubled Thoughts on Contemporary Feminism* (London, Virago, 1987); and Alison Jaggar, *Feminist Politics and Human Nature* (Brighton, Sussex, Harvester Press, 1983).

FEMINIST ETHICS AND NEW REPRODUCTIVE TECHNOLOGIES

Susan Sherwin

FEMINIST ETHICS IS A rapidly exploding field. Many diverse approaches are being taken to this subject and no single definition has yet emerged.[1] My own position is that feminist ethics is a type of ethical theorizing that is informed and motivated by a feminist analysis of women's oppression, including a commitment to the elimination of patriarchy.[2] Feminist ethics considers the interconnectedness of persons in society to be morally significant, in contrast to the assumption common to most of the leading Western ethical theories that persons are essentially separate, autonomous beings. It seeks to replace relationships of dominance and subordination with those that foster equal power, trust and respect.

Those who pursue feminist ethics do so from a self-consciously political perspective with an agenda of social change before them. Although other, more traditional ethical approaches are also political (in the sense that they have implications for the power structures in society), their political agendas and effects are often not made explicit. In fact, proponents of traditional ethical theories tend to consider the apparent political neutrality of their theories to be a mark of objectivity which strengthens their authority. As they have done for most academic theories, feminists have analyzed the oppressive implications of traditional ethical theories and have become persuaded that this claim to neutral objectivity is false, unsubstantiated and, generally, self-deceptive.[3] Feminists have argued for a distinction between truth and neutrality and developed criteria for objectivity which can be compatible with specific social interests.[4] Hence, feminist ethics is explicitly and consciously directed towards eliminating (and not just theorizing about) injustice by improving the status of women in society.

Further, the scope of the subject matter of feminist ethics is very broad in that it sees ethical problems in places traditional theorists have not. Most of the mainstream discussion on abortion, for instance, has focused on the questions of the moral status of the fetus and the mother's right to control her body. But a feminist ethical analysis demands that we also consider the social conditions which lead to unwanted pregnancies and which prevent women from choosing to see pregnancies through to term, for example, circumstances that do not permit adequate care for the child produced.[5] In the case of in vitro fertilization (IVF), those working within the traditional ethical approaches have tended to define the ethical problems associated with this practice as revolving around questions of the appropriateness of artificial intervention in human reproduction, the risks of deformed infants, the immediate danger to the prospective mothers and the costs involved. In contrast, a feminist ethics approach demands that we also consider who controls access to this technology, the degree of voluntariness exhibited by the participants in a culture that continues to evaluate women and marriages by the production of children, and the ways in which this technology (together with other social practices) changes or reinforces oppressive social attitudes about women and children.[6]

A feminist ethics perspective reflects feminist insight and analysis of the systemic nature of patriarchal patterns of oppression. Actions need to be evaluated in the context of their effect on sexist structures in society. Since oppression is created by interrelated practices, understanding individual practices requires us to look at them in the context of other patterns with which they are entwined. Traditional theories seem to assume that we can make ethical decisions about specific acts or practices simply in terms of the features which constitute them, but an understanding of the systemic pattern of oppression makes clear that we should also try to see how each practice fits into general social patterns and structures. Hence, we cannot expect to decide about the ethical acceptability of any particular reproductive product or service such as abortion, surrogacy or genetic screening just by looking at its specific features. We must also consider what social conditions have led to the development of that practice, whose interests are served by it (and whose are harmed) and how its widespread use may change power structures in society.

Since the underlying concern of a feminist ethics analysis is to reduce the forces of oppression in our society, we should pay attention to increasing the freedom of individuals in matters of central importance to their own lives. In particular, it is important that any discussion of reproductive technology include an analysis of reproductive freedom which focuses on individual control and protects against coercion (either from other individuals or from social forces generally) over central aspects of reproductive life. The norm of reproductive freedom should protect individuals' control over their own sexuality, sexual activity and childbearing and ensure adequate resources for proper childrearing. Given the interrelatedness of people in society, we must consider whether one person's freedom to raise children, for instance, is being pursued at the expense of another's right not to bear children. What is necessary is a set of social arrangements that ensures maximum – and equal – reproductive freedom for all, and not reproductive privileges for some purchased through restrictions on the freedom of others.

In reviewing the relevant social arrangements, a feminist ethics approach ought also to consider the historical structures governing women's lives. From such a perspective, it is clear that an important aspect of most (and perhaps all) known societies is the assignment of control over sexuality and reproduction; power over the sexual and reproductive activity of women within each society is concentrated in the hands of an elite through legal, religious, medical and social means. The heterosexuality and monogamy of women (except for designated sex-trade workers) is commonly commanded through a collection of social, religious and legal methods. Contraceptive information, for example, has historically been suppressed, and access to abortion is determined by the political agenda of a state's rulers. In this century in North America, medicine has contributed to the historical trend of interfering with a woman's control of her own reproductive life by wresting power from women through exclusion of midwives. Medical practitioners have institutionalized their concepts of contraception, conception and childbirth as medical events, thereby gaining authority to treat them all as processes subject to medical authority. From a feminist perspective, the new reproductive technologies appear to be another variation in a long history of external power exercised over women's reproductive lives.

With these cautions in mind, we can turn to look at some forms of new reproductive technology and consider the value constraints which an ethical perspective must add. Clearly, an important feminist concern in evaluating reproductive technologies is that each particular technology ought to be such that it increases control over reproduction available to individual women and does not serve to concentrate control with those in authority in society. Sex information, safe and effective contraceptive techniques, abortion services and guidance on conception and genetic information can serve this function. But feminism is interested in eliminating the oppression of women generally and, hence, contributing to the freedom of all women. It is an assumption of feminist theories that for any woman to be truly free, all women must be free. The apparent freedom some women derive from their specific heterosexual, class, or racial affiliation is better identified as privilege, not freedom, for they could not retain the choices they now control if they were to change their attachments to the hierarchical status quo. Hence, an important feminist consideration is that the increase in reproductive freedom be of benefit to women *qua* women and not be just a matter of privilege for fortunate women. These technologies, then, ought to be distributed in such a way as to be universally accessible, permitting all women greater control over their own sexuality and reproduction.

However, the current system of distribution governing the new reproductive technologies has medical experts performing a gatekeeper function; physicians have the power to permit and deny women's access to services connected with their reproductive lives. Since many of these forms of technology are marketed as expensive commodities, economic status is the first screening mechanism that women encounter in pursuit of them. Conceivably, the medicalization of this technology may eventually lead to its being treated as any other medical service under socialized health care, so perhaps the access question could be formally resolved in Canada. Yet, even if this technology were to be considered a medically insured service, the universality provided is likely to be merely theoretical, since in practice consumption of sophisticated medical services is generally associated with class.

Even if the affordability and distribution problems could be solved, it is difficult to envision true woman-centred control of this technology, for the medical specialists in charge would continue to exercise judgemental control in choosing among women petitioning for their services. Recognizing that there are value components in the use of reproductive technologies, the medical authorities who deliver the technology feel that they must make the value decisions attached to facilitating the reproductive control women seek. Hence, they must be persuaded that a woman has "good cause" if she seeks sterilization or abortion. Many will pick and choose among candidates, providing service to some and denying it to others according to their own moral sense of what is an appropriate choice for these women. Most medical practitioners will deny IVF or Donor Insemination (DI) to women who are not married, judged to be sexually deviant, promiscuous or irresponsible, considered to be mentally or financially unstable, considered too old or too young for medically approved childbearing, or who are mentally or physically challenged.

Certainly, it is to be expected that those involved in deciding to prevent or create human life should give serious thought to the responsibilities entailed, but we might better ensure responsible decision-making if our society were to provide potential parents with the resources necessary for making such decisions and for dealing with the consequences of their choices. In this way, we could respect individual autonomy rather than distrusting women's capacity for decision-making by putting full authority in the hands of a professional elite. There is further cause for concern about arrangements that make medical professionals the final arbiters in decisions about parenting. As a professional elite, doctors are likely to make decisions in accordance with a value structure reflective of existing social biases, including values which are sexist, homophobic, racist, capitalist and elitist. Such values are incompatible with the overall freedom of women in our society, and there is enormous danger that widespread use of reproductive technology will increase the already excessive power of medical specialists and strengthen the social acceptance of an oppressive set of values.

Within the context of a sexist society where women have yet to gain full control over their sexual and reproductive lives, much of this technology threatens to result in technological imperatives which can contribute to further reductions of individual reproductive control. For instance, women in Canada do not have much personal control over the place or circumstances of childbirth. They tend to be herded into hospitals where they are subjected to a wide range of technological interventions in the management of labour and delivery. Should the infant be born with life-threatening abnormalities, dramatic efforts will be made to "salvage" it, with little opportunity for parental input in determining the acceptability of these measures. In hospitals it is very difficult for anyone, patient or physician, to avoid the use of available technology.

For many women, fertility enhancement reflects a more subtle form of technological imperative. Research connected with enhanced fertility already goes beyond its promise of assisting those who are truly anxious to bear children and is creating a situation where women are feeling tremendous pressure to pursue all known avenues to achieve conception. They are no longer confronted with a moment when they can say, without guilt, that they tried and failed. Each failure can now be seen as an opportunity for increasingly complex and distressing interventions. Infertile couples are not helped to accept their childless status and may not have the opportunity to redirect their energies and take an interest in an existing child or to see other means of sharing love in a world where millions of people are starving – for this technology supports a view that biological connection is the most important factor in human relationships.

A feminist world-view would concentrate on seeing that all children are cared for before fostering elaborate, expensive attempts to custom-design genetically related children. In a patriarchal society, paternity in particular is extremely important;[7] hence, some men will be motivated to produce their own children in any way possible. This interest and its unquestioned acceptance by many physicians leads to a state of affairs where women are encouraged to undergo the physical and emotional rigors of in vitro fertilization if their husbands "suffer from" low sperm counts. Such advice should be evaluated in the context of a feminist analysis of the connection of paternal interest with the oppression of women.

Contractual pregnancies (so-called surrogate mothering arrangements) raise similar concerns. Women who cannot, or prefer not to, bear children may find themselves locked into contractual arrangements with a woman who can bear the child their husband seeks. As long as men maintain the economic and social power in relationships, wives may find they have little say about raising children their husbands conceive through such legal arrangements. Moreover, it is hard not to see the decisions of the mother who contracts to bear a child in surrogacy arrangements as representing the limited options of the disadvantaged in an unjust society. Surrogates frequently refer to their motivation as seeking to help others who are deprived of the joys of children. Feminists are not reassured that this altruism can be accepted as constituting a truly voluntary choice, since self-sacrifice, especially in terms of childbearing for others, seems to be a paradigm example of the ways in which feminine socialization may be connected with women's roles in an oppressive society.[8] In any event, except in cases where there is a strong personal bond between the mother and the contracting couple, surrogacy is almost always a financial arrangement where the couple purchasing the services of the mother uses its greater financial power to purchase the agreement of an economically disadvantaged woman.

Clearly, surrogacy involves significant physical and emotional sacrifices on the part of the mother. She must agree to modify her lifestyle (including her sexual activity), to seek regular prenatal care (including genetic screening, and subsequent abortion if the contracting couple disapproves of the result) and to undergo all the normal hazards of pregnancy without the usual joys of a subsequent loving relationship with a child. Surrendering an infant after pregnancy is emotionally wrenching for the mother and for any other children she may have – they must struggle to understand why she has given away a sibling of theirs. It is unclear, then, how free the choices of the women concerned are in any of these arrangements.[9] (I find it curious that states which prohibit people from selling a kidney or a cornea for paternalistic reasons seem willing to tolerate open trade in the matter of contractual pregnancies.)

An important area of ethical concern to be raised with respect to the various means of new reproductive technology is the ways in which these technologies reflect and deepen general social attitudes about women. DI, IVF, embryo flushing, embryo freezing, superovulation, genetic engineering and sex selection are all techniques that have been developed in animal husbandry and translated to human beings. Just as these techniques facilitate the use of prize animals in the breeding of genetically advantageous stock, they threaten to permit the use of certain women as instruments to reproduce children with the genetic characteristics preferred by a powerful elite. In a racist culture, the embryos produced by women of one race may potentially be flushed and transplanted to the wombs of women from another, less powerful race for breeding purposes in much the same way as embryos of prize-winning cows are now transplanted into less valuable cows, thereby maximizing the genetic output of the award winners. There is likely to be a market available for such service among those who can afford to lease a surrogate gestator when pregnancy is judged undesirable by affluent women. Clearly, consumer choice does not ensure adequate protection of the interests of all participants. It is important, then, that questions of control of a technology be discussed at the same time as it evolves.

If we consider the technology associated with genetic control of children from a feminist analysis of our culture, particular concerns arise. Sex selection of embryos, whether pre- or post-conception, is extremely troubling in a sexist society.

Where males are cherished and females are devalued, we must be very uneasy about providing prospective parents with the power to choose the sex of each offspring. Such choice might lead to little disruption in a society that did not systematically discriminate on the basis of sex, but in a society that clearly prefers the male, the implications are a matter of serious concern. Presumably, most parents will choose male offspring more often than female, thereby constituting a practice which will result in serious sex imbalances. While some futurists forecast greater power for individual women in a society where they are scarce, others anticipate that scarcity will cause women to be treated explicitly as reproductive property, being sold to the highest bidder. If couples get to exercise the option preferred by most contemporary North Americans of male child first and female second, we can look forward to further entrenchment of social attitudes that see males as stronger, brighter and more powerful, since boys will grow up with the privileges of the first born and learn to perceive them as natural. Catering to gender preferences that have been created in a world which is oppressive to women is likely to reify gender differences found in sexist society and lead to more unquestioning acceptance and exaggeration of these tendencies. And if technology develops the means to permit male pregnancy and/or artificial wombs, women could conceivably become virtually obsolete although a few would be maintained as suppliers of ova.

Feminist ethics directs caution in other aspects of genetic engineering as well. Techniques that may in time help prospective parents custom-design a child with respect to physical or mental characteristics (for example, tall, blonde, high I.Q, musical aptitude) will likely also serve to reinforce existing cultural prejudices and facilitate increased oppression experienced by those who do not measure up to the prevailing standards. Parents with the economic or political power to use these techniques to control the natural lottery of genetic endowment affecting their own children will use it to increase the power of those possessing the characteristics they favour. Thus, we can anticipate that those lacking the relevant characteristics will have even less power than they now possess, and social differences will be exacerbated.

The technology that governs genetic screening for birth defects is already being perceived as a technological necessity. Parents are being manipulated into seeking such technology and accepting medical judgement about the acceptability of offspring with certain defects. Down's syndrome, for instance, is widely identified as a defect to be screened against; women are encouraged to seek such screening from the age of thirty-five even though the risk of bearing a Down's syndrome child is less than one percent at thirty-five. Yet many parents of Down's syndrome children and many Down's syndrome adults disagree with the conclusion that this condition merits abortion. The judgements implicit in these decisions are painted as matters of medical expertise whereas they are value judgements that require no explicit technical training.

A feminist analysis committed to providing women maximal control of their own reproduction must not only ensure women the right to refuse screening and genetically determined abortions, but also help to reduce the coercive social forces that make it difficult for women to say no to these proferred services. This will require that support services be available to help parents with the special needs of children they may choose to bear despite their genetic handicaps. Hence, we must not only analyze the technique of genetic screening, we must also look at the context in which it is being sold and the likely effects of its widespread use.

A perspective of feminist ethics, then, directs our attention to the overall pattern of reproductive control in society. It advises that we seek technology that does not offer piecemeal responses to technologically induced problems such as iatrogenically induced sterility, but instead concentrate research on the search for safer, more effective and reversible means by which an individual can control her own reproductive capacity. Reproductive technologies should not be evaluated simply in terms of their immediate demand, but rather in terms of how their availability contributes to a system of improving women's reproductive control over their own lives.

Given its concern with eliminating patterns which oppress women, feminist ethics demands an approach to issues which involves strategies that support the empowerment of all women. The ethical acceptability of the new reproductive technologies must be evaluated in terms of their influence on the status of women and children in society as a whole. It is not sufficient to measure only a technology's contribution to individual happiness or even its effect on reducing individual suffering. As with any social practice, each form of reproductive technology must be examined in terms of its effect on all women's control of their own lives. For that reason, it is important to move cautiously in determining public policy which will govern the introduction and distribution of such technology while keeping the larger picture in mind at all times.

NOTES

1 See, for instance, the papers in Eva Feder Kittay and Diane T. Myers, eds., *Women and Moral Theory* (Totowa, New Jersey, Rowman and Littlefield, 1987) and in Barbara Hilkert Andolsen, Christine E. Gudorf and Mary D. Pellauer, eds., *Women's Consciousness, Women's Conscience: A Reader in Feminist Ethics* (San Francisco, Harper and Row, 1987).

2 Susan Sherwin, "A Feminist Approach to Ethics," *Dalhousie Review,* vol. 64, no. 4 (Winter 1984-1985).

3 Some biases in traditional ethics are uncovered in Kathryn Morgan's "Women and Moral Madness," in Marsha Hanen and Kai Nielson, eds., *Science, Morality, and Ethical Theory* (Calgary, The University of Calgary Press, 1987), pp. 201-226.

4 Lorraine Code presents a clear case against the pursuit of objectivity in a value neutral way. In contrast, she proposes an ideal she calls "objectivism" as a mode of contemplation that acknowledges human fallibility and enjoins us to keep in touch, as closely as possible, with ordinary experience, being vigilant against "epistemic imperialism." Lorraine Code, *Epistemic Responsibility* (Hanover, Brown University Press, 1987), especially pp. 77-78 and pp. 142-143.

5 See, for instance, Kathryn Payne Addelson's "Moral Revolution," in Marilyn Pearsall, ed., *Women and Values* (Belmont, GA., Wadsworth, 1986), pp. 291-309.

6 I have attempted to spell out the differences between traditional ethical approaches and that of feminist ethics on this issue in Susan Sherwin, "Feminist Ethics and In Vitro Fertilization," in *Science, Morality, and Feminist Theory*, pp.265-284.

7 For an analysis of why paternity is politically important, see Lorenne M.G. Clark and Lynda Lange, eds., *The Sexism of Social and Political Theory: Women and Reproduction from Plato to Nietzsche* (Toronto, University of Toronto Press, 1979).

8 Barbara Houston outlines and explains this sort of concern in "Rescuing Womanly Virtues: Some Dangers of Moral Reclamation,"in *Science, Morality, and Feminist Theory*, pp. 237-262.

9 Christine Overall spells out the evidence for questioning the degree of freedom on the part of surrogates and for general worry about how surrogacy contributes to social attitudes about the status of women in society. See Christine Overall, "Surrogate Motherhood," in *Science, Morality, and Feminist Theory*, pp. 285-305.

CONCLUSION

For Canadian women most of the important questions about the future of human reproduction still remain undecided. And many of those questions will be confronting us almost immediately:

- The introduction of new abortion legislation, if and when it occurs, could lend further support to advocates of fetal rights and may very well reduce, rather than confirm, Canadian women's recent and tentative entitlement to complete abortion services.
- Decisions about the costs and availability of in vitro fertilization and donor insemination will determine in many cases which women can become mothers and which cannot; the structuring of information about these processes and their results will determine whether or not women are able to make informed choices about their use.
- New and existing forms of prenatal diagnostic testing may further our knowledge of the condition and development of the fetus, but they may also deeply affect women's attitudes towards their pregnancies and their offspring, and contribute to the eugenic motive to produce only babies of certain specified characteristics.
- Decisions will have to be made about the practice of "surrogate" or contract motherhood. Legalization of this practice will permit the buying of babies and the commodification of women's bodies; yet criminalization may have the effect of victimizing poorer women who see contract motherhood as their only option.
- On the more optimistic side, the future of birthing choices for women looks brighter now than it has in the past few decades: the role of midwives and the value of home birthing are gradually acquiring more public awareness and approval. What is needed now are steps to legitimize home

birth, free-standing birthing clinics and the work of midwives so that these choices are available to all Canadian women.

More generally, the future of reproduction in Canada will require careful thought and concerted political action in regard to the meaning and scope of reproductive rights and freedom. More woman-centred research is badly needed to help us understand the causes and prevention of infertility, the short- and long-term consequences of the use of reproductive technologies, and the content and structure of the social systems which are now determining whether, when, and how we become parents.

A woman's body and her reproductive capacities do not belong to the fetus, to her partner if any, to the father of the fetus, to physicians and the medical establishment, or to the state. Beyond that assertion, further feminist elaboration of the ideas of reproductive autonomy and self-determination is essential. What do we, as feminists, want to include within the sphere of reproductive choice and freedom? How far do reproductive rights extend?

For feminists, reproductive behaviour and the belief systems, institutions and social practices related to it are likely to remain a significant site of theorizing and activism. The ways in which the future of human reproduction unfolds will continue to play a major role in how women are socially constructed, in what it means to be a woman, and in the continued oppression or liberation of women.

Christine Overall

NOTES ON
CONTRIBUTORS

RONA ACHILLES completed her doctorate in sociology at the Ontario Institute for Studies in Education. Her doctoral thesis, entitled "The Social Meanings of Biological Ties," is an exploratory study of participants in donor insemination programs. She is currently working as a consultant in the area of infertility and new reproductive technologies.

SOMER BRODRIBB has written some of the first feminist material on reproductive technologies, and has presented and discussed these issues with women's community groups and at academic conferences internationally. Last year, she prepared "Women and Reproductive Technologies" for The Status of Women, Canada (Ottawa). She is a member of the journals *Resources for Feminist Research / Documentation sur la recherche féministe* and *Reproductive and Genetic Engineering: Journal of International Feminist Analysis*. Currently, she is affiliated with the Section on Discourse Studies, University of Amsterdam, where she is pursuing post-doctoral research on the work of Mary O'Brien and Luce Irigaray.

CYNTHIA CARVER received her medical degree from the University of Toronto and a Masters in Public Health at Chapel Hill, University of North Carolina. She was in general practice in Toronto for eight years, and has been a public health physician for the past five. She is also a regular columnist for *Chatelaine* and has written a book and articles about the Canadian health care system, particularly as it affects women and lower income groups. She is the mother of three grown girls and grandmother to a growing number of grandchildren.

NIKKI COLODNY is a physician and psychotherapist. Involved in the women's movement for many years, she first worked as a volunteer birth control counselor in 1973. More recently she has been active in the abortion rights movement. This involvement led to her being arrested and charged in September 1986 for performing abortions at the Morgentaler Clinic in Toronto. She has performed abortions in free-standing clinics and was one of the founding members of both Women's Choice Health Clinic and Choice in Health Clinic.

MARGRIT EICHLER is a Professor of Sociology at the Ontario Institute for Studies in Education. She has published very widely on a large number of feminist issues. Her latest two books are *Families in Canada Today: Recent Changes and Their Policy Consequences* (2nd ed., Toronto, Gage, 1988) and *Nonsexist Research Methods: A Practical Guide* (Winchester, Allen and Unwin, 1988). She is founder and coordinator of the Canadian Coalition for a Royal Commission on New Reproductive Technologies.

ABBY LIPPMAN is an Associate Professor at McGill University. Her research has focused on the development, utilization and evaluation of genetic health services and on their implications for women's control over their reproduction. She is particularly interested in how genetic knowledge and technology are applied to and influence individual and societal decision-making.

BOB LEE has worked in the Ontario Coalition for Abortion Clinics in Toronto for six years. He is also a member of the Midwifery Task Force and AIDS Action Now.

THELMA McCORMACK is Professor of Sociology, York University, former President of the Canadian Sociology and Anthropology Association, Chairperson of the Graduate Program in

Women's Studies, York University, first incumbent of the E. Margret Fulton Chair in Women's Studies, Mount Saint Vincent University. Specializes in feminist studies, mass communication, political sociology and sociology of health and illness. Went from being a working mother to being a working grandperson.

KATHRYN PAULY MORGAN Ph.D. is Associate Professor of Philosophy and Women's Studies. Having survived a spinal fusion, a knee reconstruction, three laparoscopies in the context of infertility workups, and one Caesarean section, she is naturally interested in the areas of feminist medical ethics, sexuality, romantic love, feminist pedagogy and feminist theory. She is optimistically engaged in raising her child in a non-sexist cooperative setting.

PATRICIA O'REILLY grew up on Wolfe Island where Lake Ontario greets the St. Lawrence River. After studying life sciences and working in medical research for eight years, she returned to school and majored in political studies, first at Queen's University and now at the University of Toronto.

CHRISTINE OVERALL is Associate Professor of Philosophy and Queen's National Scholar at Queen's University, Kingston, Ontario. She is the author of *Ethics and Human Reproduction: A Feminist Analysis* (Allen and Unwin, 1987), and co-editor of *Feminist Perspectives: Philosophical Essays on Method and Morals* (University of Toronto Press, 1988). She is currently working on a book entitled *Women, Sexuality and Feminist Theory,* to be published by Unwin Hyman. She is the mother of two children.

DEBORAH C. POFF is the Associate Director of the Institute for the Study of Women at Mount Saint Vincent University. She is the editor of the *Journal of Business Ethics* and the co-editor of

Atlantis: A Women's Studies Journal.

SANDA RODGERS is Vice-Dean and Professor of Law at the University of Ottawa, Common Law Section. She has written widely on health law matters. She is particularly interested in the impact of the Canadian Charter of Rights and Freedoms on issues involving health and in health policy issues as they affect Canadian women. She most recently served as a member of the Fetal Status Working Group of the Law Reform Commission of Canada.

SUSAN SHERWIN is an Associate Professor of Philosophy at Dalhousie University. Her principal academic interests are in feminism, ethics and medical ethics, and she is currently attempting to pursue them all simultaneously by writing a book on feminist medical ethics. She is also involved in a variety of community and campus activities in conjunction with and support of women.

HARRIET SIMAND is the founder of DES Action / Canada, a non-profit women's health organization whose aim is to provide information and support for the 200,000-400,000 Canadians exposed to the hormone drug DES. She is currently completing degrees in Civil and Common Law at McGill University.

PAUL THOMPSON is Professor of Philosophy at the University of Toronto and is Chair of the Division of Humanities, Scarborough College, University of Toronto. He is the author of numerous articles on the structure of biological science, a book, *Theory Structure in Biology,* and a number of articles on medical ethics, especially abortion and childbirth.

VICKI VAN WAGNER has practised as a midwife in Toronto for eight years and has been active in the struggle to win legal recognition for midwifery. She is also a member of the Ontario Coalition for Abortion Clinics and has spoken and written extensively on reproductive rights.

BETSY WARLAND's most recent books include *Double Negative* (a collaboration with Daphne Marlatt), and *serpent (w)rite*. She lives on Salt Spring Island, British Columbia, and is co-editor of *(f.)Lip* – A Newsletter of Feminist Innovative Writing. She is currently editing a book of her essays, articles and prose poetry and is writing a play.

LINDA S. WILLIAMS is an Assistant Professor in the Department of Sociology at Trent University, Peterborough, Ontario, where she teaches family sociology, research methods and statistics. Her previous work has included studies of rape victims reporting to the police and couples in commuter marriages. Her current research interests are focused on a feminist analysis of the effect of in vitro fertilization on women's reproductive autonomy and consciousness.